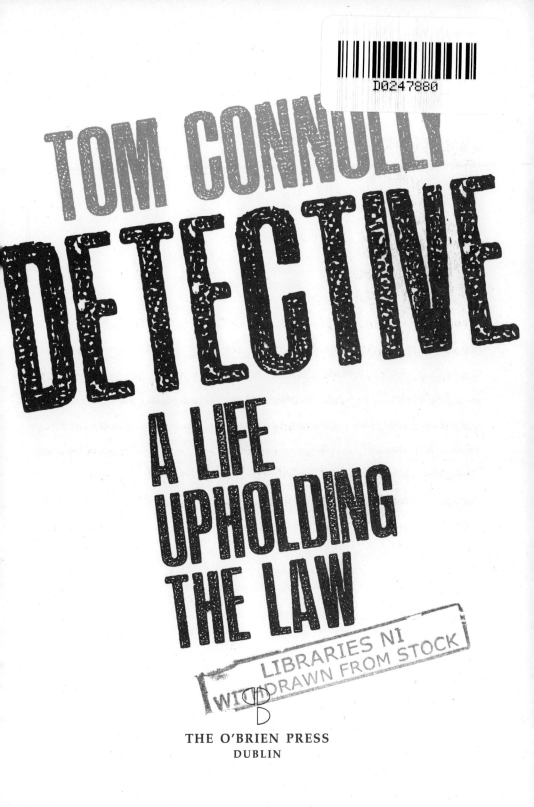

TOM CONNOLLY

DETECTIVE

A LIFE UPHOLDING THE LAW

THE O'BRIEN PRESS
DUBLIN

First published 2015 by
The O'Brien Press Ltd,
12 Terenure Road East, Rathgar,
Dublin 6, D06 HD27, Ireland.
Tel: +353 1 4923333; Fax: +353 1 4922777
E-mail: books@obrien.ie.
Website: www.obrien.ie

ISBN: 978-1-84717-772-8

1 3 5 7 8 6 4 2
15 17 18 16

Photo credits: p121 courtesy of the *Irish Examiner*,
p283 courtesy of the National Monuments Service.

Printed and bound by Scandbook AB, Sweden
The paper in this book is produced using pulp from managed forests

Dedication

I dedicate this book to the memory of my wife Maureen,

to our children Tom, Maria and David and to our grandchildren Ciara,

Michelle, Aoife and Niamh; David, Mark and Aidan; and Thomas and Ciaran.

Acknowledgements

I sincerely thank my ex-colleagues throughout the country for the assistance and support they gave me in compiling this account of various investigations I was involved in. A special word of thanks to the widows of John Morley and Henry Byrne, Frances and Anne, who shared with me their recollections and intense grief arising out of the murder of their husbands. To Derek Kelly, now the sole surviving occupant of the garda car of July 1980, for his recollection of events on the day and his trauma suffered as a result. To Jenny, my typist, for her efficient work and the professional manner in which she prepared all the material for presentation to the O'Brien Press. I want to express my heart-felt gratitude to my fond friend, Teresa, for the many hours she spent editing the book before presentation to the publishers, and for the great support and encouragement she gave me throughout the whole process. Thanks to two other people that discussed with me their recollections of a memorable day in their lives many years ago.

Thanks to all my family and friends who encouraged and supported me along the way, and to The O'Brien Press, especially Eoin, for his patience and his cooperation with me in dealing with some thorny problems.

Again, thank you everybody for your assistance and help, and I wish you and yours good health and happiness always.

CONTENTS

CHAPTER FOUR: SCENES OF CRIME EXAMINER

CHAPTER FIVE: DETECTIVE SERGEANT

CHAPTER SIX: INSPECTOR, UNIFORM SECTION

CHAPTER SEVEN: DETECTIVE SUPERINTENDENT

INTRODUCTION

In June of 1994, I retired from the Garda Síochána, with the rank of Detective Superintendent. At that time I was attached to the Investigation Section at Crime Branch in Garda Headquarters. I had served thirty-nine years, having joined in 1955. My father and grandfather were policemen, and my two sons and one of my daughters-in-law are serving Gardaí now, so you could say that police work is in my blood.

When I retired, I had no intention of writing my memoirs, or anything else for that matter. Colleagues, friends and acquaintances had urged me on occasion to do so, but I always gave them a very definitive 'no'. One reason was that I would have to write about myself, which indeed I still have reservations about. Eventually, and for various reasons, I changed my mind, and set about writing my recollections and reminiscences. It has been an interesting journey, looking back through old case notes, court records and media reports. Some of it brings back hard memories, of the faces of bereaved and distraught families, of dealing with depraved and unscrupulous criminals, and of long, tense hours at crime scenes, in interrogation sessions and in courtrooms.

This book, I suppose, is also a sort of tribute to the work of the many thousands of brave men and women who have worked with the Garda Síochána, dedicating their working lives to keeping the rest of us safe. I hope this book will give the reader a window into the work of the Gardaí – into how investigations are carried out, how evidence is gathered, how criminals are apprehended and how cases can be won or lost in Court.

Since my Garda career began in 1955, there have been many changes and advances in the technology used in policing, particularly in the field of forensics, with comparison microscopes and DNA profiling now providing concrete and indisputable evidence. However, the basics of crime investigation remain the same: diligent examination of the crime scene and interviewing of all persons in the immediate area of a crime, careful and thorough follow-up of every lead and thread of information, and impartial and cold assessment of known facts.

It has been an interesting and challenging career, full of ups and downs. I have met all manner of interesting, good, civic-spirited people, people who are willing to do their bit to keep society safe. I would recommend the work of a Garda to anyone seeking a 'life less ordinary'.

CHAPTER ONE

EARLY DAYS

MY FAMILY BACKGROUND

My grandfather, Patrick Connolly, was born in 1862 in Ballyfin, County Laois. He joined the RIC in 1882, and was stationed in Limerick. There he met my grandmother, Ellen Creagh, and they married in 1893. Ellen Creagh's father, John Creagh, was also in the RIC. A native of Cork, his first station was Waterford, and then he was transferred to Limerick. His father, John Creagh, was also in the RIC. As Ellen Creagh was from Limerick, when my grandfather married her he was transferred out of Limerick to Scariff in County Clare, where my father was born in February 1901.

My father's first job was as a telegram boy, delivering telegrams by bicycle. He then became a fireman on the railway, operating out of Limerick. He married my mother, Kate Minogue, from Ballintotty, Nenagh, in September 1921. I believe they met while my mother was working in a bar near the railway station in Nenagh.

My dad joined the Garda Síochána in November 1922. I can see by his application form that he was two years in the IRA, so that must have looked well at that time on application forms to join the Garda. His first station was Enniscorthy, County Wexford, in February 1923. He was a member of the first station party to arrive in Enniscorthy. After some time there, he became the Superintendent's clerk.

The first born in the family was Eileen; she died at a very young age, and was buried on her fifth birthday. She died in the married quarters attached to the Garda Station in Enniscorthy in April 1927. My dad was transferred from Enniscorthy to Charleville in June of 1934, and the family arrived there with six children: Kitty, Paddy, Molly, Nancy, Jimmy and John. I was the first member of the family to be born in County Cork. I was born in Newline, Charleville, in August 1934. We soon moved to Prospect Lodge, The Turrets, in Charleville.

My first real memory of Charleville is my brother John cutting off the top of my finger, the middle finger of my left hand, with a hatchet, when I was about five years old. I'm sure it wasn't intentional. Our house in Prospect Lodge was single storeyed, with a tiled floor, three bedrooms, a pantry and a dry toilet out in the garden.

My mother, God rest her, was a great provider, with a lot to do and a lot to look after. We had very little growing up really, but we survived and I think we were all the better for not having too much. My dad had a bicycle, and he was very careful with it, because it was essential for his work. We were always trying to have a go on it, but we'd have broken it up on him.

I remember some of my younger sisters being put into a tea chest in the kitchen. Once they were able to walk, to keep them out of trouble, they'd be put into the tea chest, where they could hop up and down and shout and scream. I think every one of us went through the tea chest in our time, and we all did the roaring and shouting too.

My brothers Paddy and Jimmy were great lads for hunting rabbits. They would catch them as well as hunt them, and they very often put food on the table for us. Paddy got a greyhound named Nora, from where I don't know, which was wonderful for catching rabbits. There was great affection for this greyhound, and we still talk about it.

Paddy used to set snares for rabbits, and one day I made a snare myself. I made it from a piece of netted wire, cut with a pliers to about a foot or so long, and straightened by pulling it back and forth over a railing. Down the field was a gateway and I could see a track under the bottom rail of the gate where I took it that rabbits would go through. I set my snare there, and I went back to it some time the next day. There was a rabbit in the snare, and it looked like he was just sitting down with his head resting on the bottom rail. I went over to him, and he was dead. I was terribly sorry that I had killed the rabbit, but anyway I took him out and brought him up to my mam, and of course she was delighted. To this day, any time I see a rabbit, I think of the rabbit that I killed. But I'm sure I ate part of it myself without any problem.

One of my best memories of Charleville is going up Love Lane, about a quarter of a mile from our house, to a pond where there were collies – little fish like pinkeens. We brought jam jars, and if we caught one with red under the mouth, that was a blood cock, a real prize catch.

A big, tall man on a donkey and cart used to call to us in Charleville. Tom Fisher was his name, and he would sell tripe, drisheens, black pudding and eggs. Mam would always get something from him. I always had the impression that he was so tall, when he sat in the front of the donkey and cart he had to hold up his legs to keep them off the ground.

I don't have much memory of going to the infants' school in Charleville, but I know that I did. I have little memory either of the CBS in Charleville, because I was only there a short time before my dad was transferred to Clonakilty. The world knows that De Valera went to school there, and the Archbishop in Melbourne, Archbishop Mannix. We used to go and get apples from a family down the Limerick Road who were relatives of Archbishop Mannix.

Prior to leaving Charleville, Kitty, Paddy and Molly had already flown the nest, to make their own way in the world. Kitty went to Tooting Bec hospital in London, Paddy joined the Army in Cork and Molly went to some place in England as well. While the family was in Charleville, its number increased by six. I was the first born in Charleville, and then came Sadie, Joan, Eileen, Margaret and Willie. Willie was born in October 1943, and was only four months old when we left Charleville. I remember loading all our bits and pieces, as much as they were, into the lorry on the morning of the transfer. My dad went with the lorry, and we went to the railway station with my mother and went by train into Cork and on to Clonakilty.

The railway station in Clonakilty was at the top of a hill called Barracks Hill. I remember coming down from the station and it was dark. My mam, with little Willie in her arms and eight children, walked down Barracks Hill, then down Strand Road, to our new home. We were reunited with Dad and our furniture. There was great excitement – we had a two-storey house, with an indoor toilet and many other extras compared with the home we had just left.

Having left a school that De Valera had attended, I was now in a school where Michael Collins had gone.

In May of 1944, a few months after we moved to Clonakilty, Willie died. He was only seven months old. I remember we were all gathered around him, and Mam told us that he was going to die. We were all in tears, and praying as best we could. He was buried in Darrara Cemetery, about four miles from Clonakilty, the following day. That left eleven of us in the family.

Most of us had never seen the sea, or even a boat, before we went to Clonakilty, so we had great excitement the first couple of weeks, exploring the town and surrounding area. When my dad was off duty and we were off school, we often used to walk down to Inchydoney, about three or four miles away. Inchydoney is a beautiful spot, now home to a beautiful hotel. It was a long walk, and on the return journey, we would be strung out over about a quarter of a mile along the road. Mam always seemed to be home first, and well advanced with the cooking by the time we arrived.

My dad was a great gardener, and always had every inch of the garden sown with fruit and vegetables. There wasn't sight of a weed anywhere. He always had a new plant of some sort ready to replace the one he would take out. My mam and dad were very strict on doing our lessons at night time. They made sure we did them, and did them right. We would have our books and pens and pencils ready for the morning. I can still hear someone say, who took my pencil? There'd be a bit of a squabble, looking for bits and pieces.

I got involved in sport at an early age in Clonakilty. My mam and dad would say, 'Well, it's going to keep you out of trouble anyway.' I remember the first match I went to play with Clonakilty. I was only a sub, and I was going to Ballinascarthy, four miles out the road. I knew my mother had my togs washed and nicely ironed, and they were inside in the sitting room in a press. So I put my hand in, pulled out this thing and put it in my pocket. I got my boots and joined the rest of the lads heading off to Ballinascarthy. Of course there was no dressing room or anything then; we togged out in the side of the ditch. So I took off the shoes and socks and the pants, and got this thing out of my pocket. What was it? It wasn't shorts; it was a pillowslip. It could have been worse I suppose, and anyway I wasn't playing. In fact I was relieved, when I saw the size of the opposition.

In my first real match, in 1949, I got a little medal for being a finalist. In 1952, I played with Cork minors, and we won the Munster Championship. We were beaten by Galway in the all-Ireland semi-final, and Galway were the eventual winners. In the same year in the final, I won the Cork senior football championship with Clonakilty. After a replay I was playing centre field.

In one match in Clonakilty, in the first few minutes I dislocated my left thumb. Somebody ran in from the sideline and gave it a pull and pushed it back into place, and I played on. 'Twas foolish, but I was okay after a couple of days. There were no scans or anything like that in those days.

On 8 May 1955, Clonakilty played St Nick's in the first round of the senior championships in Kinsale. The previous year, St Nick's had beaten Clonakilty in the final, so this was a real grudge match. I happened to be captain, and we won, 2-2 to 3 points. I thought, and so did others, that another county title was looming on the horizon for Clonakilty, having just beaten the previous year's champions. Macroom ended our dreams in the next match and we were gone. I received a beautiful black eye and a cut under the left eye during that match. It was the first of a few that I would get before the year was out.

The following morning, I picked up all my possessions and left Clonakilty on the train for Dublin. I shed a few tears on the way into Cork at leaving my mam and dad and the rest of my family behind, as I set out on my own in life.

TRAINING AT GARDA HEADQUARTERS, THE PHOENIX PARK

I arrived in Dublin, and made my way over to Crumlin to my aunt Jane Wheatly's house. She kept me there for the night, for which I was very grateful indeed, and I was also grateful to her son Joe who brought me on the back of his Lambretta scooter up to the depot gate the following morning. Here I joined two hundred and eighteen others joining the force that day. Joe's niece, Lorraine Wheatly, is now Chief Superintendent in charge of the Westmeath Division, based in Mullingar.

Recruits entering training had to have all the items on a list. I remember one item listed was a pair of black boots. The Connollys didn't have the price of a pair of new boots. I had been in the Forsa Cosanta Áitiúil (FCA Army reserve) for two years or so, and had been issued with a pair of brown boots. My da, who over the years was the resident cobbler for all, did a great job of changing the colour of the FCA boots to black. I wasn't surprised to notice that many of my fellow recruits were also former FCA members, with identical boots, which required plenty of black polish to keep the original brown colour from showing.

We were organised into classes of twenty-five, and soon integrated with each other. Our training lasted five months, and graduation day was 10 October 1955. During my time in training, I played with the Cork junior football team, and I picked up two more black eyes during the course of that championship. I was known to most of the fellows as the fellow with the black eyes.

As a Garda trainee, I was paid five pounds ten and a penny per week. Out of that we had to pay our mess bill, so we didn't have too much to

The fellow with the black eyes

spend out of the five pounds ten and a penny. My time off in the depot centred around the Garda sports ground, kicking a ball around with colleagues who were interested in football like myself.

I missed my passing-out parade, as I went to Birmingham on that date to play in the All-Ireland junior football final against Warwickshire. Cork County Board was very strict on Rule Twenty-seven, the rule that prevented members from playing or attending foreign games. They would certainly suspend anybody that breached that rule. However, on the Saturday, the day before the final, two teammates and I got lost, so to speak, and we attended a soccer match. I will always remember it. Birmingham were playing Sunderland, and it was a spectacular scene – such a huge crowd, a beautiful pitch, great excitement and wonderful skill on display on the field. I remember one of England's soccer greats, Len Shackleton, was playing. He was probably one of the reasons we went to the match. That was the first and only soccer match I ever attended.

We won our own match, and then I travelled back that night by boat, to arrive around six or seven o'clock in the morning. I made my way back up to the depot. All my colleagues had left, gone to their respective stations. I felt alone in the world, and missed all the lads, having missed my opportunity to say good-bye. Anyway I went straight to bed, as I was jaded tired, and the train to Kildare was leaving around seven o'clock that evening.

CHAPTER TWO

GARDA

KILDARE, MY FIRST STATION, 1955

When I arrived in Kildare Station, the electricity was off for some reason or another. There were candles lighting in the public office, one up on the counter, and another on the fireplace. I was brought upstairs to a huge big barn of a room where there were two other men staying. The Station was a hundred years old, and the floor boards were very worn. T he nails were sticking up above the timber, and fluff and dust was coming up between the boards. I got a single bed, with a mattress about two inches thick, and a few grey blankets. No wardrobe, just a chair, and a rack overhead for your possessions. No toilet upstairs, and no water, so we had to go down to the basement to use the toilet. There were two or three big windows in the room, facing out onto the street. No curtains, but there were big shutters. We didn't complain – we had a job and we got on with it.

My Sergeant in Kildare was John McGrath. A Tyrone man, he was strict, fair, fatherly and considerate. If you abided by him, as I think I did, he kept a man on the straight and narrow path at the beginning of his time of service. My Superintendent was Malcolm G. Crummey, an extremely nice man.

There were nine or ten Gardaí in Kildare at the time I arrived there. Great characters, and mostly elderly men, and I think the fact that my father was a Garda helped me greatly to associate with them. One of them, Pat Hennessey, was a great storyteller. One story he used to tell took place during the time the British were in the Curragh camp. The daughter of one of the officers was out late one night, and she was sexually assaulted by a man in uniform. She pulled a button off his uniform. The investigators were satisfied of the barracks the culprit came from. So all the barracks personnel were paraded the following morning in uniform. This button was from a particular place, an epaulette or sleeve, I don't know, and the officer went around with the button. He looked at every uniform, and each member was missing this same button. According to Pat, the officer stood out and said to them, 'A thing is done and well it's done and wise is he who did it, and let no man know who knows it not, or do again who did it.'

We'd have an inspection by the Super every month, and by the Chief every three months. And of course, the night before, young men like myself in the Station would be studying police duties in the public office beside the fire. But, as Pat Hennessy put it, 'It's too late to sharpen your sword, when the drum beats for battle.'

I wasn't too long in Kildare before I found a GAA field, and I started going up training with the local team. In 1957, I threw in my lot with Round Towers in Kildare, and I played with them up to 1960, when I was transferred to Naas and went back to playing with Clonakilty again. I won a county championship final with Towers, and we were beaten in another.

For the first couple of years of my service in Kildare, I was on ordinary duty, doing patrols and working in the public office. But after this time, I started to drive the patrol car – first came ZL 6755, an old Prefect, and then we graduated to FIK 11, a Consul. Pat Mulgrew was the other driver while I was there.

We were on night duty every second week, which was tough, because sleeping accommodation wasn't great. When we were on night duty, we'd go to a different station every night and pick up a member from that station. We'd patrol anywhere we wanted to go really, unless there was something in particular on. Of course there was no radio in that day – no radio in the car, no radio in the Station. In Kildare, if you saw the light on in the public office in the early hours of the morning, it was the signal that they wanted you for something. That was the communication system.

Coming up to Christmas every year, the Chief Superintendent would send out a circular. It was much the same every year, and the heading was 'Anticipated Outrages over the Christmas Period'. The outrages outlined were the theft of Christmas trees from the forest out around Carbury, and the theft of turkeys from farmers in the locality, who would be rearing maybe twenty or thirty for sale at Christmas. The Chief, Finionn O'Driscoll, was very regimental and formal on inspections. He had a thing about a particular criminal – John Keenan was his name, a Monaghan man. Keenan used to specialise in breaking into priests' houses and churches, and he used to travel on a bicycle. At some time or another, the Chief had circulated the number of John Keenan's bicycle – the number was on the frame under the saddle. Some Guard took it some time and sent it in to the Chief, and he circulated it so that every Guard should know the number of this bicycle. At inspection, he would ask the number, and I remember one day he issued an instruction that when Gardaí were out on duty at night time, to make sure they called by the churches and priests' houses, and look all around the area for any sign of John Keenan's bicycle.

One day I was out in Suncroft, a little village about three or four miles from Kildare, with two pubs, a church and a shop. I went into the pub for something, and there was a man sitting at the counter. Who was it? John Keenan! I knew him from his photograph. I brought him out anyway and chatted to him, got his bicycle and put it into the boot and brought him into Kildare Station. I talked to him for an hour or so. He didn't admit to any crime, but at least I was showing that I knew him.

MY BLACK BOOTS

I mentioned earlier about these black boots I got, FCA boots that I brought to the Depot. Having left the Depot, the boots were well worn in the soles, so I got protectors. Now people may not know what protectors are, but in those days they were quite common. They were like studs, in various different shapes – half-moon shapes, triangles and that sort of thing. I got two cards of them and I hammered them into the worn soles of my boots in a very irregular manner. So then I was right for the road again. I put them on when I was going on duty, and went out in the street. I wasn't gone fifty yards when I said, I can't wear these. I was like a plough horse; I would be heard all over the town. So I went back and changed, and didn't wear them any more.

A week or so afterwards, I went down the town and I saw this man with a canvas bag on his back and he looking up at the signpost. I took it that he was a travelling man, and I found out he was. I spoke to him and brought him up to the Station, because I wanted to see what was in the bag. He told me his name, and that he was from Balbriggan in Dublin. I had a look in the bag, and it contained the usual things a travelling man would have. He had a razor, a bit of a towel, soap and a whiskey bottle with an inch or two of whiskey in the bottom of it.

We chatted away, and when he was going he said to me, 'Garda, would you have any pair of shoes you'd give me?' He said, 'Look at these, they're in very bad repair.' So here was an opportunity for me to get rid of those boots. He was delighted with them, put them on and off he went.

Next morning, a shopkeeper reported that his shop had been broken into, on Station Road. I went down with Sergeant McGrath. The culprit had clearly come in through the back yard, broken a window and got into the shop and stolen a few bits and pieces. It had been raining, so the clay was soft, and out in the back yard, leading right up to the window, I saw perfect impressions of the soles of my old boots. I knew by the way I had hammered in the protectors, that they were definitely my boots. So the crime was solved. John McGrath circulated his description, and he was arrested that night or the following night, in the Ivy Hostel in Dublin. I thought I was going to be in trouble, but it didn't turn out that way. So that was my boots from the FCA and what happened to them.

NEIGHBOURLY DISPUTES

When I was about two or three months in Kildare, I was on duty one night with Garda Michael McNamara, affectionately known as Mick Mc. A lady down in Assumpta Villas, an estate in Kildare, had complained about the conduct of another lady, her neighbour. So we went down to the house. Mick did all the talking of course, as I was just the little boy.

The lady outlined the way the lady next door was behaving. The lady was putting her washing up on her hedge, and there were a number of other complaints, all silly things really. Mick listened for a while, and then he said to her, 'Do you know what you'll do now? When you are up town tomorrow, tip into your solicitor and you get him to summons the bitch, and that will keep her quiet.'

So we left, and called in to this lady who was supposed to be causing the problems, and she outlined the troubles she was having with her neighbour. The hedge was hers, and she was entitled to put her clothes on it, and so on. We listened for a while, and then Mick Mc told her exactly what he had told her neighbour – go down to the solicitor and get him to summons the bitch. Then we left, mission accomplished. I certainly didn't hear any more about it, and I doubt Mick McNamara did either. It was all a learning process for me.

AFTER-HOURS TIPPLES IN KILDARE

In Kildare at that time, there was very little crime really. Maybe at weekends, you would have a few soldiers that would be a bit late going home to the Curragh Camp. They might see a bicycle on the side of the street, and be tempted to take it, as they could then get back to the Curragh in ten or fifteen minutes. Occasionally you would have a lad coming into the Station saying, 'My bicycle is gone Garda,' and of course we would know where to find it. It would be recovered up in the Curragh Camp the following morning.

I think I had a bit of a reputation for raiding pubs, but I don't think for prosecuting really. When you're out on duty and you know there is unlawful trading going on inside a pub, it's no harm to go in and show yourself.

Now there were two pubs in Kildare at that time by the name of Nolan's – one was up at the top of the square, and was known as Top Nolan's, and the other was lower down on the Dublin Road, and that was Bottom Nolan's, which has since changed ownership several times. So one night, I went into Bottom Nolan's, and there was a crowd inside, after hours, having a few drinks. I saw a man go out the back door into the yard, and I knew him well because he played on Round Towers football team with me. I walked off out the back door, down the yard and garden, and I could hear noise down the end, in a garden shed. The door of the shed was pushed closed but the sliding bolt was open. Knowing who was in there, I closed the bolt and walked away. Back in the bar, of course, the customers had now left.

Three or four days later, I met my friend that had been locked in the shed, down training at the GAA pitch. I said to him, 'I thought you were locked up!' I'm not going to quote his reply, but he took it well. He said it was better than having his name appear in the local paper, for being on a licensed premises after hours.

THE CHILD DROWNED IN A GULLY, 1957

I was sent to the border, to Dundalk, at the very end of 1957. I was there about three months, on night duty at a checkpoint out near Hackballs Cross. I wasn't too long there, when a very sad incident occurred. There was a report of a child after falling into a gulley, somewhere north of Dundalk. It had been raining very heavily for a number of days, and there were floods all around the place. Two of us went out anyway, and I remember there was a field and half of it was flooded. Down in one corner, where the water was about three or four feet deep, it was flowing into a gully and under the road. The child, who I think was around five or six years old, had been up on the ditch over the gully, looking in at the water flowing, and had fallen in. The force of the water brought the child in under the road, where it was trapped. The water was only about an inch or two below the top of the gully.

When we arrived, the Fire Brigade was already there, frantically doing what they could. They were pumping water from one side over to the other, trying to lower the level, and meanwhile another crew was digging a hole in the road, trying to get down to the gulley underneath. We were there for about an hour, helpless. There was nothing we could do. I do not remember the body being found – perhaps we had left at that stage. It was terrible to be there, unable to do anything. I think before we even arrived, the child had left this life.

MAUREEN MCDONAGH, THE DANCE, 1958

In late 1958, I went to a dance in Ballyshannon, a little place between Kilcullen and Athy on the main road. The parish hall had a dance on, and I remember going with the crowd of lads from Kildare in a baby Ford. At the dance, I met a beautiful, loving, wonderful and saintly lady, Maureen McDonagh from Suncroft, who was later to become my wife. We got engaged on 15 August 1959, and we got married on 19 September 1961. Maureen is no longer with me.

DONEGAL ELECTIONS

From Dundalk, I went back to the Depot to do my refresher course. While I was there, there was an election, a general election I think. In those days, you would have a Garda in every polling booth in the country. Every Garda that was available was sent out, and the group on the refresher course were sent off to different parts of the country.

We went out the day before the election, up to Donegal with two or three others, including a Sergeant Moloney, the Sergeant in charge of the Garda Band at the time. We took off by train, up through the north, up to Letterkenny. We scattered there, and Sergeant Moloney and myself were heading for Churchill in Donegal.

Somewhere on the route we had to travel by narrow-gauge railway. There were only about two small carriages and about half a dozen passengers, and along the route one of the carriages become derailed. The train naturally stopped, and we got out. The driver and the guard were well prepared for a situation like this – it had clearly happened before. We offered to help, but they said, no, we will manage. They had a few crowbars, and were able to get it back on the line again. There we were, derailed, then back on the rails again and off we go.

We got a bus somewhere and arrived late that night in Churchill. We went to the Station, and there was somebody there to meet us. They had arranged for Sergeant Moloney and myself to stay in the local pub, the only accommodation available. Not alone was that the only accommodation available, but there was only one bed, a double bed, so I had to sleep with Sergeant Moloney for two nights.

I was told where to go the following morning, and was given a bicycle, perhaps one that was found or had no owner. I was rushing to be there on time, but I needn't have worried, because when I arrived, there was no one else there. It was a polling booth in a house at a crossroads, out in the middle of nowhere. Eventually people started to arrive, and I would say if there were one hundred in the whole day, it's as many as were there.

That evening I had to wait until the ballot box was collected. Then I was alone, and I had to make my way back in the dark to Churchill. I would say that the distance was around three or four miles of country roads. I started off anyway, and sure I hadn't a clue; I would come to a crossroads and didn't know whether to turn right, left, or whatever. I went to a dwelling house that had a light on beside the road, and I told them my situation. Here I was, a new Garda in uniform, a complete stranger to them, lost with no light. They gave me a bicycle lamp, and told me exactly how to get back to Churchill. They asked me to leave the bicycle lamp in the Garda Station, and they would collect it whenever they were in there. With the luck of God, I made it back to Churchill Station.

TRANSFERRED TO NAAS, 1960

I was transferred from Kildare to Naas on 16 March 1960. I was told about the transfer about a week or so before. At first I did not want to go, I wanted to stay in Kildare, but John McGrath had a good chat with me, and he advised me it was the best thing for me to do. I needed to think of my career, and not about my football. In Kildare County at the time, a GAA player had to play with the team in the parish in which he lived, and playing with the Towers was one of the reasons I wanted to stay in Kildare. In the end, I took John McGrath's advice – not that I agreed to go, but I had little say really. The Towers football team wasn't really sufficient grounds for an appeal.

My first day on duty in Naas was Saint Patrick's Day 1960. I was driving the patrol car between Naas and the Dublin border, up and down and up and down, supervising traffic going to the Railway Cup finals. I was saying to myself, if I was in Kildare, I would be off today and going to the match myself. I was sorry to have left all my friends and teammates in Kildare. I still go to Kildare regularly, and play golf with some of my ex-teammates. But I am delighted I went to Naas. I don't know what would have happened to me if I had stayed in Kildare, and no one else does either, but I am happy the way things turned out.

NAAS GARDA STATION

Naas Garda Station in 1960 was situated just beside Naas Courthouse, on the main street. A new Garda Station has been built since then, and the old Station is now the Naas Court Hotel. In 1960, there were about forty to forty-five Gardaí there, of all ranks. There was a mess in the Station, and the cook was a lovely elderly lady from the town, named Elizabeth Farrell. She was a mother to all of us who dined at the mess. She was a great character, good humoured and very fluent and well versed in all Garda terminology. There was limited sleeping accommodation in the Station, and I was one of the members who availed of it.

Duty for me at that time involved driving the patrol car, covering the Clane, Celbridge, Maynooth, Kill, Blessington and Naas area, and later Rathcoole. Night duty was every second week, and it consisted of investigating traffic accidents, stolen cars and thefts, as well as traffic supervision. At that time, of course, the main road from Cork to Dublin went through Naas. The main road from Waterford, Kilkenny and Carlow also came into Naas town, at Murtagh's Corner.

THE CURRAGH CAMP ROBBERY

I was on duty one night with Bill O'Connell from Kill. Lord have mercy on him, Bill is long gone now. Bill, as was sort of normal for him, got tired and he said, 'I'll knock off, I'll go home, you know where I live.' So Bill went off and I continued driving around, you could say aimlessly, but I was out and about with my eyes open.

About three o'clock in the morning, I was going towards Newbridge, and at a place called Jigginstown on the main road I met a cyclist coming against me. He had no light, so I stopped him, and I knew by him it was more than the light was a problem. We chatted for a while, and he told me he was after taking the bicycle in the Curragh Camp. He was an ex-member of the Defence Forces, and knew the run of the Camp very well. He told me that he went to the Curragh on the late bus, and he went to one or two billets in the Curragh. When the lads were asleep he went in to their lockers, and he had about four wallets belonging to Army chaps. I brought him back to the Station, and he was dealt with.

Around ten o'clock the following morning, I was asleep upstairs in the bed and I got a little shake on the shoulder, and who was it? Only Inspector Eamon Doherty, affectionately known as the Doc, who was Inspector in Naas at the time and later the Commissioner. He was delighted that we had got a prisoner, and wanted to know all about this soldier downstairs in the cell – how he was got and everything else. Of course, being the Doc, he said, 'Bill O'Connell was out on duty with you last night; where was he when you got this prisoner?' I said he wasn't feeling well, and I dropped him home, so that was the end of that. The Doc knew very well I'm sure; he knew Bill as well as I did.

MY FIRST ENCOUNTER WITH JAMES ENNIS, 1960

In or about the first week of December 1960, I was on duty in uniform on the Dublin Road in Naas. I saw a man on a pedal bicycle, sitting stopped and with his leg up on the footpath. He had a billycan hanging off the handlebars, and a beet knife, or a beet crowner as it is often called, strapped onto the carrier of the bicycle. I took him to be a traveller, on account of the billycan and his general appearance really. So I started to talk with him, and we had a long conversation. He told me his name was James Ennis, and he was from Kilmegue, Robertstown, County Kildare, about five or six miles from Naas. He was a farm labourer, and travelled around the country seeking work. He mentioned Cork – Watergrass Hill amongst other places. He was friendly and talkative, and we parted on good, friendly terms. I took his name and his description in my notebook.

Some days later, at about two-thirty or three o'clock in the afternoon of 12 December, Joseph Reynolds returned to his home in Clane, County Kildare. Again that would be about five or six miles from Naas. Mr Reynolds, a Health Inspector with Kildare County Council, had left home at about nine o'clock that morning and gone to work. On returning home, he found the whole place in confusion, and blood spattered around parts of the house. He went into the spare bedroom, and found his wife Mary, lying face downwards on a bed. He turned her over and her right eye was completely closed. She was bleeding from a gash on her head, and there was a stab wound under her nose. He immediately sought medical assistance, and called the Gardaí. Mary Reynolds, semi-conscious, was conveyed to St Laurence's Hospital in Dublin. She remained an inpatient there until 16 January.

Sergeant Thomas Tobin was on duty when a man called to the Garda Station at Carrigtwohill, County Cork, at about half-past six on this same night, 12 December 1960. The man gave his name as James Ennis, and said he wanted to make a report of a happening up the country that day. The Sergeant noted that he had blood on his shirt and overcoat. When asked about the blood, Ennis said he got it from the woman he had assaulted up in Clane that morning.

He told the Sergeant that he had left Kildangan at about seven o'clock, and had cycled to Clane, roughly twenty-seven miles away, arriving about half-past eleven. He had gone into a bungalow, and asked a woman there to make tea for him. He followed her into the kitchen and demanded money, but she said she didn't have any. He said he drew out the beet crowner from his belt, and again demanded money. She repeated that she did not have any, and he hit her on the head with the beet crowner. She ran out the door shouting for help, and he pulled her back into the kitchen. She ran into a bedroom and she threw a handbag at him and said, 'The money is in that.' Then she raced out of the bedroom and into the kitchen. Ennis followed her, and prevented her from going out the front door. He said he held the beet crowner in his hand all this time, but that the blade fell off as he stopped her from running out.

She fell on the floor and Ennis saw a small hatchet. He took it in his hand, and struck her a few times in the head with it. She started to moan, and he went into the bedroom, got the handbag and took five one-pound notes out of it. Then he searched the rest of the house, but got nothing else except a watch, which he handed over to the Sergeant.

Before Ennis arrived, Sergeant Tobin had already heard on the news about a serious assault on a woman in Naas that day. So he immediately contacted the Gardaí at Naas, and told them what Ennis had related to him.

At the house in Clane, the investigation had been initiated. The scene was preserved; a technical examination was being arranged; house-to-house enquiries were being made; and all the usual things that are done after a serious incident like that.

On receipt of the information from Sergeant Tobin, Inspector Ned Doherty, later Commissioner, Detective Sergeant Tom Spain and I immediately got organised. We left Naas at about half-past eight, and arrived at Carrigtwohill Garda Station at about twelve midnight.

James Ennis knew me straight away, as it was only about a week since we had met. He spoke freely about what he had done in Clane that morning. After leaving the house in Clane, he had cycled to Young's Cross, about halfway between Celbridge and Lucan. He got a bus to Dublin, and then a train to Cork. From Cork, he got on a bus towards Midleton, but got off in Carrigtwohill to give himself up.

We arrived back in Naas with our prisoner at about half-past five that morning. Later that morning, the clothing and footwear that Ennis was wearing were taken from him for examination. I was living in the Station at the time, and I gave him a pair of black shoes to replace the footwear taken from him.

Ennis appeared before a sitting of Naas District Court on 15 December 1960, charged with the attempted murder of Mary Reynolds. He was remanded in custody and later appeared at a number of sittings of the District Court, as depositions were taken in the case before Mr Justice McGrath. Dr Cleary of

Saint Laurence's Hospital in Dublin described Mrs Reynolds's condition on the day of the attack. He said she was in a state of mild shock; she had loss of memory of the events leading up to and at the time of her assault, and she didn't know where she was. He said the lacerations on her head, hands and face would be consistent with having been struck by the beet crowner and hatchet that were produced in the Court. He did not think he had ever seen as badly a lacerated head in his career. He said it was possible she had been struck on the head up to fifty times.

Inspector Doherty informed the Court that Ennis had asked him to tell the injured woman's husband that he was very sorry for all the trouble he had caused. Taking of depositions concluded on 13 February 1961. The Justice, having heard eighteen prosecution witnesses, said he was satisfied that a *prima facie* case had been established against Ennis. He asked Ennis if he had anything to say, and Ennis told the Court that he did not wish to say anything. He was remanded in custody.

James Ennis appeared for trial before the Central Criminal Court in Dublin, on 24 April 1961. On the charge of the attempted murder of Mary Reynolds, he pleaded not guilty. On the charges of robbery with violence, wounding with intent to cause grievous bodily harm, and larceny of a watch, he pleaded guilty. Counsel for the prosecution announced that they would enter a *nolle prosequi* on the attempted murder charge. The prosecuting senior counsel, Mr Darcy, outlined the actions of Ennis in the commission of the assault on Mrs Reynolds. Describing the injuries she sustained, he told the Court that although Mrs Reynolds had recovered physically from the assault, mentally she had not recovered. He said this was as bad a case of robbery with violence as one could contemplate.

Inspector Doherty was called and outlined Ennis's three previous convictions. The surgeon once again outlined the injuries Mrs Reynolds had received.

He also described her condition a week after being discharged from hospital, and said that, due to a brain injury she received, she was still childlike. His view was that she would continue to have residual brain damage.

James Ennis told the Court he had no intention of killing Mrs Reynolds. He said if he had had that intention, he could have killed her with one or two strokes. Having heard the evidence, Mr Justice Kenny, on the charge of wounding with intent to cause grievous bodily harm, sentenced the accused to three years' penal servitude. On the charge of larceny of the watch, he sentenced him to one year. On the charge of robbery with violence, the sentence was four years, the sentences to run concurrently.

In his comments after sentence, the Judge said, 'This woman was doing an act of kindness, and you then attacked her in this savage manner. In your favour it has to be said that you pleaded guilty and you called to the Gardaí in Cork, and admitted your guilt shortly afterwards.' The Judge told Ennis that he could have got life imprisonment on the robbery charge, and only the fact that he had expressed his regret and pleaded guilty had led to the lighter sentence of four years.

As Ennis was led away to commence his sentence, little did I think that the pair of black shoes I gave him at Naas Garda Station, in December 1960, would literally walk Ennis and me back into Court later, he to face an even more serious charge than he had just been sentenced for.

PUT IN MY PLACE IN THE WITNESS BOX

In about 1960 or 1961, when I was in Naas, I got a good roasting in the witness box one day from the presiding Judge. It was in relation to a man who had overturned his car at a bend somewhere near Naas. He was arrested and brought to the Station, where I saw him with a number of other members. At that time there was no breathalyser or blood test; we only had our observations.

The man was charged in the District Court with driving while drunk. The other members gave evidence that in their opinion, he was unfit to drive, as a result of the consumption of alcohol. I gave evidence that I could not say that his condition was as a result of the consumption of alcohol, as he had suffered a fairly serious head injury in the accident. I conceded, of course, that there was a smell of drink from him, but I couldn't in all conscience swear that alcohol had caused inability to drive.

He was convicted, and he appealed to the Circuit Court. At the appeal, we all gave our evidence, the same as we had in the District Court. But the Judge gave me a rough time. I stated that I couldn't say definitively that the man's condition had resulted from the consumption of alcohol. His head injury may have been the cause. Anyway, the driver lost his appeal.

I considered that I was being strictly impartial, and I have always endeavoured to be so when giving evidence in Court. I gave my honest opinion, and that's that. That Judge was not impressed by me, however.

CHAPTER THREE

TRAINEE DETECTIVE

NEWBRIDGE GARDA STATION, 1961

In April 1961, I was transferred to Newbridge as a trainee Detective. I was to replace a Detective Garda Brian Brennan, who was promoted to Sergeant and transferred to Baltinglass. I was back to my old district again, covering Kildare, Monasterevin, Rathangan, Carbury, Robertstown, Kilcullen and Newbridge. There was no car in Newbridge – the only patrol car was in Kildare, available to each sub-district station when required. I always used my bicycle for duties in the Newbridge area. But if I had to travel further, I would get the patrol car if it was available.

The Curragh Military Camp and the Curragh Racecourse are in the Newbridge area, and a good deal of my time was now spent up and down to the Military Camp. I would liaise with the Military Police on enquiries there, mostly in relation to larceny, and an odd house breaking.

THE CURRAGH

The main road from Cork to Dublin passes through the Curragh plains, with the Curragh Racecourse on one side and the Military Camp on the other. Thousands of sheep graze on the Curragh plains, and there was no fence or barrier to keep the sheep off the main road. They used to wander into the road, disrupting traffic and causing many fatalities among the sheep. You would often see one, two or three sheep lying dead on the road, having been struck by a vehicle.

The County Council had decided to erect a concrete fence the whole way across the Curragh plains, on both sides of the road, to keep the sheep off the road. The sheep owners protested, and on occasions at nighttime the fencing would be broken down. This, of course, brought the Gardaí into the picture, and special night patrols were performed to prevent and identify the culprits. The new Detective naturally got the job of investigating these incidents, and I must say that he didn't make any great headway in the matter. Anyway, this dispute settled down after a year or so, and the fence still remains.

MY FIRST ENCOUNTER WITH ATTEMPTED SUICIDE

During my time in Newbridge, I charged one particular youth with house breaking and larceny. He was charged in the District Court, convicted and sentenced to a term of imprisonment. He appealed to the Circuit Court, and the appeal was refused. The youth went home after the Court appearance. He wasn't in custody, but a committal warrant was issued by the County Registrar, to come into force a week or so later.

In due course, the warrant came to me for execution, so one morning I went to the youth's home and met him and his mother. She was naturally upset at her son going to prison. He asked me if he could shave. I knew to look at him that he didn't need a shave, and it immediately crossed my mind that perhaps he had in mind doing some harm to himself. I said, 'No, you're all right.' I took him into custody, and walked him to the Garda Station, half a mile away. In the public office, I handed him over to the Station orderly, informing him that the youth was a prisoner, and would be going to Saint Patrick's institution later that day.

As it was near lunchtime, I left the Station and returned about an hour later. I went to the cell to see the youth, and I found that he was unconscious. He had his tie pulled very, very tightly around his neck, and his face was blueish in colour. I called the Station orderly, and we immediately loosened the tie, with great difficulty. We called the doctor and an ambulance, and I rang Superintendent Crummey in Kildare. The doctor arrived quickly, and he didn't give us great hope of the youth's survival. He pricked the youth with a pin, and there was absolutely no reaction. The ambulance team put an oxygen mask on the youth, and rushed him to Naas hospital. There was great news that evening – the youth had recovered consciousness in the hospital. He was released that night and brought to Saint Patrick's institution.

The incident was a shock for me, and a lesson learned in relation to searching prisoners, and removing items that they could harm themselves with. I had been sort of warned when he had wanted to shave, and you have to learn to pick up on these signals.

A HAPPILY MARRIED MAN, 1961

Maureen and I had agreed to get married in September 1961. On arrival in Newbridge in April, I immediately set about looking for a house. I eventually found a two-storeyed house on Eyre Street in the town. For months prior to

September, I busied myself, painting, papering and cleaning. Maureen would come from Dublin some afternoons on the bus, roll up her sleeves and do her part, then return to Dublin on the late bus, and by September, we were well pleased with ourselves and the work we had done.

We got married on 19 September in Suncroft, with a reception in Lawlor's Hotel in Naas, and the first stop on our honeymoon was Wicklow town. We spent several days in Donegal, Sligo, Mayo, Galway and Ennis, and wound up in Clonakilty on a Saturday evening. I had stopped at a few football fields around the country, togged out and run a few circuits of them, in preparation for the big event on the Sunday – the Cork County Senior Football Championship Final, Clonakilty verses Avondhu. I was playing centre half back, number six, for Clon.

It was high-emotion stuff. We missed two penalties, in the fourth minute of the game and in the dying minutes of the game. In the end, it was another shattered dream for the Clon team and supporters, as we were beaten 1-7 to 1-5. When playing with Towers, I played on the Kildare Senior inter-county team for a few years, and on return to Clon, I played on the Cork senior team for some time.

The honeymoon continued for five or six more days, and all further information in relation to it will remain with me. Back to our house in Eyre Street then, to get on with our lives. We had as our immediate neighbours Tony and Anna McCarthy, and three children I believe at the time. A Captain in the Defence Forces stationed in the Curragh, I was to meet Tony years later, many miles from home, when he was the Commanding Officer of the 52nd Irish Battalion, serving in the Lebanon.

Maureen was very fond of animals, particularly dogs. I got her a small terrier pup after a few months in Newbridge. She really loved it, and we brought it with us on our walks. One evening Maureen came with me to Devoy Military

Barracks in Naas, where I was playing in a seven-a-side football game with the Garda team. We brought the dog and during the course of the game, the dog got poisoned and died. Maureen was heartbroken, as was I, but more for Maureen than for the loss of the dog.

NAAS GARDA STATION, DETECTIVE BRANCH

In August of 1962, Pat Marron, a member of the Detective Branch in Naas, retired. I transferred from Newbridge to Naas to fill the vacancy. I became very interested in crime investigation, and in Naas, twenty miles from Dublin, you had plenty of practice. The most prevalent crimes in the area at that time were houses out in the country being broken into, particularly at three, four or five o'clock in the afternoon. Houses would be temporarily unoccupied, with people at work, gone shopping, bringing kids to or from school, or whatever.

Now, how does a criminal know when a house is unoccupied? There are many, many ways, such as the post heaping up in the porch, or milk uncollected outside the door. I learned of a new one, when one day a house was broken into around the outskirts of Naas, and property stolen. A neighbour saw a car parked a short distance from the house, and was able to provide the make and colour and a portion of the registration number, which turned out to be an English number. I investigated the case, and circulated this information throughout the country. A week or so later, I got a telephone call from the Gardaí in Nenagh. They had arrested an English man down there, who was caught after breaking into a house, and was in possession of a motor vehicle matching the description I had circulated. I travelled down to Nenagh and interviewed him.

As he had been caught red-handed in Nenagh, there was no difficulty in getting him to admit the crime in Naas. He had some property out of the Naas crime in the car. I asked him how he knew there was no one in the house in Naas that he had broken into. 'Well,' he says, 'I know my job, and you know yours.' He told me he had stopped where there were a number of houses together, and he watched them for a while. There was a line of washing out in the garden of one of the houses. It started to rain, and no one came out of the house to take in the washing. He took it that there was no one in the house. Criminals have many ways of sizing up situations and targeting houses for attack and plunder, there's no doubt about it.

ROBERT HOWARD, 1962

Robert Howard was born in April 1944, in Wolfhill, County Laois. He is now serving a life sentence in Frankland prison in Durham in England, for the murder and rape of a fourteen-year-old girl, Hannah Williams from Kent. Miss Williams disappeared on 21 April 2001, from Deptford in southeast London. She had gone shopping, to a market just around the corner from her home, and her mother, Bernadette Williams, became worried when she didn't return at the normal time, and didn't answer her mobile phone. When she hadn't returned home by five o'clock the following morning, she reported her missing to the police.

In 2001, Robert Howard was living with a woman named Mary Scollom, in her house in North Fleet in Kent. Scollom had formerly been in a relationship with the father of Hannah Williams, and had remained friendly with the girl when the relationship ended. Howard had met Hannah through Scollom, and had shown great interest in her.

Almost a year after Hannah Williams disappeared, a workman was using a digger to clear dense undergrowth on land near the Blue Lake at North Fleet, as part of the Channel Tunnel development. He found the badly decomposed body of a young girl, wrapped in a blue tarpaulin, with rope wrapped around her neck. The body was identified as that of Hannah Williams. Howard was arrested in March 2002, and eventually charged with murder. He was found guilty, and sentenced to life imprisonment. Reporting of that trial was restricted somewhat, because Howard was at this time also charged with the murder of Arlene Arkinson in Northern Ireland.

Arlene, Robert Howard, Howard's girlfriend Pat Quinn, and Pat Quinn's daughter Donna Quinn went to a disco at the Palace Hotel in Bundoran, on 3 August 1994. Arlene disappeared that night, and there has been no trace of her ever since. Howard was driving the car that night, and after the night out in Bundoran, Howard dropped off the others before driving away with Arlene. He claimed that he dropped her off in Castlederg, and that he had seen her in a car in town the next day.

After a prolonged investigation, Robert Howard was arrested and charged with the murder of Arlene Arkinson. The trial was held in Belfast Crown Court in the summer of 2005, eleven years after her disappearance. He was acquitted.

Now, why am I writing about this man? Because Robert Howard and I met, on the Rathasker Road in Naas, some time in 1962. Then aged eighteen, he had already made quite a name for himself in the field of crime. When I say crime, I mean the commission of crime.

A house had been broken into on Rathasker Road. I went there and met a strange young man, walking into Naas. I questioned him, and we wound up in Naas Garda Station. After questioning, he admitted that he had broken into the house. He had some property stolen from the house in his possession. He subsequently appeared at Naas Court, and was convicted and sentenced to eight months' imprisonment. Other charges, from stations outside of Naas, were also brought against him, and he admitted those.

Howard had started committing crimes at the age of thirteen. He has a long list of convictions in Ireland, and some in England. The Irish convictions included housebreaking, larceny, malicious damage and sexual assaults, all at different stages of his career, because he was a career criminal really. He appeared in courthouses in Portlaoise, Urlingford, Abbeyleix and Athy, which were not too far from his own home, and also in Roscrea, London, Cork, Sligo, Durrow, Naas, Monaghan, Omagh and finally Maidstone, where he got the sentence of life imprisonment.

The sexual cases that he was convicted of include attempted intercourse with a girl who was six years of age, in London; attempted rape in Durham, for which he got six years; rape of a woman in Cork, after breaking into her house, ten years; and unlawful carnal knowledge of a girl under the age of seventeen, in Northern Ireland, one year. Finally, murder and rape, life imprisonment. A lot has been written about Robert Howard, about what he did and didn't do. It is reasonable to assume that he hasn't been charged with every crime he has committed.

Around 1974, Howard was examined by a psychiatrist, when he was charged in Cork with rape and robbery. Describing Howard as a dangerous psychopath, the psychiatrist stated that he was surprised by Howard's extremely courteous demeanour. He said that he was a very refined man, but having seen his record he knew he was also very dangerous. I sensed and feared that he had already killed someone. I knew his violence was likely to get far worse, especially towards women. I believe him to be an explosive psychopath. I doubt that Robert Howard will ever again gain his freedom. I believe it would be in the best interests of the public if he never does.

MURDER OF GEORGE APPLEBY,
WATERGRASSHILL, 1964

I mentioned earlier that James Ennis was sentenced to four years penal servitude for robbery with violence, assault and theft, perpetrated on Mary Reynolds of Clane, in December 1960. I mentioned a pair of shoes that I gave him when his own were removed for forensic examination, and that they would appear again.

On 22 April 1964, at Portlaoise Prison, having served his sentence, James Ennis was about to be discharged from custody. Prior to leaving the prison, he was handed some items by the prison authorities – an overcoat, a peaked cap, a two-piece suit, a pair of black shoes and a suitcase. He was also given a travel voucher, allowing him to travel by train from Portlaoise to Cork. On 23 April, he went to Portlaoise Railway Station, produced the travel voucher to the booking clerk, and was given a single-journey ticket to Cork. He travelled on the 10.45am Dublin–Cork train, arriving in Cork at 2.35pm, and booked into a lodging house at Parnell Place. He did not occupy the bedroom in the boarding house on the night of 24 April. He knocked at the door the following morning, Saturday, at 6.45am, went in and looked for his breakfast. That evening, he went to another lodging house, on Glanmire Road in Cork. He left there on Sunday morning, 26 April, and travelled to Dublin by train.

On arrival in Dublin, Ennis purchased the Sunday newspaper, and read an account of a murder that had occurred on the night of 24 April, in Water-grasshill in County Cork. George Appleby, a fifty-one-year-old farmer, had been clubbed to death in his bed, with his wife beside him. His wife was also seriously assaulted, but survived. The report stated that the Gardaí were anxious to interview a man named James Ennis, who had previously worked for Mr Appleby. Having read the report, Ennis went to Store Street Garda Station and presented himself to the Gardaí there.

George Appleby, the deceased, had lived in a substantial house with his wife, their two sons Eric and Ivor, and a workman named Thomas Gailey. The Applebys were substantial farmers. On the night of 24 April, Eric Appleby and Thomas Gailey went to a dance in Upton, roughly fifteen miles away, and did not return until 5am. Ivor and his parents remained at home; they watched television until 10.30pm, then retired for the night.

On his return, Eric, twenty-six years of age, went straight to bed. He got up at 8.30am, went to his parents' room, and found his father dead in bed and his mother lying on the floor. She was badly injured, and mumbled a few words. The Gardaí and medical assistance were called immediately.

The usual scene preservation, examination and investigation commenced straight away. There was a roll-top desk in the drawing room in the house, in which Mr Appleby kept some private papers and his wallet. It had been forced open, and the wallet was missing. A pair of gents' black shoes were found in the drawing room of the house, which did not belong to anybody in the house. A pair of shoes was missing from Mr Appleby's upstairs bedroom.

Dr John Healy from Carraignavar went to the Applebys' house in response to a phone call. On arrival, he saw a man lying on the bed, with severe head wounds. He was dead. There was an iron bar, and a pool of blood on the floor. Mrs Appleby was in another room; she had serious injuries and was semi-conscious. He organised for her to be moved to hospital.

James Ennis immediately became a suspect for this crime – he had worked there; he used to sleep in the house; and he had been convicted of a violent robbery in 1961. He had just been released from Portlaoise Prison a day or two before the murder, and had a voucher to travel by train from Portlaoise to Cork.

On Ennis's arrival at Store Street Station, the incident room in Cork was immediately notified. Ennis was brought to the Detective Branch office, and was interviewed by Chief Superintendent Barney McShane of Dublin Castle.

The Chief Superintendent commenced to take a statement from Ennis, in which he said he arrived in Cork on 23 April, and booked into a lodging house. He went around the city, met a girl aged twenty, and stayed with her until 10:30pm. They arranged to meet at noon the next day in Patrick Street, and did so. They remained together, according to Ennis, until 7am on Saturday, 24 April. He then went to the Parnell Place lodging house, and had his breakfast. Of course, we had no name for this lady.

Ennis and the Chief Superintendent took a short break for tea. When the interview resumed, Ennis said, 'Tear up that statement, it is not all the truth.' He said he would make a true confession. Ennis then described walking from the city out to the Applebys', and mentioned all the places he passed en route. He stayed in an old ditch in the Applebys' land until it got dark. He continued:

I picked up an iron bar in the yard, and a screwdriver. There was no light on in the house, I got in a window and I had the iron bar in my hand. I forced open a drawer of a desk and I got a wallet. I went upstairs to Mr Appleby's room, and I was opening the press in the room when he shouted. He was in bed and I was beside the bed. I struck him with the iron bar on the head a number of times. Mrs Appleby was beside him, and I think she got struck too. I don't know how many times I struck her. I was in my stocking feet and I put on a pair of men's shoes I found in the room. I left the bar after me and I took a coat and a hat from the house when I was leaving. I got about £10 in the wallet and I walked back to Cork, and went to the lodging house. I got tea and I went to bed. I then put all the clothing I was wearing in Appleby's house, and the shoes, coat and hat that I took there, into my suitcase and I left the suitcase in the bus office in Parnell Street. I stayed in another lodging house in Cork on Saturday night, and I came to Dublin this morning on the eight o'clock train.

Ennis was found guilty of the murder of George Appleby. He gave evidence himself, a slightly different version from that in his statement. He said that when he was in the bedroom, Mr Appleby had jumped out of the bed and punched him a number of times. He was afraid, and tried to get away. He struck out with the iron bar, and pushed him back down on the bed, and struck him again, though he didn't know how many times.

In evidence for the defence, Dr Thomas Murphy, the medical officer in Mountjoy Prison in Dublin, described the accused as a belligerent psychopath. Such people, said Dr Murphy, would generally be outcasts from society. They are shiftless, and emotionally unstable. They do not profit from experience, and lack prudence and good judgement in ordinary affairs. They react violently in ordinary situations. He said that while in Mountjoy Prison, the accused had made two suicide attempts, once by suspending himself from the window in his cell with a sheet, and a few days later by suspending himself from the bars of a passage on the cell landing. Both attempts were demonstrative, having been made in the presence of other people. Ennis, said Dr Murphy, was a man of unstable personality, whose actions will be completely unreliable under stress. In cross-examination, Peter O'Malley, counsel for the prosecution, asked Dr Murphy whether the accused was insane, or was insane at the time he committed this act. Dr Murphy replied, 'No.'

During the course of the investigation, Gardaí in Cork needed to identify the shoes Ennis left in George Appleby's house on the night of the murder. They brought them to me, knowing that I had given Ennis a pair of shoes. I examined them, and I was reasonably satisfied that they were the same shoes that I had given to James Ennis, at Naas Garda Station in December 1960. But I was not sufficiently sure to go to Court and give evidence under oath. I brought the shoes to a shoemaker in Kildare town who used to repair shoes for me when I was stationed there. I asked if he could tell me who owned them. He examined the shoes and said, 'I have no idea whatsoever. But I can tell you this much: it was I who repaired them.' That was sufficient for me to be able to go to Court, and give evidence that they were the shoes that I gave to Ennis.

James Ennis is, without doubt, the longest-serving prisoner in the Irish prison system. He has been in custody since he entered Store Street Garda Station on 26 April 1964, up to the present time. From 24 April 1961, up to the day he went to Store Street, he had only been at liberty for four days. He has now been in custody for a continuous period of fifty-one years.

LARCENY AT LAWLOR'S HOTEL, NAAS, 1968

In October 1962, I went to the Technical Bureau for a month on a Detectives' course, relating to Detective duties, evidence and procedure. From July to September 1967, I went on a three-month course to the Technical Bureau, this time a Scenes of Crime Examiner's course. Some time after that, putting my newly acquired Detective technical skills into operation, I examined the scene of a crime at the rear of Lawlor's Ballroom, Store and Kitchen, Naas. Five large copper pots had been stolen, with a capacity of ten gallons each. The pots were used by Lawlor's in catering at races, horse shows and like events around the country. They were years old, but had a very high replacement value.

On the bank of a small stream at the rear of the premises, I found what I took to be boot impressions in soft clay. It appeared that the culprits had entered the premises by that route, and had left by the same route. I took a wax impression of the best prints that were there. When I lifted the impressions and cleaned them up, the pattern could be seen very clearly. There were three or four travellers' caravans parked on the Racecourse Road at that time.

I suspected that the men folk were involved in the larceny of the copper pots, which would likely be sold as scrap.

I visited the caravans, and inspected the footwear of the men folk. One man was wearing boots with the very same pattern that was on the wax impression. I brought him to the Station, and showed him the wax impression that I had taken at Lawlor's. I convinced him that the impression was verifiably from one of his boots. To be honest, all that I could see was that it was the same pattern. Maybe I could have taken it a bit further if he denied it, and had the boot and the impression brought to the Technical Bureau for some expert to take a closer look at. Anyway, he eventually admitted taking the pots and, luckily for Lawlor's, he had them hidden in the ditch, not too far from the caravan. We went to the field and returned with the pots intact. I brought him and the pots to Naas Garda Station, where he was charged.

Superintendent Tom Corbett was the Super in Naas at that time. He took a particular interest in this case, as he was a frequent visitor to Lawlor's Hotel. He was delighted with the recovery of the property and the charging of the culprit, and of course he had to be the first person to Lawlor's, to tell them of the pots being recovered intact.

HOUSEBREAKING AT A RESTAURANT IN NAAS, 1968–1972

I was involved in an interesting case of theft involving a restaurant in Naas. One evening, the owner and his wife closed up the restaurant, and went to visit relations in Sallins, two or three miles away. When they got back to the restaurant, they discovered that a large amount of cash had been stolen from a room downstairs in their absence. The door into the room was locked, but there was a window that faced the street at ground level, and that window had been pushed up at the bottom. I went to examine the scene.

Immediately inside the window was a geranium, a large one, on a large timber stand. There was very little room to either side of the geranium. I moved the geranium to get at the window from the inside, and upon doing so, a lot of petals and withered leaves fell off onto the ground. Before I moved it, there were very few petals and leaves on the ground. I was satisfied that no one had come in that window, even though it had been pushed up a foot or so. Although it looked as though somebody had got in that way, I was satisfied that no one had, because of the lack of geranium petals and leaves on the ground.

A few years later, the restaurant owner and his wife were again absent from the restaurant for a few hours one afternoon. Again the restaurant was closed. On their return, they discovered that a large amount of cash had been stolen in their absence from an upstairs room, with a locked door. There was one window out of the room, about ten or twelve feet above ground level. A ladder that belonged to the premises was standing up against the windowsill on the outside; the glass was broken at the window catch, and the window was wide open. It appeared that somebody had put the ladder up to the window, broken the glass, opened the catch, got in the window and stolen the cash.

I examined the scene, being particularly cautious on account of what had happened on the previous occasion, with the window and the geranium. I very carefully examined the window for fingermarks, but didn't get any. Next, I examined the broken glass. Now, when you break glass, there are cracks that run straight out, maybe five or six of them from the point of impact. They are known as radial cracks. If you come out from the centre of the point of impact, you will find what are called concentric cracks, forming complete circles around the damaged area where the force was applied.

Before glass breaks, however, it bends. At the edge of the cracks, where you can see the thickness of the glass, there are marks called striations. When I examined the glass in this window, I was satisfied that the window was not broken from the outside. It was broken from the inside, which put a completely different complexion on the thing altogether. Sellotaping together the remaining pieces of glass in the window, to keep them in position, I removed the pane of glass and brought it up to the Ballistics Section, and they confirmed that the glass had indeed been broken from the inside.

A few days afterwards I met the owner. I told him about the glass situation, about the window having been broken from the inside. We had a nice little row between us, because he accused me of suggesting that he was setting this thing up to claim money off the insurance company. But I told him I was merely informing him that the glass was broken from the inside. Anyway, we fell out.

About two years later, he rang me and I went to see him. He told me that he had made a discovery: that a relative of his, who had keys to every door in the restaurant, had stolen the money. No person was charged in relation to the thefts.

MURPHY AND GUNN ROBBERY, NAAS, 1970s

This wasn't my case really, but my involvement in it didn't go too well. Murphy and Gunn had a filling station on the Dublin Road in Naas, when I was stationed there. They advertised for a petrol pump attendant, and employed a man with a Dublin address. He told them he was a native of Cork, and had spent some years in England. During conversations with staff, over a period of five or six months, he mentioned that he was a plumber by trade; that he had lived in a particular part of London; that he was a member of a particular health club; and a few other things about himself, including pubs he used to drink in in England.

They found him to be an excellent worker. The petrol pump attendants used to work shifts, and they were open twenty-four hours. One bank holiday weekend, he asked another attendant to switch shifts with him. The newly employed attendant took up duty at 10pm on the bank-holiday Monday, and was due to finish work the following morning at 8am. When another attendant came to work on Tuesday morning to relieve him, there was no sign of the man, and the place was locked up.

The filling station had a kiosk on the forecourt, used as an office. In it was a safe, built into the floor, the door of it facing the ceiling. All cash the attendants received was deposited in this safe. The attendants had no key to the safe; they simply dropped the money in. The management eventually opened the kiosk on the Tuesday morning, but they couldn't open the safe. The takings from Saturday evening up to Tuesday morning should have been in the safe. Very small stones had been dropped into the keyhole of the safe, and the key could not be inserted into the lock. When the stones were eventually removed and the safe was opened, of course it was empty. All the money was gone, and so was the petrol pump attendant. He had fled, and had also fled from his address in Dublin.

This was reported to Gardaí in Naas, and a uniformed Sergeant from Naas was investigating the crime. He got in touch with police in London, and sent detailed information about the culprit, from what the man had told his fellow employees – his name, his occupation, the area where he had lived, where he had drunk, the health club he had belonged to, and so on. The London police had picked out a suspect, and sent over a photograph of him. The photograph fitted the man that had been in Naas – same name, occupation, height, build, native of Cork – so things were looking good.

There was one thing about the man in the photograph, however – he did not have a beard. The man in Naas had a beard, a very short beard. The Sergeant brought the photograph down to the employees and one of them said, 'Sure this lad had a small beard.' So the Sergeant got a biro, and he gave the photograph a small beard. Then he showed it to the rest of the staff, and they said, 'Oh that's him, no doubt, that's him.' So the Sergeant communicated with London and said he was satisfied that the photo they sent over was of the man. He prepared an extradition warrant and it was sent to England, with the man's name and all the particulars about him.

In due course, the police in London went out and arrested the suspect, and put him in custody. Then they got back to the sergeant in Naas and said the man was going to contest his extradition, as he denied that he was ever in Naas. They asked if they had anybody over there to identify him. So the Sergeant went to the Murphy and Gunn management and staff, but no one was willing to go to England to identify this fellow. The Sergeant couldn't identify him himself, because he had never seen him, so he enquired from other members at the Station whether anyone could identify him. So idiot here of course said, 'Well, I know him, I got petrol from him several times, and I think that I could identify him.' Of course, I had seen the photograph that the Sergeant had, with the pencilled-in beard, and to me it was a great likeness. I thought I would be able to pick him out, so I agreed to go to London to view the identification parade, and to give evidence before the Magistrate's Court.

So off I went anyway to London. At the police station concerned, I met the member who was in communication with the Sergeant in Naas, and was dealing with the extradition application in London. An identification parade was arranged for later that morning. Prior to the parade and over a cup of coffee, the member threw a photograph across the table to me and said, 'There's your man.' It was the same photograph that he had sent to Naas. Anyway, as soon as I went into the room to view the identification parade, I could see the man that was in the photograph, and that I thought was in Naas. I took my time and looked at all the others, and eventually came back, and I picked him out.

Later that morning, I went to the Magistrate's Court, where the hearing was to be held. I told the Magistrate the whole story – about meeting the petrol pump attendant in Naas; about the photograph sent to Naas, and the Sergeant putting a beard on the photograph; and that I had looked at it, and was satisfied that he was the man that worked at Murphy and Gunn. I told him that I was shown a photograph that morning. I wasn't going to hold back anything, because I knew that showing me a photograph was not the thing to do. I told him that I believed the man that I picked out in the parade, irrespective of the photograph, was the man named in the warrant. I was questioned at length by the solicitor for the prisoner, who said that he had never even been in Naas.

The Magistrate asked me if there was any possibility that the prisoner's fingerprints could be found at Murphy and Gunn in Naas. I replied that the possibility existed that his fingermarks might be found on documentation handled by the petrol pump attendants during the course of their duties. The Magistrate adjourned the case for some weeks, and released the man on bail. The idea was to have the documentation in Naas examined, to see if the prisoner's marks were on it. I returned, met the Sergeant and brought him up to date with what had happened in England. I was finished now with the investigation, my job having merely been the identification parade.

About two weeks after I returned, the Sergeant in Naas got a telephone call from his counterpart in England that was dealing with the case. It was discovered that the man charged for the Naas crime had been stopped somewhere in England on the bank-holiday Monday, travelling on foot on a highway. He could not possibly have been at work in Naas on that same day. The wrong man had been arrested, and, of course, I was wrong in my identification.

That's not the end of the story. Some weeks afterwards, I was discussing the case with one of the employees at Murphy and Gunn, and mentioned the identification parade. He said to me that it was very easy to identify that fellow – he had a very big scar down one side of his neck, and he always wore a poloneck jumper to conceal it. That was a shock to me. The scar was a vital clue as to the man's identification, and it had not been discovered in the initial part of the investigation. I accept that I was not blameless in this matter. I believe I should have better informed myself of the suspect's description, prior to going to England. I could have spoken to the staff myself, instead of relying on my casual meetings at the petrol pumps with the culprit.

Visual identification evidence in Court is fraught with danger, so much so that at a trial where evidence of visual identification is being given, the trial Judges must warn the Jury of the dangers of wrongful identification. In the event of a witness being shown a photograph of a suspect and subsequently picking him out in an identification parade, a Judge will disallow this evidence.

CHAPTER FOUR

SCENES OF CRIME EXAMINER

ROBBERY AT LEIGHLINBRIDGE, 1973

Having completed the Scenes of Crime course at Garda Headquarters, I was appointed Scenes of Crime Examiner for the Carlow and Kildare division. Prior to my appointment, a Scenes of Crime Examiner would come out from the Technical Bureau when a scene required examination. That continued to be the way in serious cases, such as murders. It was a duty I really enjoyed, and I approached every scene as a challenge. If the culprit left a clue to his or her identity – and there was a 'her' once or twice – I was determined to find it. I have had a good many successes, resulting from clues such as fingermarks, head hair, shoe impressions and paint flecks, among many others.

One Tuesday, after a bank-holiday weekend, I went to Leighlinbridge in County Carlow to examine a crime scene. A furniture factory had been broken into over the weekend. During the examination, I found that drawers had been broken open in the office, and that the culprit had opened a tin of salmon he got in the canteen. He consumed most of the salmon, having cut it open with some sharp instrument. I collected up all of the materials that I suspected would have fingermarks, and brought them back to Naas, examining them later in a room that I had for that purpose.

I found good fingermarks on the broken drawers, and I found one good one on the salmon tin. In crime investigation, prints found at the scene of a crime, left unintentionally by a culprit, are referred to as fingermarks. Fingerprints are impressions taken intentionally from a person, which can then be compared with fingermarks found at scenes.

During the course of my examination of the salmon tin, I discovered the top of a penknife blade at the bottom of the tin, among some uneaten salmon.

One night, about two weeks later, I called to Naas Garda Station. I was in the habit of calling to the Station most nights, just to enquire what was happening around the area. Some lads would go out for a pint or two; I used to go to the Garda Station. On entering the public office, I saw a number of items up on the counter – razor, soap, a few coppers, the usual things that a travelling man would have. It was obvious there was a prisoner in the cell. One of the items on the counter was a penknife. I picked it up and my heart started to accelerate a little – was it possible I had the penknife used to open that salmon tin, forty miles away and two weeks ago? I opened the penknife, and yes, the top was missing from one of the blades. I went up the stairs straight away, and retrieved the top of the blade from the salmon tin. I put the two together. No doubt about it, the blade was united with its tip. I told the Station orderly that I wanted the prisoner in the cell, Michael Deniffe, a Kilkenny man, for a crime, and to ensure he was not released until I was informed. The prisoner had been arrested for being drunk, and was not in a condition to be questioned at that time.

Early the next morning, I discovered that Mr Deniffe had been released. No great harm had been done, because I knew who he was. I brought the items bearing fingermarks, and the piece of blade that I found in the salmon tin, to the Garda Technical Bureau. The Ballistic Section confirmed that the portion of blade found in the salmon tin was in fact the piece missing off the penknife blade. The fingermarks I found on the other items were also identified as belonging to Michael Deniffe. I passed the information to the Sergeant in Leighlinbridge, and Deniffe was arrested somewhere that week. Deniffe admitted the crime at Leighlinbridge, along with many others that he had committed. I did not have to attend Court; in fact I never had the pleasure of seeing or speaking to Michael Deniffe.

THE MURDER OF FRANCIS NOEL BARRY, NAAS, 1975

During my service, I have been involved in investigating a number of cases where a wife had killed her husband. In most of these cases, the husband had beaten, abused, insulted and tortured her mentally and physically. Out of fear for her own safety, she made him pay the ultimate price. No one knows how many women are driven to breaking point, with no place to turn for help, or afraid of retaliation if they do seek help. Domestic violence is a big problem, a huge problem, and alcohol is one of the main factors in it. This is one such case, that brought home to me what some women have to endure.

In March 1975, I was a Detective Garda in Naas. I went to the home of Mr and Mrs Francis Noel Barry, on Pacelli Road in Naas, at about eight or nine at night. The body of Mr Barry was lying on the landing upstairs. He was dead, having suffered a number of stab wounds. I learned that the deceased's wife, Rosanna, had been in the house at the time that Mr Barry received the stab wounds. Rosanna Barry was not present when I was in the house. She had been taken to Naas General Hospital, and was detained there.

I went to the hospital to speak to her, but could not do so until 1am. The doctor treating her told me that she was then in a condition to be interviewed, and he had no objection. I spoke to her for about two hours, and she related to me what had happened in the house, and admitted that she had stabbed her husband. She also told me that her life had been hell with her husband for the last sixteen years.

In her statement to me, she said she was forty years old, and had five children, two boys and three girls. She was watching television that night, when her husband came home drunk. He was aggressive, and started to mess with her. She knew he was waiting for her in his bedroom, so she got a butcher's knife with a black handle, that she had left on top of the press in her bedroom. She had brought the knife from the kitchen a few nights before, to use on her husband. When she got the knife that night, she left her bedroom with it and went out to the landing, put off the light in the bathroom and went into Noel's room. He was lying on his back in the bed, in his shirt and underpants, not covered with bedclothes. She could see him from the streetlight. She went to the side of the bed, and Noel said something to her that she couldn't make out. She had the knife in her right hand, and she stabbed him with it. Then she ran out of the room and down the stairs screaming, to her father's house.

She said she had had a life of hell with her husband for sixteen years. He was a very heavy drinker, and often beat her. One time two years ago, he took off his tie and tried to strangle her. She left him about eleven years earlier and went to England, because she could not stick the beatings. There were a number of times over the previous few years that she stood over him as he lay drunk, with the knife in her hand, preparing to stab him. She couldn't go on living with him, with the way he was treating her.

Rosanna Barry was released from Naas Hospital at 11am that morning. She was arrested and brought to Naas Garda Station. She appeared before the Central Criminal Court in Dublin, charged with her husband's murder, and she pleaded not guilty. Rosanna's father, William Keogh, described in the Court how his daughter ran to his house nearby, and she was very hysterical and in her bed clothes. The five Barry children were in their beds in the house at the time of the stabbing. Some neighbours took the children to their homes for the night.

Two Naas curates, Reverend Joseph Shorthall and Reverend Patrick Ramsbottom, gave character references in the Court for Rosanna Barry. The Court heard that any one of the three stab wounds inflicted on Mr Barry was sufficient to cause death. Mrs Barry told the Court that she just could not cope. There were good times in her marriage, but the majority were bad times. She could not forgive herself for what she had done. This deed, Mr Justice Gannon said, was committed out of loss of self-control. It was one of the tragedies of our country that many people live their lives suffering from worries and frustration. The consequences of Mrs Barry's actions, he said, must be a great burden on her, and she brought it on herself.

Having heard the evidence, the jury found her not guilty of murder, but guilty of manslaughter. The Judge imposed a suspended sentence of seven years on Rosanna Barry. She was bound over for four years on her own surety of £100, and was allowed to go home. I think justice was done.

APPREHENSION OF MICHAEL BOYLE, PUNCHESTOWN, 1975

Punchestown Racecourse is situated in the Naas Garda area in County Kildare. On 1 May 1975, I was on duty there, at the annual Punchestown Racing Festival. During the afternoon the Gardaí received a report – a dangerous criminal named Michael Boyle, who had escaped from the Central Criminal Court on 15 April, by producing a firearm to the prison officers that were escorting him, had been observed at the races that day.

The late Detective Pat Burke and I commenced to search the course, the buildings and the crowd for Michael Boyle. What followed is best described in the following excerpts from a report made by the late Superintendent Richard Gilpin, Superintendent in Naas at the time.

On the 15th of April 1975, Michael Boyle appeared before the Central Criminal Court, Chancery Place, Dublin, on charges relating to Armed Bank Robberies at Dundrum in County Wicklow, and Enniskerry County Wicklow. During the period when the Court had adjourned for lunch, the Prisoner Michael Boyle escaped from the custody of the Prison Officers, by producing a pistol. Boyle had not been recaptured up to the 1st of May 1975, on which date members of the Gardaí on duty at the Punchestown Racecourse in County Kildare, received information to the effect that Michael Boyle had been seen at that race meeting. On receipt of the information, all members on duty at the race meeting were alerted.

Arrangements were made to have all exits manned by Gardaí, and a search of the racecourse area carried out. This Race meeting was the biggest of the year at this venue, and there was a very large crowd in attendance. This meant, that carrying out a search for an individual was an extremely difficult task. Detective Garda Thomas Connolly and Garda Patrick Burke, both of Naas Station were on duty at the race meeting. Both were unarmed and in plain clothes. The two members commenced carrying out a search of the public bars within the Racecourse enclosure. Detective Garda Connolly and Garda Burke, entered one of the bars which was crowded, and they observed a man wearing, a red tartan cap and long fair hair, standing near a counter. Detective Garda Connolly knew Boyle, and this man bore a strong resemblance to him. The members kept this man under observation from a distance. The man appeared to be behaving suspiciously, and after a few minutes he left the bar, by pushing his way through a crowd of people towards an exit. At this stage, Detective Garda Connolly recognised the man as Michael Boyle.

When Boyle had left the bar, the two members followed him. When the members reached the exit they observed Boyle, walking at a fast pace towards a crowd of people on one of the stands. At this stage he had gone a distance of twenty-five to thirty yards from the bar exit. Boyle was only a similar distance away from the crowds on the stands. Detective Garda Connolly, fearing that Boyle would reach the crowd, and make good his escape, ran after him. Garda Burke followed him and when Detective Garda Connolly got to within ten or twelve yards from Boyle, the latter turned around in the Detective Garda's direction. The Detective Garda pretended that he was not interested in him. Boyle then continued to walk towards the stand.

Detective Garda Connolly reached him, and placed his left hand on Boyle's right shoulder. Boyle turned swiftly and freed his shoulder, he muttered something to the member and immediately drew a pistol from inside his jacket. He made a movement to point the gun at the Detective Garda, who grabbed the muzzle of the gun. The member caught the wrist of the hand which was holding the gun, and forced the gun away from the Detective Garda's body. At the same time the Detective Garda shouted a warning to Garda Burke who was following. Boyle tried to force the gun towards the Detective Garda, who forced the gun above their heads, placed his right foot behind Boyle's knees and knocked him backwards onto the ground. The Detective Garda fell on top of him and continued to hold on to the gun.

Garda Burke had arrived on the scene at this stage, and a violent struggle took place between the members and Boyle. During this struggle, the gun was at different times pointed at Detective Garda Connolly and Garda Burke. The members eventually succeeded in wrenching the gun from Boyle's hand.

When the gun was taken from Boyle, he succeeded in getting free, and he ran in the direction of the catering building. The members followed him and Detective Garda Connolly was holding the gun. During the course of the chase, both Boyle and Detective Garda Connolly collided with some members of the crowd, and both persons knocked over some of them. The chase continued to the back of the stands, where Detective Garda Connolly managed to trip Boyle. Boyle stumbled and was immediately tackled by Detective Garda Connolly, who brought him to the ground. Detective Garda Connolly was still holding the gun, and Boyle endeavoured to get it. The Detective Garda and Boyle struggled on the ground, and Garda Burke gave assistance to the Detective Garda. Fearing that Boyle might succeed in getting the gun, the Detective Garda threw it along the ground out of Boyle's reach. Following the struggle, the two members mentioned, with the assistance of other members, subdued and arrested Boyle. The gun was immediately recovered, and found to be in a cocked position. It was loaded with nine rounds of ammunition in the magazine, and there was one up the breach.

Boyle was taken to Bridewell Garda Station Dublin that evening of the 1st of May 1975, and on the following day he appeared at the Central Criminal Court again, to face the charges on which he appeared before that Court at the time of his escape. He was subsequently found not guilty of the charges relating to the bank robbery at Enniskerry.

During the struggles with Boyle, the two members suffered the following injuries, but were not non-effective for duty for any period. Detective Garda Connolly: cuts and abrasions to the backs and knuckles of both hands, abrasions in the forehead and the left knee. His clothing was also damaged. Garda Pat Burke: cuts to both hands and knuckles and the right wrist, injuries to his right knee, and ankle.

Michael Boyle, aged 29, native of Dublin, is a former member of the Defence Forces, is married and resides at number 18 Scott Park, Bray, County Wicklow. Is five foot nine in height, and a man of good physique. He has been detained for different periods in the Central Mental Hospital at Dundrum, and escaped from there on two occasions. He is presently serving a period of five years' imprisonment at the Curragh Military Detention Centre. This sentence was imposed at the Central Criminal Court on charges of house breaking and larceny, committed in the Bray and Cabinteely areas. There is no doubt that Boyle, apart from being mentally unstable, is a dangerous and ruthless criminal. To achieve his freedom, he would have no hesitation in shooting any person, particularly members of the Garda Síochána.

In effecting the arrest of Boyle, the members displayed exceptional courage and heroism, involving risk of life in the execution of duty. I am satisfied that the action in each case, was one of exceptional duty, that they performed it in an intelligent manner and that there was imminent risk to the lives of the members. The members had full, previous knowledge of the risk involved and their actions were the subject of very favourable comment, by many members of the general public, who actually witnessed the event.

Detective Garda Connolly displayed Detective ability of a high degree by recognising Boyle, who was disguised by wearing a wig of long, fair hair; his normal hair is black. He tenaciously followed and struggled with Boyle, knowing the risk of life involved, and disarming him. His actions deserve the highest award. Garda Pat Burke, whilst his actions were of a supporting nature to Detective Garda Connolly, nevertheless displayed a high degree of bravery and tenacity. His actions merit an award, perhaps not equal to, but closely aligned to that deserved by Detective Garda Connolly.

As a result of all that, Garda Pat Burke was awarded the Silver Scott Medal, and I was awarded the Gold Scott Medal. The presentations were made at the Garda training centre in Templemore on 16 July 1976, by Patrick Cooney, Minister for Justice at the time. Not alone did I get the Gold Scott Medal, but also a very generous monetary reward, and I am sure Pat Burke got the same. It was a big day for the Connollys – my wife Maureen, my three children and some of my brothers and sisters and nieces and nephews were there. We had a great day, though my mother, God rest her, was ill and could not attend. Two or three days after the presentation, I went to Clonakilty and brought down the medal, because she wanted to see it. She was very proud indeed, and she died, God rest her, on 15 August that year, 1976.

A citation was also presented, which read as follows:

While on duty at Punchestown Races on Thursday 1st May 1975. Detective Garda Thomas W. Connolly 12622E and Garda Patrick J. Burke 14100C, both unarmed and in plain clothes, arrested a much wanted man, who in resisting arrest, drew a gun and pointed it at Detective Garda Connolly. Detective Garda Connolly, unhesitatingly grabbed the gun and with help from Garda Burke, succeeded in disarming and arresting him after a violent struggle. Before attempting the arrest, the Gardaí had been informed, that the man was dangerous and likely to be armed. Subsequent examination of the gun showed that it was a .22 calibre star pistol. The hammer was cocked, the safety catch was on, it had one round in the breach and nine rounds in the magazine. For exceptional courage and heroism, involving risk of life in the execution of duty, the Scott Gold medal is awarded to Detective Garda Connolly and the Scott Silver medal is awarded to Garda Patrick J. Burke.

Signed Commissioner Edmund Garvey, 16 July 1976

A presentation was made that same day to Garda Michael Reynolds, posthumously, as he was shot dead following a bank raid in Dublin. He was off duty, with his wife,

The Gold Scott Medal for valour, awarded to me on 16 July 1976

and he didn't know there had been a raid, but he saw the car and knew there was something wrong. He followed the car to St Anne's Park, out along the coast. Then, leaving his wife in the car, he followed the raiders on foot. After a short distance, one of them turned around and shot him dead. They were charged with capital murder, but it had to be reduced to murder at common law, as he was in civilian clothes, and the raiders did not know he was a member of the Garda at the time he was shot. There was a lady involved in that case, Marie Murray, and herself and her husband Thomas were both convicted of the murder.

Michael Boyle was eventually dealt with, for the crimes that were outstanding against him at the time he was arrested in Punchestown, and for the Punchestown incident. Nine years later, when I was an Inspector in Store Street and Boyle was serving a sentence in Mountjoy, he drank something in the prison, stain or thinners or something, and was brought to Jervis Street

Hospital in Dublin. The prison officers thought he did it so he would be brought to hospital, where it would be easier to escape from. Anyway he was there for a couple of days, and there were two prison officers and a member of the Garda there with him at all times.

One morning early, when one of my unit was on duty at Jervis Street Hospital, minding Boyle, I dropped in to see the Garda, and of course I went in to see Michael Boyle as well. I walked in, and there he was, sitting up in the bed. I said, 'How are you, Michael?' He said, 'I am all right.' I said, 'Do you remember me?' He looked at me for about half a minute, and he said, 'Punchestown.' He remembered, though he hadn't seen me in uniform before.

Michael Boyle was eventually released and, of course, committed more crime. His favourite one was kidnapping, taking somebody out of a house, bringing them out to a wood, tying them to a tree, contacting their well-off husband and demanding money. He was charged with one or two of those, but I don't know how many he got away with.

The last I heard of Michael Boyle was some years ago now. Gardaí in Dublin got information that he had gone to England, to assassinate some English criminal. The information was passed to the police area concerned. The Gardaí in Dublin had passed on the name of the man that he was intending to shoot, and the police in England set up surveillance on the man's house. One morning, when this man came out his front door, Michael Boyle appeared from some distance away and fired a couple of shots at him. As he did, the police fired a couple of shots at Boyle, and seriously injured him – he was lucky to survive. Anyway, he did survive, and had to face the Court again on a number of charges. He got a very long sentence, more than ten years I believe, and that's the last I heard of him.

MURDERS OF ELIZABETH PLUNKETT AND MARY DUFFY, BRITTAS BAY AND CASTLEBAR, 1976

On the night of 28/29 August 1976, twenty-three-year-old Dubliner Elizabeth Plunkett was abducted from the Brittas Bay area of County Wicklow. She was brought to a nearby wood by her two abductors, and raped and abused, God only knows how many times, over a considerable length of time. She was then strangled, stripped of her clothing and dropped out of a boat, a considerable distance out to sea, her body weighed down with a stolen lawnmower. Her body was washed ashore at Lacken, Duncormack, on the Wexford Coast on 28 September. The lawnmower had become detached from her body, which had drifted approximately fifty miles south.

On the night of 22 September 1976, Mary Duffy, twenty-four years old, of Deerpark, Bellcara outside Castlebar, left a coffee shop at Ellison Street in Castlebar, where she was employed as a waitress. She had finished work around 10 or 10.30pm, and was trying to get a lift home. She telephoned her brother, who would often collect her, but failed to contact him. She was in touch with another person, and left a message for her brother to collect her. She said she was going out the Breaffy Road, which was on her way home, and hoped that he could collect her there. Unfortunately the brother didn't get to collect her, and Mary did not make it home that night, or ever again. She was abducted by two men, who both raped her in the car as it travelled. They drove about sixty miles from where she was abducted, to a wood.

They kept her alive in the wood for at least twenty-four hours. The unfortunate girl was subjected to brutal rape and abuse, on many occasions. She was finally strangled, stripped naked and dropped overboard from a boat in Lough Inagh in County Galway. Her body was recovered by divers on Sunday, 10 October, eighteen days after her abduction. The body was weighed down by an anchor, a cavity concrete block and a sledgehammer.

These were two of the most shocking crimes of rape and murder the country had ever experienced, committed by two brutal, sadistic and depraved men. Much has been written about these horrific crimes, including a lot of conjecture and inaccuracies. I will only write about the facts known to me, as a result of my involvement in the investigation.

I was stationed in Naas at this time, and I travelled to Wicklow to assist in the investigation into the disappearance of Elizabeth Plunkett. I had, prior to this, assisted members of the Investigation Section, Crime Branch of Garda Headquarters, on investigations into serious crimes in Kildare and the surrounding counties.

The background to Elizabeth Plunkett's presence in Brittas Bay on the night is already in the public domain. I am not going to dwell on it, other than to say she was with a crowd of friends in McDaniels' pub in Brittas Bay around 11pm. She left alone after a trivial disagreement with her boyfriend. She did not have any transport, and walked away from the pub towards Dublin. She did not return home that night to Pembroke Cottages, in Ringsend in Dublin.

The following morning, her family and the boyfriend's family went to Brittas Bay. They searched all day, but found no trace of her. Her disappearance was not reported to the Gardaí for quite a while. Search parties were eventually organised, and a great number of her friends, relations and Gardaí participated. After a day or two, items of her property – a shoe and a wristwatch – were discovered in Castletymon Wood, about half a mile to the rear of McDaniels' pub. The worst was then feared. In a more thorough search, other items were found, including a homemade cardboard label with the name Jeffrey Murphy written on it, and a pair of black boots, with steel tips on the heels kept in place with brass screws.

When the cardboard label was discovered, the late Detective Garda Joe Nealon of Wicklow produced his notebook. He had an entry in it from Monday, 30 August. He had spoken to two men near McDaniels' caravan park on that morning. They had a fire, and were burning some material, and there was some clothing on the ground. They said that the clothing had got wet in the recent rain, and they were endeavouring to dry it. At this time, Detective Garda Nealon was unaware of Elizabeth Plunkett's disappearance. He took the names as given to him by the two men, John Murphy and Jeffrey Murphy. They said they were brothers. Detective Garda Nealon remarked that they did not look like brothers, and the man who gave the name Jeffrey said they were stepbrothers. Anyway he wrote their descriptions in his notebook. They had a car, and he had a description of it, and the registration number. They said they worked in a forest in Fethard in County Tipperary. The car was subsequently traced to a man in Fethard, by the name of Frank Walsh.

Inspector Reynolds, as he was then, and three others, including myself, went to Fethard to continue investigations there. That led us to an Englishman named Chris Outrum, who was living in Fethard. He told us that while he himself was serving a sentence in Mountjoy Prison he met two other men there. He named them as John Shaw and Jeffrey Evans. He said they used the names John Murphy and Jeffrey Murphy on arrival in Ireland, about two years previously. He was shown the black boots found at Castletymon Wood, and identified them as the property of Jeffrey Evans. He said it was he who put the brass screws on the tips of the heels, while they were in prison. He had left prison before Shaw and Evans, and on their release they came to stay with him. On Saturday, 28 August, they borrowed a car in Fethard and went to Dublin, returning on Tuesday, 31 August. The car was the one recorded in Detective Garda Nealon's notebook, that he had seen the two men with at Brittas Bay on Monday, 30 August.

Some days before our arrival in Fethard, Chris Outrum said he drove Shaw and Evans to Limerick. He did not know their present location, and had no way of communicating with them. We stayed around Fethard for a number of days, making enquiries and hoping that they would return to Outrum's, but they did not. From Tuesday, 31 August, to the time Outrum drove them to Limerick, Shaw and Evans had committed burglaries and larcenies around the Tipperary, Cork and Waterford areas.

Back in Wicklow, the search for Shaw and Evans had escalated. It was discovered that both men had arrived in Ireland two years previously, and commenced to commit crime in the Cork and Tipperary areas. They had been arrested and charged with upwards of sixteen burglaries and larcenies, and eventually appeared at Cork Circuit Court on 5 February 1975. Both were sentenced to two years' imprisonment.

Shaw, an ex-miner, was a native of Wigan. He was thirty-one, married, separated and had three children. He had upwards of twenty previous convictions in England, including one for attempted rape, for which he was sentenced to six or seven years, and one for indecent assault on a young boy. Other convictions were for robbery, house breaking and larceny, things like that. Evans, a native of Tyldesley in England, was thirty-three, and was married and separated. He had upwards of thirty previous convictions in England, for house breaking, robbery and other offences.

At the time of their arrival in Ireland, both Shaw and Evans were wanted by police in the Greater Manchester Police area, for the rape or attempted rape of three young girls. One of the girls was a daughter of a police officer in Manchester. An extradition warrant was waiting in Dublin when Shaw and Evans were released from Mountjoy Prison, having served the sentence imposed at Cork Circuit Court in February 1975.

Shaw was released first, on 5 August 1976, and he was immediately arrested on foot of the extradition warrant. The Justice at Dublin District Court adjourned the case for some matter to be clarified in relation to the warrant. He released Shaw on bail, in spite of Garda objections, and set a date for the hearing. Shaw then travelled to Chris Outrum's in Fethard, County Tipperary.

Evans was released on 26 August, and was immediately arrested on the extradition warrant, just the same as Shaw. He also appeared before Dublin District Court, and again the District Justice sought clarification on some issue relating to the warrant, and adjourned the case to a later named date. Evans was also released on bail, again in spite of objections. Evans then travelled to Fethard to join Shaw and Outrum, arriving there on 27 August. The day after Evans arrived in Fethard, he and Shaw borrowed a car from Mr Walsh, went to Dublin and then on to Brittas Bay that night.

The Gardaí had sought all the information about Shaw and Evans in the possession of the English police, and were furnished with previous convictions, photographs, descriptions, and so on. A special information bulletin was compiled, and circulated throughout the force, giving all available information that could help in identifying the wanted men. Their descriptions were also made available to the media, and they got widespread coverage.

Up to 22 September 1976, there was no information as to the location of Shaw or Evans. The possibility existed that they had separated or returned to England. There was a certain amount of apprehension and fear among the investigation team, that Shaw and Evans would abduct another female, which could have tragic consequences. All available resources were concentrated on tracing their whereabouts. The general public also felt uneasy, believing that two dangerous criminals were roaming the country, likely to abduct a female and commit rape or murder.

The watch found in Castletymon Wood, and identified as that of Elizabeth Plunkett, was examined at the Garda Technical Bureau for possible fingermarks or palm marks. A small part of a palm mark was developed on the glass face of the watch. The fingerprints and palm prints of John Shaw and Jeffrey Evans were already available, and were compared with the palm mark found on the watch face. In this jurisdiction, for a fingerprint expert to give evidence in Court that a fingerprint or palm print matches a fingermark or palm mark requires that there be at least twelve points of similarity between them, with no dissimilar points. The number of points required vary from country to country. Our fingerprint expert will be reasonably satisfied that a particular fingermark or palm mark matches a particular fingerprint or palm print if he can find eight or nine points of similarity, and of course no dissimilar points.

Our fingerprint expert expressed the view that the palm mark on the face of the watch found at Castletymon Wood was made by one of the palms of Jeffrey Evans – he had found eight or nine points of similarity. This, of course, could not be given in evidence in Court, because the number of points did not reach the magic twelve. However, it strengthened the suspicion that Shaw and Evans had contact with Elizabeth Plunkett.

On Wednesday, 22 September, matters turned very much in favour of the investigators in their search for Shaw and Evans. Unfortunately, another abduction, rape and murder would be perpetrated by them before they were arrested. On that evening, a shopkeeper and publican, who also had petrol pumps outside on the forecourt, saw a black Ford Cortina car stop at his petrol pumps, at Maam, Connemara, County Galway. There were two men in the car; the passenger got out and requested three pounds' worth of petrol, and the driver remained in the car. The alert shop owner noticed that the Cortina car had very obviously been hand-painted black. He spoke to the passenger, who had an English accent. They got the petrol, and drove away in the direction of Leenane. That was about 7pm.

There was something about the occupants of the car that made the shop owner suspicious. He wrote down the registration of the car – SZH 562 – and made a mental note of their descriptions. He remembered reading in a daily paper some day recently that two English men were wanted in connection with the disappearance of a girl in County Wicklow. The thought occurred to him that he should make a report to the Gardaí about the two men and the car. He considered contacting Garda Whelan, who was stationed in Maam, or Garda Sommerville in Leenane, and he decided against it. But not for long; the following morning he had second thoughts. He contacted the Gardaí and gave them whatever information he had.

Shaw and Evans had gone on to Leenane that evening, then on to Westport, and late that night they arrived in Castlebar. They saw Mary Duffy walking alone towards home outside the town, some time just after 11pm. Shaw got out of the car and approached her. He punched her in the face, brought her back to the car and forced her into it. She screamed, and her screams were heard by residents in houses nearby, but they did not realise that the screams were from somebody in distress. When Mary did not arrive home that night, her family presumed she had spent the night in town with friends, and would go straight to work on Thursday. However, she didn't have work on Thursday. It was Thursday night before any concerns were raised about her whereabouts. Her family made efforts to locate her, through her friends and relations, but no trace of her could be found. Her sister Kristina contacted Castlebar Garda Station at about 11.45pm, and reported Mary's disappearance. She made the report to Garda John Duggan, and she outlined to him Mary's last known movements, and the efforts they had made to find her.

House-to-house enquiries were commenced, out along the route that Mary would take home. It was then that the people who had heard screams on Wednesday night came forward and spoke to the Gardaí. A search of the roadway, in the vicinity where the screams were heard, was carried out. Mary had a denture, and when the roadway was searched, a portion of a broken denture was found. It was examined by the dentist who had supplied the denture for Mary. The portion of the denture found on the roadway exactly matched a portion of the cast taken for Mary's denture. There was no doubt that it was hers. This indicated strongly that Mary had been assaulted and possibly abducted from this location on the night of 22 September.

Searches for her and for Elizabeth Plunkett continued, with negative results. The Gardaí in Castlebar were in contact with the incident room in Wicklow dealing with the disappearance of Elizabeth Plunkett. Comparisons between the two disappearances were obvious, and it appeared that there was a genuine possibility they were abducted by Shaw and Evans. Another alert was circulated to the Garda force, this time with a registration number and description of the hand-painted black Ford Cortina.

The following Sunday night, 26 September, Gardaí Jim Boland and PJ Corcoran of Salthill went on duty in the patrol car in the Salthill area of County Galway. Prior to leaving on duty, they entered particulars in their notebooks relating to the recent disappearance of Mary Duffy, to Shaw and Evans and to the black Ford Cortina.

They drove around Salthill, and up and down the promenade a number of times. There was a large amount of people and traffic around at the time. At about 11.30, they saw a black Ford Cortina parked on the side of the street, near the Ocean Wave Hotel. They checked the registration number – SZH 562. Yes, it was the right car, the one the whole country was looking for.

Garda Boland parked the patrol car out of sight in a laneway. The Gardaí had no radio communication with Salthill Garda Station, for some reason or other, that night. He communicated with the Garda Headquarters in Galway, a few miles away, for assistance. Garda Corcoran got out of the car and went on foot to Salthill Garda Station, to inform them of the finding of the car.

Some minutes after Garda Corcoran had departed, Garda Boland saw two men approach the car from the direction of the Ocean Wave Hotel. They got into the car, and started it up. At that stage the Galway patrol car contacted Garda Boland, telling him they were at Salthill Garda Station. He told them what was happening, and to come immediately to his location. Garda Boland then drove the patrol car up to the rear of the black Cortina, preventing it from reversing out or driving away.

Garda Boland jumped out of the patrol car, opened the driver's door of the Cortina, and pulled out the driver, who was Evans. The patrol car arrived then, and also Garda Corcoran, and they pulled Shaw out of the car. Evans gave the name Roy Hall when arrested, and Shaw gave the name David Ball. Shaw and Evans were brought to Salthill Garda Station, and later to Garda Headquarters at Eglington Street in Galway. The search was over for the two wanted men, and great credit must go certainly to the shopkeeper in Maam, and Gardaí Jim Boland and PJ Corcoran, for their alertness, observations and subsequent actions.

At about 1am the following morning, 27 September, I was at home asleep in bed when the phone rang. It was Detective Inspector John Courtney, with the news that Shaw and Evans had been arrested in Salthill. He asked me to be in Galway as soon as I could that morning, and to bring Detective Garda Kennedy of Kildare with me. I rang Tim Kennedy shortly after the phone call, and agreed to pick him up at 5am. I twisted and turned in the bed I don't know how many times that night, and I doubt if I slept a wink. Anyway I collected Tim and we headed for Galway, and arrived there at about 7.15am. We went to the Station; all was quiet and the prisoners were asleep. We were the first there from the Crime Investigation Section in Dublin. We were brought up to date about the circumstances of the arrest.

We were told that when Evans was searched, in his coat pocket was found a receipt for £300, in respect of the purchase of a caravan in Barna House caravan park in Galway. I enquired if anyone had searched it, to see if Mary Duffy was in it. I was told by the chap I was speaking to that he didn't know. I went to the caravan site, and there was a Garda there; the caravan was being preserved. He didn't know whether or not it had been searched before he took up duty. Fearing that Mary Duffy could be detained in the caravan, tied up or whatever, I opened the door and searched, and was satisfied that Mary Duffy was not there, dead or alive.

I went back to the Station, had breakfast and waited for the lads to arrive from Dublin. Some time later, I learned that Jim Boland had indeed had the good sense to search the caravan before I arrived. Along with Detective Inspector John Courtney, I interviewed Jeffrey Evans that day, from 11.30am until 7pm. At the end of that period, Evans admitted to being at Brittas Bay on the night of Saturday, 28 August, but had not admitted any crime in relation to Elizabeth Plunkett.

He was interviewed by other members of the Gardaí after that, and very late at night he admitted the abduction and murder of Elizabeth Plunkett and Mary Duffy. He made a written statement admitting his involvement, and implicating John Shaw.

Shaw was interviewed many times throughout that day, up to 11.30pm, when he was put to his cell for the night. He had made no admissions. Having become aware of the contents of the statement made by Evans, Detective Garda Gerry O'Carroll and I took Shaw from his cell at 4am, and continued to question him. After a short time, he admitted murdering Elizabeth Plunkett and Mary Duffy. The interview concluded at 7am.

The following is the statement he made:

Statement of John Shaw born 6 July 1945, of Barna house, Salthill, County Galway, made to Detective Garda T. Connolly of Naas, County Kildare, at Galway Garda Station on 28 September 1976. The caution is incorporated in the statement.

He says; I am married and I have three children. I am separated from my wife who lives in England with my children. I was born in Wigan, Lancashire in England, and came to Ireland about two years ago with Jeffrey Evans. He is also English. On 5 August 1976, I went to live with another English chap called Chris Outrum, at Fethard in County Tipperary. Jeffrey came to stay at Outrum's, on Friday, 27 August 1976.

On Saturday, 28 August, I got the loan of a car from Frank Walsh of Fethard. Walsh is a friend of Outrum's. The car was an Austin. Jeffrey and I left Fethard in the car on the Saturday and we drove to Dublin. We went there to collect suitcases of Jeffrey's at the railway station, along the quays. We collected them at about four or five o'clock in the evening. We had a meal in the city and decided to go to Brittas Bay, County Wicklow, to break into some caravans. Somewhere outside Arklow, we went into a pub on the main road and had a few drinks. I don't know the name of the place; we left it after a few hours. We then drove on towards Brittas Bay.

We were talking about girls, and Jeffrey said he was going to pick up a bird and have it off with her. He said he wanted a small bird. Jeffrey was driving. We drove around the roads for a small while, looking for a bird. We saw one standing at a corner. Jeffrey stopped and asked her if she wanted a lift? I got out of the car and walked up the road at the time. This girl told Jeffrey that she was waiting for somebody, and he picked me up again.

Shortly after that, we saw another bird on the road. Jeffrey said, she will do. She was walking down towards Arklow. We passed her out and Jeffrey stopped. I got out and he turned the car and went back and picked up the girl. He then picked me up. I sat in the back and the girl was in the front seat. She was wearing a pants, and a jumper with writing on it. We drove to the woods with her. She told us she had a row with her boyfriend, and she started to scream in the car, and we stuffed tissues into her mouth.

When we got to the woods, we dragged her out of the car, we climbed over a wire fence that was across the road there. We went into the woods with her, we had a hold of her, we told her to lie down and she did so. We took the suitcases out of the car and put them on the ground beside her. Jeff told me to take the car away. I went away in the car, and left Jeff with the girl. I parked the car in a carpark, on the main road near a pub. I walked back to where Jeff and the girl were. I was gone about five hours, and it was becoming bright when I got back. I saw people coming along the road, trying to stop cars, and I got in over a gate.

When I got back to Jeff and the girl, I saw that the girl's hands were tied. Her clothes were on. I took off her pants and had intercourse with her. She was struggling all the time. Jeff went a short distance away while I was having intercourse with her. He then returned, and he had intercourse with her. Jeff said he would go and get back the car, and he told me to kill her while he was away. He said to me, remember what happened in England.

Jeff went off for the car, and I had intercourse with her again. When Jeff came back he said, why haven't you killed her? He said again, remember what happened in England. I took a nylon shirt out of one of the suitcases, I put the sleeve around her neck and choked her. She was dead. It was then about six in the evening of Sunday. We left the body in the forest and went to the caravan site, and we broke into a few caravans. Some time after midnight, we returned to the forest with the car. We carried the dead girl to the car, and put her into the back seat. I think Jeff had her shoe and watch. We drove down to the caravan site again, and we got a lawnmower out of the shed at the caravans, and a rope. We put her into a boat; we tied her on to the lawnmover with the rope. Jeff and I rowed out into the sea, Jeff threw her out and she sank.

We came back in again, and went to a pit in the field behind the caravans. There was a fire there, and we burned the girl's pants and jumper. We stayed in Brittas Bay that day, Monday. The police came along and spoke to us. We stayed around the caravan park until some time late that night, or Tuesday morning. We then returned to Fethard.

We stayed with Outrum again until 10 September. While we were there, we done a few strokes around the area. We left Fethard on 10 September 1976, and Chris drove us to Limerick. We came on to Salthill then, and we bought a caravan. We stayed in this caravan and pinched a car in Clifden. Jeff pinched it, not me.

A few days after that, we were in Castlebar one night, it was about twelve o'clock, and Jeff was driving. We saw a girl on the road walking along. Jeff stopped the car and I got out and went over to the girl. I grabbed a hold of her and dragged her to the car. She started to scream. I put her into the back of the car and sat in beside her. She told me her name was Mary. We headed for some place near Clifden. While Jeff drove the car along the road, I had intercourse with the girl. I only took off her pants. Somewhere along the road, I started to drive, and Jeff got into the back of the car with her. She didn't scream, but she said, don't do me any harm.

We got to a forest and we stopped. We pulled her out of the car. Jeff pulled off her clothes and we both had intercourse with her. Jeff gave her some pills to take. He gave her five or six pills, she took them and she got a bit dizzy. Jeff told her they were sleeping pills, and that he would take her home. I wanted to let her go, and Jeff said we couldn't. I got a cushion out of the car, and put it over her head, and put my hands around her neck, and I killed her. We threw her into the back of the car with her clothes, and Jeff said he had picked a spot to dump her.

When she was alive, Jeff drove off in the car and came back again to me in the forest. He went to our caravan and got some food and the pills. We gave her some sandwiches and barley water. When Jeff returned, he had a cavity concrete block in the car. There was also a rope. Jeff was away about four hours. He went away in the morning after we took the girl, and he returned that evening. While Jeff was away, I had intercourse twice with the girl. I saw men fishing, close by on the river. Jeff had intercourse again with her when he came back. The girl was with us more than twenty-four hours before I killed her.

We brought her up the road a short distance from where I killed her. We took her out of the car and I tied the concrete block on to her with the rope. Jeff tied an anchor and a brick on to her. We broke into a shed beside the lake; we took two oars out of it. There were a number of boats on the lake. We put the girl into a boat, and went out on the lake. It was dark and we dumped her into the lake, and I think she sank. I will show you to the spot today.

We burned all her things on the road somewhere on the way back to the caravan. We left the boat back in the same place, and put the oars in the shed. The girl had big leather boots and wore two rings. We took off the rings and threw them away somewhere in the forest. We returned to Salthill and went to our caravan. The night we picked up the girl Mary in Castlebar, we had a roof rack on our car. We took it off a car somewhere.

I am sorry for what I have done, and I want to help in every way to find the two girls that I have killed. There must be something wrong with me. I have heard this statement read over to me, and it is correct. I do not wish to make any changes or alterations to it, as it is correct.

It is signed with an x, John Shaw. It is witnessed by myself and Gerry O'Carroll.

In the early afternoon of the same day, I spoke to John Shaw, and he agreed to accompany members of the Garda on a trip around Connemara, to point out the places they had been when they murdered Mary Duffy. I was present when Inspector John Daly of Galway cautioned him in relation to the trip, that any place he pointed out would be given in evidence. He agreed to go.

The following is from my statement of evidence to the Court:

A short time later, John Shaw accompanied Inspector John Daly, Garda Christopher O'Reilly, Detective Garda Brendan Moran, both of Eglington Street Garda Station, and I, in a Garda car to a point about three miles outside Galway. Shaw was asked to direct us where to go from there. He directed us to Lough Inagh. On arrival he kept looking out the window towards the lake, as we drove along. When we arrived at a place were some boats were moored beside a boat house, he said; that's the place we got the boat. He pointed out a red buoy in the lake and he said; I remember we bumped into that on the way out. We went on down the lake to our right, and we dumped her in. When standing on the shore of the lake opposite Lough Inagh Lodge, John Shaw pointed to a spot around the centre of the lake, and about 400 yards on the boathouse side of lough Inagh lodge, as the spot where they pushed the body out into the lake. He said, I'm not sure, it was dark.

John Shaw then directed us to a spot beside the roadway at Attery in Recess, County Galway. We got out of the car, and John Shaw looked along the left-hand side of the road. He pointed out a spot below the level of the road at some rocks and he said, that is the spot we burned her things. At that spot, I saw the remains of a fire. On examination of the remains of the fire, I saw it contained small portions of clothing which remained unburned, two safety pins, part of a zip fastener and two metal strips. I saw Detective Garda Colm Dardis of the Ballistic Section, Garda

Technical Bureau, Dublin, take possession of all the articles remaining from the fire.

John Shaw then directed us to the old railway station, beside a wood and river, at Ballynahinch, County Galway. On arrival, he said, this is it, in that gate. We entered through the gate, and Shaw directed us along the old railway line to a spot under the platform at the old station house. He pointed out a spot, where I saw the remains of a fire. I saw a navy pullover, which was burned, a bottle and some cartons. Shaw said, that's my pullover. Detective Garda Colm Dardis and Detective Sergeant Martin Hogan, Fingerprint Section, took possession of all the articles from this spot.

John Shaw then led us over a wire fence, and into a wood. We travelled into the wood about 100 yards, along the river bank, until we came to a spot about 10 yards from the river bank, where the grass had been trampled down. Shaw said, this is the spot. He pointed out a spot to us where he had killed the girl, and pointed out a fallen tree that she had sat on, when the fishermen had been fishing beside them. He pointed out a piece of cloth on the ground, as being the cover of the cushion he had used. Detective Garda Colm Dardis and Detective Garda Martin Hogan took possession of the piece of cloth, and a soft cushion in a plastic bag, at this location, and a plastic ground sheet of some sort.

John Shaw then directed us to a bridge where a river flows into the sea, near Clifden in County Galway. He told us that was the bridge where they had thrown away two sleeping bags.

We then returned to Lough Inagh. Shaw brought us along a wire fence that runs from the roadway to the lake. On the right-hand side as one looks towards the lake from Lough Inagh Lodge, he indicated a spot along by the fence, about 300 yards from the road, and on the Lough Inagh side of the fence. He said, I threw her rings around here somewhere.

We then accompanied Shaw to the moored boats beside a boathouse. He examined the boats and said, the one we had did not have water in it, and it had two glass jars. He pointed to one boat and said, I think that's it, I think that's the one, because there is no water in it. There was one glass jar in this boat, and there were two glass jars in one of the other boats. We then returned to Eglington Garda Station, and on the route, John Shaw was given tea and sandwiches.

Late that night, Shaw and Evans were brought to Wicklow Garda Station. I travelled back home with Detective Garda Tim Kennedy. I was driving, and about four or five miles from Galway, coming into a right-hand corner, I drove up on the footpath on the left-hand side. I was falling asleep, and I had to stop and hand over driving duties to Tim Kennedy. I got into the back seat and fell asleep, and I only woke up when the car stopped outside Tim Kennedy's house in Kildare. Then I drove back home to my good wife, and got there around three or four o'clock in the morning.

On the following day, Wednesday, 29 September, I accompanied Detective Inspector Hubert Reynolds of the Investigation Section, Garda Mark Carroll of Carlow, Garda Jeremiah Hallaghan of Rathdrum and John Shaw to the Brittas Bay area of County Wicklow. Before we travelled, I reminded him that he had said he would point out certain places in Brittas Bay if he was brought up there, and was he willing to go now? He said, yes. We travelled from Wicklow Garda Station in a car driven by Inspector Reynolds. I heard the Inspector caution Shaw that what he would say or point out during the course of our trip, may be given in evidence. He agreed to go.

As we travelled along the roadway from the car park at Brittas Bay towards McDaniels pub, Shaw said, we came along this road. When we reached the spot on the roadway, about 400 yards from McDaniels, where there are gateways into a field on the left-hand side of the road, Shaw said, it might have been around here, one of these gateways. As we approached McDaniels, he indicated to a roadway to the left at McDaniels. He said, we went up here. We continued on up the roadway as directed by Shaw, and we passed a water pump on the left-hand side of the roadway. Shaw said, I remember turning in left after that water pump. When we reached the entrance to the laneway, on the left-hand side at Castletymon Forest, Shaw said, I think this is the place. He indicated to a laneway and he said, we went down there.

We all got out of the car and walked down the laneway, as far as where a wire fence had been across the laneway. Shaw said, we stopped around here some place and climbed over a wire fence; we lifted her over. We walked down the lane about halfway, and Shaw looked around and indicated a spot in the forest to the left of the laneway and said, we went into the wood somewhere around here. He looked around and said, it's all changed. When returning up the laneway towards the roadway, Shaw said, I threw her shoes somewhere, but I don't know where, I don't know where it was, and some underwear as well.

Having left the forest, Shaw directed us to return to McDaniels. He showed us through a gateway, and along a lane, to the seafront overlooking the strand. Shaw said, we parked near here somewhere. We got out of the car, and Shaw looked around and saw a small river, which was running into the sea just below us, and he said, the boat was over there, we carried her over and put her into the boat, and we rowed out to sea, out as far as you can see. He indicated a spot where they left the boat on the beach, up near the top.

Shaw then directed us to a spot in the second field of McDaniels caravan park and said, up there somewhere. We drove up by the row of caravans, and on reaching the last one at the top corner, which I knew to be the property of Michael O'Keeffe of Foxrock in Dublin, Shaw said, this is the one all right. We got out of the car, and Shaw went to the store at the rear of the caravan and said, this is a shed, we got the lawnmower in this shed, two oars and a bucket I think.

He said, we got a clothes line up in one of the sites somewhere. He indicated to an area behind the caravan park and said, we burnt our clothes in one of these fields in the tip.

We then returned to Wicklow Garda Station; it was 3.45pm. Later on the same afternoon, 29 September, I saw John Shaw at Wicklow Garda Station. I took samples of pulled and cut hair from his head. I also took samples of pulled and cut pubic hair from him. The following day, 30 September, I handed the four samples of hair over to Sergeant Bill Wright of Wicklow Garda Station.

During Shaw's detention, on the morning of 27 September, he requested to go to the toilet. Having entered the toilet he locked the door, and a Garda remained outside the door. The window of the toilet, on the ground floor, looked out onto the back yard of the Garda Station. Another member was looking out from some observation point in the building, where he had the toilet window in view. He saw Shaw squeeze himself out through the small window to the rear yard of the Station. A door led from the yard out onto a laneway. The door was open, and Shaw went out that way, and a chase ensued. Shaw was captured on the street about 100 yards away, and returned to his cell.

The situation on that morning of 27 September was that the two suspects were in custody for possession of a stolen car. There was no evidence available that they had abducted, raped or murdered anybody. Suspicion, yes, but no actual evidence. There was a District Court sitting in Galway that morning at 10.30am, which continued until late in the afternoon. They were not brought before the Court that day, and did not appear before a Justice of the District Court until 29 September, in Wicklow. Therefore, they were held in unlawful custody from 10am on the 26th until their appearance three days later before the Court in Wicklow. The law at that time did not permit a person to be detained in custody for the purpose of questioning, except those arrested under the Offences Against the State Act. There were many Superior

Court judgements on this issue at the time, which stated that no person may be arrested, with or without a warrant, except for the purpose of bringing that person before the Court at the earliest reasonable opportunity. Arrest was simply a process of ensuring attendance at Court. The one exception was arrests under the Offences Against the State Act.

The Criminal Justice Act, 1951, provides that a person charged with an offence shall, on arrest, be brought before the Justice of the District Court, having jurisdiction to deal with it. If the District Justice is not immediately available, the person shall, as soon as is reasonable, be brought before a Peace Commissioner in the district. Another judgement from a Superior Court states that no person may be arrested, with or without a warrant, for the purpose of interrogation or the securing of evidence from that person. Any arrest of persons for the purpose of assisting police with their enquiries is unlawful.

Considering the duty imposed on the Gardaí by Court judgements and the law at the time, John Shaw and Jeffrey Evans were in unlawful custody when they made statements to the Gardaí and the trips around Connemara and Brittas Bay. Detective Inspector Hubert Reynolds and Detective Inspector John Courtney, the officers leading the investigation, were very well aware of this, and they took a conscious decision not to bring the two men before the Court. They considered it more important to continue the questioning, in the hope that, in the case of Mary Duffy especially, she might still be alive somewhere, held captive by Shaw and Evans. The possibility existed that their actions might save her life. Their decision in this instance was ultimately to lead to a landmark decision in Irish law, delivered on 17 December 1980 by five Supreme Court judges: Judges J Walsh, J Hennessy, J Griffin, T Kenny and P Park.

Elizabeth Plunkett's body was washed ashore on the south Wexford coast on 28 September. Visual identification of the body was not possible. Fingerprints were taken from the body, and were compared with fingermarks from her home. The fingerprints expert was satisfied that one of the fingerprints that came from the body was from the same finger that made a mark on a hairbrush in her bedroom, and that satisfied the identification of Elizabeth Plunkett.

Mary Duffy's body was recovered by divers on 10 October, lying face downwards among rocks, connected by means of a rope to a concrete cavity block, a brick, an anchor and a sledgehammer. At the post-mortem, a pubic hair that was not hers was found on the body. It was compared with samples of pubic hair of John Shaw and Jeffrey Evans by the Forensic Science Laboratory. The forensic scientist who carried out the comparison found that John Shaw's pubic hair was the same as the pubic hair found on Mary Duffy's body.

John Shaw, on his tour of Connemara, had pointed out a spot at a wire fence, near the lake, where he said he'd thrown away Mary Duffy's two rings. A search of that area was carried out, and two rings were found, which were identified by Mary's family as belonging to her.

Shaw and Evans were eventually charged with the abductions, rapes and murders of Elizabeth Plunkett and Mary Duffy. They were given separate trials, before the Central Criminal Court. During Evans's trial, as expected, the defence objected to the admission of his statement, and to the journeys around Brittas Bay, during which certain places were pointed out and certain admissions were made. The Judge, having heard legal arguments on both sides in the absence of the jury, decided not to admit this statement in evidence, saying that Jeffrey Evans was in unlawful custody at the time he made the statement and at the time of the journey around Brittas Bay. The jury heard the rest of the evidence and retired, and their verdict was anxiously awaited. In the end, the jury could not reach agreement, and retrial was ordered.

John Shaw's case was heard in January and February 1978. The presiding Judge was Mr Justice Declan Costello. Again, as expected, the defence objected to the statement and the trip around Connemara and Brittas Bay. They argued that Shaw was in unlawful custody at the time he made the statement, as he had not been brought before the Court as soon as was possible after his arrest. During my evidence, there was an objection when I commenced to give evidence in relation to taking pubic hair from John Shaw. The defence said that I had breached John Shaw's constitutional right to bodily integrity, that a doctor should have taken the samples. The Judge agreed. The evidence was disallowed, which was another lesson for me.

Judge Costello, having heard arguments by both counsels, decided to admit the statement made by Shaw, and remarks made by him on the journey around Connemara. The Judge said that, even though Shaw was in unlawful custody, he would admit the evidence due to the 'extraordinary excusing circumstances' of the case.

Shaw was convicted, and applied to the Court of Criminal Appeal for leave to appeal. During the hearing on the application, the Court asked counsel to discuss whether the necessity of protecting the right to life of Mary Duffy, pursuent to Article 40 of the Constitution, prevented the detention of Shaw from being unlawful. The application was refused, but the Court granted a certificate of leave to appeal to the Supreme Court. The certified point of law of exceptional public importance was whether the continued detention of Shaw after 10.30am on Monday, 27 September 1976, being the approximate time at which the District Justice was available, was unlawful, by reason of the obligation of the Gardaí to attempt to vindicate the right to life of Elizabeth Plunkett and Mary Duffy. Following on from this, they examined whether the statements made by the accused on 27 and 28 September 1976 were admissible for that same reason.

One of the five judges stated in his judgement:

... that article 40 provides that the State shall in particular by its laws ... vindicate the life, person, good name and property rights of every citizen. There was therefore on the State a duty to protect the life and person of

Mary Duffy. This function of the State in this case fell to be discharged by the Gardaí, lawfully established Police force of the State. For the purpose of this case, that duty devolved upon the members of the force investigating her disappearance, and in particular upon Superintendent Reynolds.

The real question which arises in this case is whether there were circumstances in which the rights to personal liberty, conferred by Article 40, may be said to have been limited or qualified. In this case, on 27 and 28 September 1976, unless there was justification for limiting, or qualifying the right of the appellant to personal liberty, there was on the facts proved a reasonable prospect that the competing rights to life and person of Mary Duffy would be seriously and irretrievably endangered. In my opinion, where such a conflict arises, a choice must be made and it is the duty of the State to protect what is the more important right, even at the expense of another important, but less important, right. ...

Although the right to personal liberty is one of the fundamental rights, in my view, in any civilised society, if the balance is to be struck between the right to personal liberty for some hours, or even days, of one person, and the right to protection against danger to the life of another, the latter right must in circumstances such as these, which confronted Superintendent Reynolds in this case, prevail. Applying these principles to this case, Superintendent Reynolds therefore had to make a choice between vindicating the right of the appellant to personal liberty, and endeavouring to save the life of Mary Duffy, which had the necessary consequences of continuing the detention of the applicant. He made that choice, and viewing that matter objectively from the point of view of foresight, and not hindsight, in my opinion he made the correct choice, and indeed made the only choice which he could reasonably have made in the circumstances.

Accordingly in continuing the detention of the appellant, he was not acting unlawfully, but was doing what was necessary to protect the constitutional rights of Mary Duffy, under Article 40 of the Constitution.

With regard to the statements made, and the evidence given in relation to what was pointed out by the appellant, and what was found as a result of the places visited on the Connemara journey, it is in my view irrelevant whether the appellant was in lawful or unlawful custody, at the time of this journey he made. This was a journey undertaken at his own expressed request. He volunteered to go and point out the different places, to which he and the accompanying Gardaí subsequently went. In this respect he was, the trial Judge found, a free agent, and all the evidence connecting him to the offences, which was obtained on that journey, was discovered directly as a consequence of his own voluntary acts. There was therefore, in my view, no ground upon which that evidence could have been excluded at the trial.

However, I should like to add that in my view, his detention was not unlawful at that time. The explanation of Superintendent Reynolds for permitting that journey was that, although the appellant had confessed to the killing of Mary Duffy, the Superintendent could not take the risk of accepting the accuracy of the statements of the appellant and Evans. He believed that, notwithstanding the admission of the appellant, there was still a chance that Mary Duffy might be alive, and that her life might be saved. The trial Judge fully accepted his explanation.

I agreed with the Court of Criminal Appeal, that it was the duty of the Superintendent to pursue, even with a remote chance that she might be alive; and that the chance that she was still alive, though remote, was sufficient to render the continued detention of the appellant lawful. Indeed if he had not permitted the journey when the appellant volunteered to undertake it, and if subsequently the body of Mary Duffy was found, not in Lough Inagh, but was tied up in a wood or remote building, it would surely be said that, with hindsight, the Superintendent had neglected his duty to the State, and to Mary Duffy.

Accordingly, my answer to the question of law set out in the certificate of the Court of Criminal Appeal, would be that the continued detention of the appellant after 10:30am on Monday, 27 September 1976, was lawful. The statements made by him, on 27 and 28 September 1976, were admissible.

Three Judges issued a written judgement, and the other two Judges approved it, and the appeal was refused. Evans's trial went ahead on 8 December 1978, and he was convicted of murder, false imprisonment and rape, and sentenced to penal servitude for life.

Jeffrey Evans died in the Mater Hospital in Dublin in 2012. He had been in a coma for over a year, and was continually in the custody of prison officers. From 26 September 1976 until the day he died, he was in custody as a result of the terrible deeds he had committed. John Shaw is still serving out his sentence in Arbour Hill, in Dublin.

If any case deserved life imprisonment, I think certainly this was one. I think both men deserve every minute of the time they have served. These crimes must have had a terrible effect on a lot of people, particularly the mothers and fathers, brothers and sisters and other relations of the two unfortunate girls. In spite of what Shaw and Evans said happened, we really will never know what torture the girls went through.

I would say that all of the Gardaí involved in this investigation were affected in some way. It affected me for a long, long time. You can't just go home and switch off, and forget things like that. You wake up at night, and these things come back to you.

THE MURDERS OF FIVE GARDAÍ,
1976, 1980 AND 1983

During my service, I have been involved in the investigations of the murders of five members of the Garda Síochána. The first of these was the murder of Michael Clarkin. Michael was stationed in Portarlington in County Laois, and he had only four years' service. He had previously been stationed in Portlaoise.

On the night of 16 October 1976, the Gardaí received a phone call to the effect that there was suspicious activity taking place, in a disused house at a place called Garyhinch in Portarlington. Detective Garda Tom Peters and Detective Garda Ben Thornton of the Detective Branch in Portlaoise, and Sergeant Jim Cannon, Garda Jerry Bohan and Garda Michael Clarkin from Portarlington, responded to the call. They all went to the disused house.

When they arrived it was pitch dark, and they endeavoured to establish what was going on in and around this house. They made their way into the house somehow, and while at least some of them were inside, there was an explosion within the house. A booby-trap bomb exploded, and it killed Michael Clarkin outright. All the others were injured in some way. The worst of these injuries was sustained by Detective Garda Tom Peters – he was blind and deaf for the rest of his life. All the others' hearing was affected for the rest of their lives.

I was one of a number of Gardaí from outside the Laois/Offaly Garda area that went to assist in that investigation. Chief Superintendent Dan Murphy, Superintendent John Courtney and Detective Inspector Pat Culligan, who was later Commissioner, were also there. Over the next month or two, a lot of local members of the provisional IRA were arrested and questioned. Some firearms and some bomb-making equipment were found. However, no person was charged in relation to the murder or the explosion.

I was involved in investigating the murder in 1980 of Detective Garda Seamus Quaid, stationed in Wexford. Seamus, from Castlemahon in County Limerick, had twenty-two years' service. He joined the Gardaí in 1958, and in 1979 he joined the Detective Branch. Seamus was a very prominent hurler, playing with Faythe Harriers. He won an All Ireland Senior Hurling medal with Wexford in 1960. He was married and he had four children.

On 13 October 1980, there was a bank raid in Callan, County Kilkenny. Seamus and a colleague of his, Detective Garda Donie Littleton, also of Wexford, became involved in the investigation. They were checking up on suspects that lived in their area. After a day going around checking on suspects, late in the evening they came across Peter Rogers, a member of the provisional IRA, whom they had been looking for. They were on their way back to Wexford on a country road, and just happened to meet him. He was driving a van, selling vegetables. They knew him, having met him on previous occasions.

They approached the van and the driver got out. As they were examining the van, Rogers produced a gun. Seamus Quaid had his firearm with him, but Donie Littleton's gun had been left in the Garda car. Rogers ordered them at gunpoint into a quarry nearby. Seamus Quaid drew his weapon, and there was an exchange of shots between Seamus Quaid and Peter Rogers. Donie Littleton escaped, Peter Rogers was shot in the left leg, and Seamus was fatally injured. He died shortly afterwards.

Rogers got into his van and drove away to a house, the occupants of which he knew. From there, he went to another house, which happened to be the house of a colleague of Seamus Quaid's, on the 1960 All Ireland-winning hurling team. Seamus Quaid's colleague on the team persuaded Rogers to give himself up to the Gardaí. I interviewed Seamus Quaid's colleague from the hurling team, and he was very cooperative, and that was my involvement.

When members were examining Rogers's van, they found a large quantity of explosives and a firearm, and of course Rogers had a firearm himself. Seamus Quaid was posthumously awarded the Gold Scott Medal, on 16 December 1982.

Rogers was subsequently charged with capital murder, convicted, and sentenced to execution. The sentence was commuted by the president to forty years' imprisonment without remission. Subsequently, as a result of the Good Friday Agreement, Rogers was released from prison. Peter Rogers was from Belfast, and he was one of a number of men that escaped from the *Maidstone*, a prison ship moored in Belfast Lough. Seven or eight of them escaped, and the following morning they appeared in Dublin at a press conference.

Rogers was in the news recently, involved in a war of words with Gerry Adams. Adams was denying that he was in the IRA. Peter Rogers stated that in 1980, he got verbal directions from Gerry Adams to bring explosives to England, and that Martin McGuinness was present at that meeting. Rogers said he had complained that the explosives were unsafe, but that they directed him to bring them to England anyway.

The third member whose murder I was involved in investigating was Sergeant Pat McLoughlin, from Patrick Street, Mullingar. Pat McLoughlin was well known to me, as he was stationed in Clane, County Kildare, and he was stationed with me in Naas for a number of years. He had joined the Gardaí in 1961, and at the time of his death had been a Garda for twenty-one years. He had been in a number of other stations before he came to Clane and Naas. In 1975, Pat was promoted to Sergeant and went to Omeath, and from there to Dunboyne in 1977. At the time of his death, he was married with four children. Pat's wife was from Prosperous, very near Clane, and her name was Price.

For many years, I used to sit in the church in Naas beside Paddy Price from Prosperous, at Saturday night Vigil Mass. We didn't get much of a chance to talk inside the church, but one night outside we had a chat. He told me who he was, and then he told me that his brother-in-law had been in the Garda, and was shot dead in Dunboyne. I knew straight away who he was – Pat McLoughlin's brother-in-law.

On 11–12 April 1983, Pat McLoughlin was in a place that you might think was the safest place anybody could be at night time – in his bed asleep, beside his wife. At that time, Pat was living in the married quarters at the Garda Station in Dunboyne. His bedroom was situated right over the front door. Pat was awakened after twelve o'clock by knocking at the front door. He got out of bed and lifted up the window. As he put out his head to see who was there, one of the two people at the front door shot him dead with a shotgun. He fell back into the room beside his wife.

Myself and Pat Culhane became involved in that investigation the following morning. There were two prisoners detained in Trim that morning. Pat and I spoke to one of them, and he admitted that he was involved in the murder of Sergeant Pat McLoughlin. This young man had recently joined the Defence Forces, and shortly afterwards had come to the notice of Pat McLoughlin. Pat found him in possession of a small amount of drugs for his own use. He wasn't arrested or summonsed, but it lingered on his mind, what was going to happen. Was the Sergeant going to tell the Army authorities? If he did, he would be dismissed from the Army.

On the night of 11 April 1983, himself and a friend were at some function or party somewhere, and they discussed what was likely to happen to him. One of them had a motorcycle, and the friend's father had a shotgun. They decided that they would shoot the Sergeant. They drove to the Garda Station, and knocked at the door. Pat opened the window upstairs, and one of them shot him dead. The other person also admitted his part, and was also arrested. Both were charged with murder. That was a wasted life, over a small thing, and Pat had not contacted the Army about the small drugs find.

I was also involved in investigating the murders of Garda John Morley and Garda Henry Byrne in County Roscommon in July 1980, which I will discuss in a later chapter.

EXTORTION, BANK OF IRELAND, CARLOW, 1979

In the spring of 1979, I went to Carlow town, and examined the scene of a housebreaking at the home of James Syme, manager of the Bank of Ireland in the town. Someone had entered his dwelling house through a downstairs window, and had taken some small items of property, which were discarded in a field to the rear of the dwelling. No clues were found as to the identity of the culprits.

On the morning of 5 April, Mr Syme was in his office in the bank, and he received a telephone call from a man calling himself Willis. He told the manager to ring his home immediately. Mr Syme did so, and a male voice instructed him to get the sum of £40,000 from the bank, go to a layby on the Carlow to Leighlinbridge Road, and put the money at a particular spot in the layby. He was told that his wife had been kidnapped, and not to tell anybody in the bank or contact the Gardaí. If he complied with these instructions, his wife would be released, unharmed.

The manager complied, but only brought the sum of £37,500. He left it as instructed, then returned to his office, and was not too long back when his wife walked in. He asked her if she had been harmed. She asked him what he was talking about. He discovered that she had not been kidnapped at all. She had been downtown, shopping, and had then gone for a cup of coffee.

The banking authorities were then told what had transpired, as were the Gardaí. The Carlow Gardaí and the manager returned to the layby on the

Leighlinbridge Road, and of course the money was gone. I was one of a number from the Detective Branch in the Carlow and Kildare Division that went to Carlow that day to investigate the crime. We remained there for a week or so. Particulars of the crime were circulated to surrounding Garda divisions, as was usual.

On the morning of the crime, 5 April, an observant, civic-spirited person was in the vicinity of the Carlow Regional College, on the Leighlinbridge Road. He observed a large Datsun motorcar, maroon coloured, with a Northern Ireland registration number, come to the gates of the college, then turn and go in the Leighlinbridge direction. The car did this a number of times. There was only one person in the car. The time coincided with the manager depositing the money at the layby. He would have had to pass the Regional College on the way. One thing that caught this observant person's eye about the car was that the glass was missing from the fly window of the rear right door.

In a day or so, information was received from the Gardaí at Newross. They were aware that a car matching the description of the car seen at the Regional College, with the glass missing from the rear right door fly window, had been seen recently, at the home of a man who was known to the Gardaí, and believed to be active in subversive activity. It was established that the car seen at this man's house was in the possession of a Hugh Meenan from Derry. He also was known to be involved in subversive activity. Enquiries continued, and the man who owned the car and a close associate of his, from Newross, who was another person involved in subversive activity, were arrested and detained under Section 30 of the Offences Against the State Act. They were questioned about the money extorted from the bank manager. They were asked to give accounts of their movements on the morning of 5 April. They said they had nothing to say, and they didn't account for their movements. They were released without charge.

At the time the information about Hugh Meenan was received, he had left the area and his whereabouts were not known to the Gardaí. Meenan's photograph, description and past history, and the registration number of his car, were passed on to the investigating Gardaí in Carlow. The Gardaí were satisfied, from their enquiries and their knowledge of these men, that Meenan and the other two men were involved in the crime. Meenan was then sought for questioning.

It turned out that the telephone wires into the manager's house had been cut. The culprits had connected incoming wires to their own phone, so that they could make the call to the manager, and take his call when he telephoned his house.

After a week or so, the Gardaí reached a stage where they couldn't take the investigation any further, in the absence of Meenan, and I returned to Naas.

Another week later, on 18 April, I was going to a Garda rugby match, along with Detective Garda Noel Long of Naas. As we drove through Longford town's main street, traffic was coming from a street on our left-hand side, and merging with us. The first car in the line of traffic, trying to turn on to the main street, was a large Datsun, maroon coloured, and, would you believe, it had no glass in the fly window of the rear right door. There were two men in the car, and I immediately recognised the driver as Hugh Meenan, from photographs I had seen a week previously.

I drove across the road, and parked my car directly in front of the Datsun. I jumped out with my official firearm drawn, and ordered the two occupants of the Datsun out of the car. When I had them lying on the ground, I identified myself to the two men, and to the crowd that seemed to have appeared out of nowhere. I asked somebody in the crowd to contact the local Garda Station, and to tell them that we needed assistance. The local Gardaí arrived shortly. I arrested the two men under Section 30 of the Offences Against the State Act, and searched both of them. They and the Datsun car were brought to the Garda Station.

I organised with the Crime Investigation Branch at Garda Headquarters for assistance in questioning the two men. We also needed somebody from Ballistics and the Fingerprint Section to come down and examine the car. Hugh Meenan gave his address as Liscloon Drive in Derry. The passenger gave his name as McLoughlin, also of Derry. McLoughlin said that they were on their way from Cork to Derry when they were arrested. He claimed to be involved in collecting funds for the republican prisoners' dependent fund. Meenan gave the same account, and denied any involvement in the fake kidnapping. Detective Inspector Michael Caravan and Detective Sergeant Pat Cleary arrived from Dublin, and they took over the questioning of Meenan. He told them the same story, denying any involvement in what had happened in Carlow.

The car was examined, and cash to the amount of £10,800 was found, hidden in the panels of the two front doors. On being told of the discovery of the cash, Meenan admitted his involvement in the crime. He now made a statement, saying the manager's house had been broken into only so as to obtain the house phone number off the telephone itself. His two associates and himself had then tapped into the telephone line. They collected the money from the layby, and drove to a wood at St Mullins, in County Carlow, immediately after. They divided up the money and separated, and each of them hid their share. Meenan then drove back to Derry. He left Derry again on 17 April, drove back to the wood and recovered his share of the cash, and was returning to Derry when he was arrested in Longford.

There was no evidence against Mr McLoughlin, and he was released without charge. Hugh Meenan, aged thirty-four and father of three children, was finally dealt with in the Special Criminal Court, on 29 May 1979, on charges of demanding £40,000 with menace and intent to steal on 5 April 1979. He was also charged with stealing £37,500 on 5 April 1979, and receiving £10,800 between 5 and 18 April 1979, the property of John Syme, knowing that it had been stolen. He pleaded guilty.

Meenan had previously served a sentence of five years, for the armed robbery of a bank in Cobh in 1972. He was now sentenced to four years' imprisonment by the Special Criminal Court.

There was a sort of sequel to the events at Carlow. In the statement made by Hugh Meenan at Longford following his arrest, he named his two accomplices. After Meenan was released, having served his sentence of four years, he returned to New Ross on 18 September 1980, and walked into a pub owned by one of the men. The former associate took exception to Meenan for naming him in his statement to the Gardaí as being involved in the Carlow crime. It was alleged in Court that he got a hurley, and assaulted Meenan. He was charged with wounding Meenan, with intent to cause him grievous bodily harm, with causing him actual bodily harm and with assault. John Mahoney, a surgeon in Wexford Hospital, said that when Meenan was admitted to hospital, he was semiconscious, disorientated, and had a deep cut in his head. An X-ray showed a depressed fracture in the skull, and he was hospitalised for three weeks. The case against Meenan's associate was dealt with in Wexford Circuit Court, and he was found not guilty.

One night some years later, I happened to turn on the 'Late Late Show'. Gay Byrne's guest was a man launching a book about his life. Who was it? Hugh Meenan, talking about his bank robbery and other deeds. That was the last I heard of him.

CHAPTER FIVE

DETECTIVE
SERGEANT

MURDER AND BANK ROBBERY, TRAMORE, 1979

By 1979, I had completed twenty-four years in the Garda Síochána, and I was quite happy in the Detective Branch in Naas. My wife Maureen was only thirteen miles from home. At the time, members of the Uniform Section were not allowed reside within thirty miles of close relatives. That regulation did not apply to members of the Detective Branch. I did not have any great ambitions for promotion, until one day a circular came out from Garda Headquarters, requesting applications for the position of Detective Sergeant, at Crime Branch in Garda Headquarters. The position was open to Sergeants throughout the country, and to members of Garda rank who had an aptitude for crime investigation. I discussed it with Maureen, and we agreed that I should apply.

I went for interview, and was one of three members who were successful. One was selected for Administration Section, one for Handwriting Section and one for Investigation Section. I was selected for promotion to the only one that would suit me really, the Investigation Section. That was 8 June 1979, but up until 7 August, I got no word of my transfer.

On Tuesday, 7 August 1979, the Tuesday after the August bank holiday, at 10.15am, five armed and masked men arrived at the AIB bank in Tramore in Waterford, in a stolen Cortina car. One man, carrying an Armalite rifle, stayed outside the bank. One stood immediately inside the door of the bank. One took charge of customers in the bank, one jumped over the counter and fired two shots into the ceiling, and one stayed in the getaway car outside. They robbed the manager, Thomas Barrett, of £4,700.

During the course of the armed raid, the Gardaí were alerted, and they arrived outside the bank in a marked Garda car, while the raiders were still inside. There was a Sergeant and a Garda in the car. The raider outside the bank with the rifle ordered the Gardaí out of the car, and he put them lying on the ground. He discharged a shot from the Armalite rifle, puncturing one of the tyres of the Garda car.

Inside the bank were ten staff members and fourteen customers. Some of the customers tried to leave, and were prevented from doing so. One of the customers was shot dead.

The incident was described later by a taxi man, who was just about to enter the bank. He said, when he was within a few feet of the bank door, he heard somebody shout, 'Get fucking in there quick!' He saw an armed and masked raider, struggling at the door with a man who was trying to get out. The raider pushed the man into the hall, forcing him to fall forward onto his face, and kicked him twice. The taxi man saw that the raider had a gun in his hand, and he pointed it at the man and fired a shot, from a distance of about one foot, striking the man around the left shoulder. The raider kicked the man he had shot in the thigh as he lay on the ground. The man who was shot was Eamon Ryan, married, thirty years of age, a civil servant in Dublin, living in Leixlip in

County Kildare. He was visiting his native town, Tramore, with his wife Berna-dette and their two young children – Dorothy, aged five, and Peter, two-and-a-half. Peter was with his dad in the bank when he was shot. The raiders escaped.

That morning I received a telephone call from Garda Headquarters, to join up immediately with other members of the Investigation Section, who were on their way to Tramore. My transfer from Naas to Crime Branch took place that morning.

The public gave great assistance to the Garda investigation. Within a few days, it became known that a seventy-nine-year-old man from Waterford had met the culprits at a prearranged location very shortly after they left Tramore, and the culprits handed over to him the cash and firearms they had used in the bank. The raiders then went to a house in Bunmahon in County Waterford. They stayed there all day and that night. The following morning, they went to a house in Killmacow in County Kilkenny, and from there some of them went on to Limerick.

The seventy-nine-year-old man was Walter Morrissey, a retired taxi driver from Waterford City. He and members of two families were arrested, under Section 30 of the Offences Against the State Act. When questioned, Morrissey admitted receiving the cash and firearms from the raiders, which were recovered by the Gardaí. He made a written statement to Detective Sergeant Jim Hurley of Waterford. I interviewed him on two occasions in Waterford. This is what he said at the first interview:

I cannot help you, I am a member of the army, sorry about what hap-pened, I'm finished with them now, nothing more to do with them. I would die first, nothing more to say.

In the interview of the following day, 13 August, he said:

I was approached by a man about ten days before the robbery, I don't know his name. But being a soldier of the Republican Army, if I knew him I wouldn't tell. I was told an armed raid was going to take place on

Tuesday, 7 August. I didn't know if it was a bank or Post Office. I agreed to take the arms and cash after the raid. I drew a sketch and I gave it to the man ... I told the man that I would take the stuff from them, and that I would bury it in a heap of sand ...

On the morning of 7 August, I went to the spot and travelled in my wife's car. I stood beside it and waited, and a car came from Tramore direction with a number of men in it. I took the arms and the cash from them; they put it into the boot of my car. I put it into plastic bags ... and I buried it in the sand. I saw the Armalite rifle; it was in two parts; I knew it was Army property and I would guard it with my life.

When asked who was to remove the cash and firearm, he said, 'I am not going to say another thing; I am not going to let anybody down.'

Morrissey was charged before the Special Criminal Court, and was dealt with before that Court on 13 May 1980. He pleaded guilty to the charge of assisting others to commit an armed robbery. He was sentenced to three years' imprisonment. The presiding Judge, Liam Hamilton, said, 'What is done nowadays in the name of republicanism, would make true republicans turn in their graves. It is not republicanism. It is pure terrorism and subversion.'

Along with a member of the Detective Branch in Waterford, I interviewed a young man from one of the families that had been arrested. The young man wasn't so cooperative at the beginning. Then he began to open up, and he told us about the men that came to his house after the robbery. He was nervous talking to us in the Garda Station, with other prisoners around. So we brought him into a car in the yard. He described what he saw and heard, and described the men as best he could. I asked him about accents, and he said that there was a young man definitely from Cork, with a great Cork accent.

That was a great help, because I had been in the Bridewell in Cork a short time previously, and had looked through a large photograph album of criminals, ordinary and subversive. Our man said that he believed he could identify this man if shown a photograph. I have spoken about photographs before, about the trip I had to England, incorrectly picking out a man in an identification parade. But there is no problem showing an album of photographs to a prospective witness, when you yourself do not know the identity of the culprit you are endeavouring to identify.

In the early hours of the following morning, a member from the Bridewell arrived in Waterford with the album, and we began to go through it. There were hundreds of photographs in the album, but when we came to a particular page he said, 'Hold on, that's him, that's one of them, as sure as I'm sitting here.' The man he picked out was Patrick Aaron O'Connell, from Ballyfehan in Cork. The investigators knew the names of most of the culprits, within a few weeks, but all were gone to ground and couldn't be located. O'Connell was known to the Gardaí in Cork as a subversive, and he was missing from home as far as they knew. It later transpired that seven men in total were involved in the raid – five at the bank, and the other two quite a distance away with cars to pick people up and drop them off.

The Gardaí in Dublin were investigating another robbery on 13 October, and had taken possession of and examined a motor vehicle in connection with it. They found, concealed in that vehicle, a number of documents, which appeared to be an account of the robbery and murder in Tramore on 7 August. The documents were in the handwriting of the participants, and were codenamed. One such document was codenamed Abba. In the Abba report, the author called himself Number One. These reports appeared to have been obtained from the culprits by the IRA hierarchy, in their own investigation into what had happened in Tramore.

On 16 October, Gardaí in Cork arrested Patrick O'Connell in Cork City, under the Offences Against the State Act. Members of the Investigation Section

Crime Branch, including myself, and Detective members from Waterford, went to Cork to interview O'Connell. I arrived in Cork late that night, and interviewed O'Connell with Detective Sergeant John McGerty of Cork, from about 2am to 4am. He denied any involvement. We interviewed him again from about noon till about 2.30pm the following day, and got the same response.

Later that night, I was interviewing O'Connell, when Detective Sergeant Charlie Gaffney from Garda Headquarters produced a number of documents to O'Connell, which had been seized in his home. These were hand-written documents, anything with his handwriting on it, like his schoolbooks and an application for a driving licence. These were produced to O'Connell, and he was asked who had written them. He admitted that the handwriting shown to him, most of it, was his. Some time later, the document codenamed Abba was produced to him. He was told that, according to the handwriting expert, the document codenamed Abba was written by the same person that wrote all of the other things. The questioning continued, by Detective Superintendent John Butler and myself, and he finally said that he had written the Abba document, and that what was in the report was correct.

O'Connell was charged before the Special Criminal Court with murder and robbery. He was convicted, and sentenced to life imprisonment, in January 1980. O'Connell gave evidence in his own defence. He said he was at home all day on 7 August, and some family members corroborated what he had said. He admitted writing the Abba report, but said it had been dictated to him, by a person he wouldn't name, and he wouldn't name the location where it was written. He said he did not know what the report was for.

Another man stood trial with O'Connell – William Hayes, twenty-three years of age, of Ferrybank in Waterford. He was charged with robbery and as an accessory after the fact. One of the reports found in the vehicle in Rathmines, codenamed Airport, was found to be in his handwriting. He refused to recognise the document, which stated that he was was four or five miles away from Waterford on the day of the robbery, waiting in a red Cortina car to pick up some of the raiders. He had nothing to do with the murder, but was charged with being an accessory after the fact. He helped out these people, knowing they had committed a crime. He was convicted, and sentenced to twelve years.

Another man was charged in relation to the raid in Tramore. Eamon Nolan, of St John's Park in Waterford, was convicted of the murder of Eamon Ryan, and the robbery of £4,700 from the bank. He had also written one of the reports found in Rathmines. He said that he had written it on request from a friend, and denied that he was involved in the murder and robbery. He was sentenced to life imprisonment. I did not have any dealings with either Hayes or Nolan.

BANK ROBBERY AND MURDER OF TWO MEMBERS OF THE GARDA SÍOCHÁNA, BALLAGHADERREEN, 1980

Around 3pm on Monday afternoon, 7 July 1980, three armed and masked men pulled up to the Bank of Ireland on Main Street, Ballaghaderreen, County Roscommon, in a stolen blue Ford Cortina. Two of the raiders entered the bank, and they shouted, 'Everybody down!' The staff heard them shout, 'Kill anybody that gets in your way. If anybody moves, kill them.'

They ordered the acting manager to get the keys, and open certain drawers and presses. They discharged some shots while they were there, and stole a considerable amount of money. The third raider, armed with a pump-action shotgun, stayed outside the main door of the bank, and it is believed that he discharged a shot into the bank during the raid.

The Gardaí at Ballaghaderreen learned that an armed robbery was in progress at the Bank of Ireland. Two unarmed Gardaí, Garda Brendan Walsh and Garda Kilmore, went there immediately in a patrol car, and parked opposite the bank. They were approached by a hooded man, who they described as six feet tall or more and of good build. He pointed the shotgun directly at Garda Walsh, ordered both Gardaí out of the car, and put them lying on the ground, saying, 'Don't try anything.'

Having robbed the bank, the three raiders got into the blue Cortina, did a U-turn on the road and drove away, shouting and cheering in great jubilation. One of the raiders had his hand out the window, waving a gun in the air. They drove off in the direction of French Park.

Information regarding the bank robbery was immediately circulated throughout the surrounding counties, with a description of the blue Cortina, registration VLI 168, and descriptions of the raiders. The information was received in Castlerea Garda Station within minutes. Castlerea is about twelve miles south of Ballaghaderreen, with Loughglinn situated about halfway between the two towns. Sergeant O'Malley of Castlerea Garda Station responded quickly. He, Garda Derek Kelly and Detective Garda John Morley, who was in possession of an Uzi sub-machine gun, left the Station with the intention of intercepting the raiders. As they drove down the street in Castlerea they met Garda Henry Byrne, who was making his way on foot to the Garda Station. He joined his three colleagues in the patrol car, and they headed in the direction of Loughglinn, believing it to be a likely route for the raiders to take. Sergeant O'Malley occupied the front passenger seat, Detective Garda John Morley sat immediately behind Garda Kelly, who was driving, and Garda Henry Byrne sat behind Sergeant O'Malley.

As they approached the junction known as Shannon's Cross or Ahaderry Cross, Garda Kelly was slowing down to negotiate a right turn, when a white

Cortina car appeared, approaching the junction from the road he was turning on to. The cars collided. The white Cortina, VZM 208, had been stolen in Taylor's Hill, Galway, on the night of 2 July. It contained the three raiders who had robbed the bank in Ballaghaderreen. They had already abandoned the blue Cortina, setting it on fire and transferring to the white Cortina.

No one was injured in the collision. The three raiders, still masked and armed, jumped out of the car. The windscreen of the Garda car was shattered by a shotgun blast, and there was indiscriminate firing at the patrol car, from what Sergeant O'Malley considered were revolvers. Detective Garda Morley discharged shots from the Uzi, from within the patrol car. The raiders returned to the white Cortina, got in and reversed back the way they had come. They didn't get far. One of the left-hand doors of the car was wide open, and as it reversed, the open door crashed into a telegraph pole. The car stalled, and the raiders jumped out. At this stage, one of the raiders separated from the other two, and escaped across a field. That was Patrick McCann.

Garda Henry Byrne had been shot in the back of the head, and his colleagues found him lying out on the road. He was bleeding profusely, and one of his colleagues said an act of contrition into his ear. He died within minutes. Detective Garda Morley and Garda Kelly got out of the patrol car. Garda Morley shouted at the raiders, 'Hold it, hold it,' a number of times. He went up the road a short distance, and there was a blast from a shotgun. Garda Morley discharged three or four shots from the Uzi, and then fell backwards onto the roadway, mortally wounded. He died later that evening.

Just then, a red Volkswagen Beetle car, drawing a trailer, arrived at the scene. The two raiders that remained at the scene came out in front of the car and stopped it. One of these men was the tall man with the shotgun, and the other man carried a handgun. The red Volkswagen, registration YAI 895, was driven by Michael Kneafsey, who happened to be a retired member of the Garda

Síochána, and his son Michael accompanied him. The raiders ordered the two men out of the car. Michael senior grappled with the man with the shotgun, and a shot was discharged into the rear of the Volkswagen. The masked men detached the trailer from the Volkswagen, and drove it away in the direction of Loughglinn.

Shortly afterwards, a local resident saw two men walking from the Loughglinn direction. Both were masked; one had a shotgun, and the other had a handgun. They walked into Andy Gallagher's house, and drove off in Andy Gallagher's car, a white Volkswagen, registration 968 2IZ. Mrs Noreen Gallagher was at her home when the men arrived. They forced her at gunpoint into her house, before taking the car.

At about 3.25pm, Garda D. Keigher, unarmed and operating a checkpoint at Ballinlough Cross, observed a white Volkswagen stop a few hundred yards from him, on the Loughglinn road. It turned around, and then drove back towards Loughglinn. Garda Keigher followed it in his private car. The white Volkswagen stopped, and the driver of it pointed a repeater shotgun at the Garda. At first, the gun was pointed upwards, but as the Garda approached, it was borne down and levelled at him. The Garda retreated and the white Volkswagen drove away. The Garda saw Mr Kneafsey's red Volkswagen, YAI 895, crashed in a ditch nearby.

At about 3.45pm, another local resident saw a white Volkswagen car come from the Cloonfad direction and turn right into Derrylahan Road. The resident continued up the same road, and discovered the white Volkswagen, 968 2IZ, in a wood, covered with branches. Colm O'Shea was sitting on a wall nearby, and he had a bullet wound in his chest. The Gardaí soon arrived, and due to his condition, they immediately conveyed O'Shea to the Regional Hospital in Galway. A portion of a bullet was removed from his chest, and he made a good recovery. He was released from the hospital on 14 July, and immediately arrested under the Offences Against the State Act. He was conveyed to Eglington Street Garda Station for questioning.

On the day of these crimes, 7 July, I was involved in the investigation of a murder in Ballybay, County Monaghan. On 28 June, William Elliott, forty-eight, a Protestant farmer and an ex-Ulster Defence Regiment member, was shot dead while attending Ballybay cattle mart. The main suspect was himself later shot dead during the course of an IRA attack on the RUC Station in Loughgall. In that raid, on 20 August 1988, all eight members of an IRA unit were shot dead by SAS and RUC personnel, who were waiting for them.

On the afternoon of 7 July, I received a phone call from Crime Branch at Garda Headquarters. I was informed of the bank robbery, and the shooting dead of the two members, and instructed to proceed to Castlerea immediately. I arrived in Castlerea around 8pm, and, as expected, found a great air of despondency and gloom throughout all the Gardaí present. Indeed I have no doubt the whole local community felt likewise.

Select members of the Garda from the surrounding counties were arriving in Castlerea, and technical support groups from Garda Headquarters were also on their way. Local Garda officers were joined by the late Detective Chief Superintendent Dan Murphy, and Detective Superintendent John Courtney from Crime Branch at Garda Headquarters. Frantic efforts were being made to identify and preserve all crime scenes, including the bank, the scene of the shooting, all cars used by the raiders and the areas in which they were found. Witnesses from the bank and around Ballaghaderreen were being interviewed, to establish exactly what had occurred. A number of men were posted at the hospital, keeping Colm O'Shea under observation.

There was much work to do. At a conference that night, members were brought up to date with the known facts, and tasks were allocated to members. I well recall at that conference, we were told how Garda Derek Kelly held

John Morley in his arms on the road, trying to console him and telling him that medical assistance was on the way. John Morley whispered to him, as he was only able to whisper, 'Say goodbye to my wife and kids for me.'

That night, and throughout the following days, thousands of expressions of sympathy were received at Castlerea Garda Station, at Garda Stations in Mayo, and I am sure throughout the country, to the families of the deceased members and to the Garda Síochána at large.

Meanwhile, a search party was organised, to commence the following morning, to search the woods and fields around where O'Shea was found, with Detective Inspector Christie McCaffrey in charge. A group had already been tasked with patrolling the roads in the vicinity of the search area during the hours of darkness, to endeavour to prevent the culprits from escaping the area.

A technical examination of the bank commenced on the evening of the crime, and it went into the following days. Where one of the raiders had stood on the polished countertop, it was found that he had left a beautiful impression of the sole of one of his shoes. That impression was preserved, and then photographed, and then the piece of timber was cut from the countertop. The photographs of the impression, and the piece of countertop bearing the impression, eventually found their way to Dr Jim Donovan, Director of the Forensic Science Laboratory, together with the footwear that Colm O'Shea was wearing when he was arrested. Dr Donovan examined the impression on the countertop, and compared it with impressions that he made of the soles of the shoes that O'Shea was wearing.

All cars known to have been used by the culprits on that day were taken possession of and brought to safe locations, where they were subjected to thorough technical examinations. The first car was a white Ford Cortina with a black roof, registration VZM 208, which was the one that crashed into the patrol car immediately prior to the shooting. It had been stolen in Taylor's Hill in Galway on 2 July. Car number two was a blue Ford Cortina, registration VLI 168, used by the raiders at the bank and later burnt out by them. It had been stolen in Athlone on 3 July. Number three was a red Volkswagen Beetle, registration YAI 895. It was commandeered at gunpoint at the scene from Michael Kneafsey and his son, and crashed in the Loughglinn area shortly afterwards. Car number four was a white Volkswagen Beetle, registration 968 2IZ. It was commandeered at gunpoint from Noreen Gallagher's home at Ballinlough shortly after the shooting, and found at a spot in Derrylehane Wood, near to where O'Shea was found. Number five was Peter Pringle's car, a Renault 4L, registration XZM 311, found in the Maam area of County Galway, and known to have arrived at that location between 10am and 4pm on 7 July. Number six was a Ford Escort, registration 897 GZO, found at Cloonabinna House hotel in Galway. That was Colm O'Shea's car, believed to have been at the hotel all day on 7 July. Number seven was the Garda patrol car, a blue Ford Escort, involved in the crash at the shooting scene. All materials and samples taken possession of during the technical examination of these six cars were sent to the Forensic Science Laboratory. Comparison was made with materials in, on or from all clothing and footwear taken from persons arrested in connection with the crime, along with head hair, and so on. The examination of those vehicles took quite a number of days.

Around 8am on Wednesday 9 July, Gardaí at French Park in Roscommon received a telephone call from a good citizen. The caller told them that there was a strange man on the roadway at a particular location, and that they might have an interest in him. Gardaí rushed to the location and located the man. That man was Patrick McCann, thirty-four, and originally from County Waterford. Having spoken to him, they formed the opinion that he could be considered a suspect.

McCann was arrested under Section 30 of the Offences Against the State Act, and brought to French Park Garda Station. His clothing and footwear were taken possession of, and other clothing and footwear were provided for him. He was photographed and fingerprinted, and head hair samples were taken. McCann had noticeable scratches on the backs of both hands and both wrists. On his forehead, over his right eye, was a long scratch, and there was another under his left eye. He was questioned all day by different members, but denied involvement in the crimes under investigation. It was quickly established that O'Shea and McCann had booked into Cloonabinna House hotel, outside Galway, on 1 July, using the false names Colm O'Dea and Patrick Ryan.

Detective Garda Matt Moore and a colleague at the Special Detective Unit at Dublin Castle contacted the incident room at Castlerea with important information. About two months previously, they had stopped three men who had left a Dublin licensed premises known to be frequented by members of subversive groups. It was late at night, and two of the men gave their names on request – Patrick McCann and Colm O'Shea. The third man, who was around six-foot-two, with long hair and a long beard, refused to give his name. The members knew the other two men, and the Gardaí were aware of their subversive activities and connections. They arrested the man who refused to give his name, and brought him to the Bridewell Garda Station. On arrival at the Station, he gave his name – Peter Pringle. He told them that his father had been a member of the Garda Síochána. Pringle was then released.

After O'Shea and McCann booked into Cloonabinna House hotel on 1 July, they were observed on a number of occasions at the hotel, in the company of a tall man with long hair and a long beard, later identified by members of staff as Peter Pringle. He was at the breakfast table with them on the morning of 2 July, the morning after they arrived. He was again in their company on Saturday night, 5 July. Pringle was now a suspect for the crimes, as the tall man outside the bank with the shotgun. The search for the tall, bearded man continued until Wednesday evening, 9 July, with negative results.

As I write about the events of 7 July 1980, I am very conscious of today's date. It is Monday, 7 July 2014, exactly thirty-four years since John Morley and Henry Byrne were murdered. Events in relation to that investigation are very clear in my mind. Something else is very clear in my mind – yesterday was the Munster Football Final, and Kerry hammered Cork by 24 points to 12 points.

On 9 July 1980, the investigation was continuing apace. McCann was being questioned, forensic tests were ongoing and members were out taking statements and interviewing people. Senior officers in charge of the investigation were never too far from a phone, waiting for a break in relation to the search for the missing man.

At 8pm on 9 July, the day Pat McCann was arrested, I questioned him at French Park Garda Station, with Detective Garda Dennis O'Shea of Galway. McCann recognised me as soon as I went into the interview room, as we had met some months previously in Waterford, when I had questioned him in relation to another crime. He denied any involvement whatsoever in the bank robbery and the murders, and he didn't account for his movements on 7 July. After quite some time, he said, 'I want to tell the truth, but I want to see my solicitor first.'

At 11.25pm, his solicitor, Mr Siev from Dublin, telephoned French Park Garda Station. I spoke to him on the phone, and he asked to speak to the prisoner McCann. I agreed to allow him to speak to Pat McCann, and following their phone conversation, McCann told us that he was sorry over the deaths, as sorry as anyone over what happened. He said, 'I will be satisfied getting away with ten or twelve years over this. Between us here now I am saying I wasn't involved in the bank robbery or the shooting, but there are a few things I want to discuss with my solicitor about the best deal he can get for me over this.' He shook hands with me and said, 'I am sorry over it all; you don't know how I feel. I want to tell the truth and in the morning when I see my solicitor, I will.'

I asked him how many robberies he had committed over the previous three or four years. He said to me, 'Guess.' I guessed about fifteen, and he said, 'More.' I kept upping my guess – twenty, twenty-five, and I came to thirty. He said, 'Yes, and a bit more. That does not include post offices and frauds I was involved in.' He said, 'They don't matter now.'

He went to the cell at 1.30am. At 2am, I went to the cell to see him. He was awake, and he told me he could not sleep, and hadn't slept since it happened. I asked him if he was all right, or if there was anything I could get him. He said, 'Yes, but I don't think you will get it for me.' I asked what it was, and he said, 'Arsenic. That is the way I feel about it now.'

McCann's solicitor came the following morning at about 11am, and had a number of consultations with him, up until 1pm. The solicitor then departed, and we asked McCann would he now tell us the truth. He replied, 'My solicitor told me not to say anything.' Throughout that afternoon he made many verbal statements that could be construed as admissions of guilt.

Around 9.30pm, when McCann was about to be brought to the Special Criminal Court to be charged, he came to me and shook hands with me. He said, 'I am sorry over what happened.'

There was a huge attendance at the funeral of the two Gardaí, a joint State funeral at Knock. Thousands of colleagues, along with representatives of every branch of State, Church leaders, GAA representatives, and thousands upon thousands of civilians, attended the requiem Mass and the burial. Great respect was shown to the two Gardaí, and the greatest sympathy to the ones they had left behind. In a tearful grieving farewell, John and Henry were buried very close to each other at the cemetery in Knock, only three or four hundred yards from Knock Shrine. Both John and Henry were posthumously awarded the Gold Scott Medal for Valour, at a special ceremony in 1982 at the Garda Training Centre in Templemore. The awards were presented to their two widows.

The funeral of Detective Garda John Morley and Garda Henry Byrne

John Morley was born in 1942, a farmer's son from the Knock area in County Mayo. He was married and had three young children, two sons and a daughter. John was well known not alone in Mayo and Connaught, but throughout the whole country, for his great powers and achievements on the Gaelic football field. He represented his native county on 112 occasions in the National League and Championship, between 1961 and 1974. He was playing club football up until the time of his murder.

Henry Byrne was born in 1950 in Knock. He was married and had two young sons, and his wife was pregnant with their third child when Henry was murdered. Henry also had close connections with the GAA. He was the twenty-first member of the Garda Síochána, and John was the twenty-second, to be murdered since the foundation of the State.

In the days following 7 July, teams of Gardaí were operating in a wide area surrounding Ballaghaderreen, seeking information in relation to the movements of the stolen blue Cortina VLI 168, and the stolen white Cortina VZM 208, used by the raiders. Gardaí spoke to council workers working in the area of Kilgarriff village, near Knock, that day, and gained some vital information.

At 1.20pm, three Council workers were working on the public road, and had closed it to traffic in both directions, loading a hut of some description onto a trailer drawn by a tractor. Two cars came from the Knock direction together. The first was a blue Ford Cortina, driven by a man they all described as big, with long, greyish hair and a long, greyish beard. The driver spoke to one of the workers, asking how long the road would be closed. He was told ten minutes or so. There was a front-seat passenger in the blue car, and the driver of the white car behind was alone. The workers described the white car as having a black roof. The bearded man remained looking straight ahead, and did not make eye contact with the man that he spoke to, or look in his direction.

Other information helped to track the probable movements of these cars all the way to Ballaghaderreen. At 1.30pm at Ballyhaunis, a man and some of his relatives saw a blue car passing by, driven by a man aged thirty or more, with a full beard with a good bit of grey in it. It was followed by a white car with a dark roof. At 2pm, a lady at Lisacol in Castlerea saw two cars passing by, a blue car and a white car. After 2pm, the driver of a truck outside Ballaghaderreen saw two cars approaching at high speed. They then stopped and reversed. The first car was a blue mark 4 Cortina, and he got most of the registration number: VZI 16. He said that the man sitting behind the wheel had the longest face he ever saw on a man. There was a passenger in the front seat of this car. The second car was white, with Galway registration plates, and he thought the registration began with NZM.

Colm O'Shea was released from hospital on 14 July, and was immediately arrested under the Offences Against the State Act. He was brought to Eglington Street Garda Station in Galway, and interrogated in relation to the bank robbery and the murders. He maintained his right to silence throughout his detention in relation to questions about the crimes. I questioned him for some time with another member, and the only time he spoke was when I asked him if he knew that McCann had been arrested. He said, 'No, how is he?' He was charged with the bank robbery and the capital murder of Garda Henry Byrne. He appeared before the Special Criminal Court and was remanded in custody.

Around 4pm on the afternoon of 9 July, a man matching the description of Peter Pringle appeared on the roadway at a place called Knockatee, a short distance outside the village of Dunmore in County Galway, four or five miles from where O'Shea was found in the woods. This man was seen by a lady who resided in that locality, walking on the roadway towards Dunmore. The lady went into Dunmore some time afterwards, and she saw him again, in the square in the village. A father and son who also lived in Knockatee, two adults, saw him pass their house on foot, walking towards Dunmore. A resident of Dunmore also saw him in the square. He entered a small shop in the village, and purchased a box of matches and a bottle of orange squash from the lady behind the counter.

There was another customer in the shop at the time. Her name is Margaret Boyle, and I hope she is still with us today. When she saw this tall, bearded man, she immediately remembered that the Gardaí were looking for a man of that description in the woods a few miles away. The reason she was so alert to this fact was that her husband was a Garda, stationed in Dunmore. Mrs Boyle immediately left the shop, and passed on the information to him. He jumped into his car and drove around Dunmore, and he learned that the tall, bearded stranger had got a lift in a lorry, heading out the Tuam road. While this tall, bearded man was basically a stranger in the area, one local man that saw him thumbing a lift happened to know him personally. He said that he believed that this man was Peter Pringle, and that he was a fisherman.

Garda Boyle pursued the lorry, overtook it and stopped it. As it stopped, the suspect jumped out of the lorry, got over a ditch, and ran away across the fields. That was at 6.10pm. The lorry driver described the man he had picked up as tall, with a big beard and long hair, and tired-looking. A significant thing he noticed was that he was wearing a maroon-coloured jumper, the same colour as the Galway flag. That was to be significant at a later stage.

A little later that day, around 6.30pm, James Meehan, who lived in the locality, arrived home from work. He parked his car near the back door of his house, leaving the keys in the ignition, and went into the house. Shortly afterwards, he heard the car starting up. Rushing outside, he saw it reversing out onto the road and taking off at speed on the Dunmore–Tuam road. He saw that there was a big, tall man behind the wheel, with a big beard and a good head of long hair. His car was a brown Ford Cortina, 9401 IM.

At 7.30pm, Sergeant Dennis O'Connor and Garda Pat Conroy of Galway were at a junction at a pub called the Green Briar, outside Galway city. They saw the stolen car, 9401 IM, heading towards Galway. It passed right in front of them, and both of them recognised the driver, who was well known to them for quite some time. They both later stated in Court that the driver was Peter Pringle. Garda Conroy turned the Garda car and followed the stolen car, but they could not locate either it or its driver. The car was found somewhere in Galway city at 8am the following morning.

When reports were received that a man matching the description of Peter Pringle was seen in Dunmore, the Gardaí went there and took statements and made enquiries. They learned that this man was seen sitting down somewhere drinking from the bottle of orange squash he had purchased. The Gardaí searched the area, and found an orange squash bottle. It was handed over to a fingerprint expert, who developed a fingermark found on it, and according to the results of the test, discovered that the mark on the bottle had been made by Pringle.

The following morning, 10 July, members searched for Pringle in Galway city, augmented by Gardaí sent from Castlerea. Before this, when it became known that Pringle was a suspect, all known haunts of his in Galway city were visited on a daily basis, and well-disposed persons were spoken to and asked for cooperation and assistance. Enquiries continued until 19 July, but there was no sign of Peter Pringle.

On 18 July, Gardaí in Galway received information from one of the well-disposed persons that they had been keeping in touch with, that the one person Pringle would be in contact with would be his girlfriend. She therefore became the subject of some covert attention. She was seen in a local licensed premises with Peadar Shevlin, a man known to the Gardaí. He was known to deal in drugs in a small way, and also to use drugs himself. He and Pringle's girlfriend went to a quiet place in the licensed premises, and had their little chat, and that information was passed on to the Gardaí. The following morning, Detective Sergeant John Tharpy brought this information to the attention of a conference being held in Galway Garda Station. It was felt that perhaps Pringle might be staying in Shevlin's house. Shevlin lived alone, in a house out near the racecourse at Ballybane Cottages. It was decided that Shevlin's house should be searched.

Detective Sergeant John Tharpy applied for, and was given, a search warrant under the Misuse of Drugs Act, 1977, which empowered him to search Shevlin's house. He went there that afternoon, accompanied by Detective Gardaí O'Reilly, Boyle and Sweeney. They arrived at the house at 2.45pm, knocked at the front door and got no response. One of the members went to the rear of the house, and saw that there was a window open. He got in through it, which, under the warrant, he was entitled to do. Then he opened the front door and let in his colleagues.

A search commenced downstairs, and Detective Garda O'Reilly went upstairs into a bedroom, where he saw Peter Pringle, sitting on a bed alone. In fact, he was the only occupant of the house. He was asked his name, and he gave it as Pringle. He said he was 'clean', presumably meaning not a threat to Gardaí. He was clean-shaven, and his hair was short and dyed reddish. Detective Garda Christie Reilly had seen Pringle on 2 July in the city. At that time, Pringle had long hair and a beard down to his chest.

Pringle was arrested under Section 30 of the Offences Against the State Act, and brought to Eglington Street Garda Station. On the way from Shevlin's house to the Garda Station, he was shivering and trembling in the car. The Gardaí took it that he was frightened. He was searched, and was found to have two £20 notes, a comb and a bunch of car keys. Pringle was put into a cell, and while in the cell he was asked to remove his shoes and socks, to make sure he didn't have anything hidden in them. He took off his socks, they were searched, and he put them back on again. I happened to be in the Garda Station at the time, and I am absolutely certain that nothing else happened to Peter Pringle when he was brought into the Station.

The late Chief Superintendent Pat Culhane and I commenced interviewing Pringle at 4.05pm that day. I am going to set down in detail what was said in our interviews that afternoon, and again the significance of this will become apparent at a later stage.

The following is from my statement of evidence, which I gave before the Special Criminal Court at Pringle's trial:

At 4.05pm on the afternoon of Saturday 19 July 1980, the day that Pringle was arrested, Detective Inspector Pat Culhane and I saw Pringle in the Garda Station in Galway. Pat Culhane introduced both of us to Pringle, and we told him we were investigating the bank robbery in Ballaghaderreen and the shooting dead of two Gardaí shortly afterwards.

We told him that we believed he could help us in some way in our investigations. He did not reply. When asked to account for where he was on 7 July, which was the date of the crime, he said, 'I will account for where I was when I see my solicitor.'

I saw, and so did Pat, that he had numerous scratches on the backs of both hands, and also on the backs of his wrists. They appeared to be some days old, and he was continually brushing off loose scabs off the backs of his hands. He pulled up the legs of his pants on request, and we saw numerous scratches and scrape marks from his knees down to his instep of his shinbones. The scabs had formed on them. I asked how he got all the scrapes and scratches, and he declined to answer.

He was wearing blue jeans, light-coloured ankle-high boots, socks, a red-to-maroon-coloured jumper, and a fawn-coloured cardigan. To me, I did not see anything unusual about Peter Pringle; he was alert and cautious.

At 4.50pm, Pringle's solicitor, Mr Silke, arrived in the Garda Station to see his client, and he did see him. At 5.35pm, Pringle returned to the office after the consultation with his solicitor. Pat Culhane and I resumed questioning him. We asked him if he would now give us an account of where he was on Monday, 7 July. His reply was, 'On the advice of my solicitor, I am not saying where I was.'

I asked him what was he trying to hide, or why he was so secretive about where he was on Monday 7 July, if he was not involved in any crime. He said, 'I know where I was.' When asked if he could get anybody to account for where he was from 12 noon on 7 July, up until Wednesday afternoon, 9 July, his reply was, 'I know where I was, I cannot back it up with witnesses now.' I asked if he could at any time, and he said, 'No.'

Sergeant Anglum, a uniformed Sergeant in Galway, came into the office and he had new clothing and footwear for Peter Pringle. I asked if he would hand over his clothing that he was wearing and his footwear, in exchange for new clothing and footwear, as we wanted to have his clothing examined. He agreed and he removed his boots, socks, cardigan, the red-to-maroon-coloured jumper, a vest, a jeans, and he handed them over to me. What transpired next turned out to be of great importance. As he handed over each item of clothing, I placed them in separate new brown exhibit bags. I did not put my hands into the pockets of Peter Pringle's jeans, nor was I in contact with discharged firearms for many months prior to that day. I asked Pringle was he wearing the boots on 7 July and he replied, 'I don't know.' I asked him if he was wearing the cardigan, and he replied, 'I don't think so.' I asked if he was wearing jeans, and he replied, 'Yes I was.' I asked if he was wearing the red-to-maroon-coloured jumper, and he replied, 'Yes I was.' I asked what else he was wearing, and he replied, 'I cannot remember.' I took a note of his exact replies about each item.

We asked him if he knew Pat McCann and Colm O'Shea, or if he had any association with them. He denied any association with them, and he said, 'I think I know them all right; they are not friends of mine.' I asked when was the last time he met them, and he said, 'It could be a few months or so ago, I'm not sure.' When questioned about when he arrived at Shevlin's house, he said, 'Friday week last.' Which was 11 July. When asked why he shaved off his beard and cut his hair, he said, 'The way I would not be recognised. I knew you were looking for me. I was going to go into town to contact my solicitor, and I didn't want to be picked up on the way in.' I asked why was he hiding in the house and afraid of being picked up, and he said, 'Look, I had nothing to do with the robbery and the shooting of the Gardaí.' When asked again where he was on 7 July, he said, 'I have nothing to say, on the advice of my solicitor.'

When he was asked when he had heard about the bank robbery and the shooting of the Gardaí, he said, 'I heard it on Wednesday afternoon,' which was 9 July. I told him, from Monday afternoon, 7 July, it was head-lines on television, radio and newspapers, and checkpoints were set up all over the west of Ireland, and it was the talking point of the general public all over the country. He was asked where he was from Monday afternoon until Wednesday afternoon, that meant he was not in touch with anybody to hear about it. I asked him how he had heard about it on Wednesday afternoon, and his reply was, 'I have nothing to say to that.' He was told Garda Boyle of Dunmore had seen him in a lorry in Dunmore on 9 July. He was asked what he was doing there, and he said, 'I have nothing to say to that.'

The solicitor came again to see him at 8pm, and remained until 8.20pm. When he was gone, Pringle was again asked to tell us where he was on 7 July, and he said, 'On my solicitor's instructions, I have nothing to say about that.' When asked why, after fifteen years or so, he would suddenly shave off his beard and cut his hair, when Peadar Shevlin could have con-tacted his solicitor for him, his reply was, 'I have no comment to make.'

At 9pm, Detective Sergeant Ennis came into the office, and took swabs of Peter Pringle's hands, combings of his head hair and head-hair samples. At that stage, I handed over to Pat Ennis the clothing and foot-wear given to me earlier that day by Peter Pringle. I left the office with Pat Ennis, and returned again to the office at 9.30pm. Peter Pringle was refusing to account for where he had been on 7 July to Detective Inspec-tor Pat Culhane and Detective Inspector Joe Madigan.

At 10.05pm, his solicitor, Mr Silke, was back again to speak to Pringle.

At that stage, Pat Culhane and I finished our interviews with Peter Pringle for the day. I had recorded all the replies that he had made to Pat Culhane and I, during our interviews with him that day.

Later, certainly after that interview with Pringle, Peadar Shevlin, the man in whose house Pringle was arrested, was in the station. Shevlin gave us an account of the movements of Pringle and some information that he claimed Pringle had told him, up to the time he met him, which he said was on 11 July.

We resumed interviewing Pringle the following day, Sunday, at 2.50pm. Pringle was being interviewed by Detective Inspector Joe Madigan and Detective Garda Ennis at that time. When Pat Culhane and I entered the office, those two members left. We began by asking Pringle where he was from Monday, 7 July, up to the time he went to Shevlin's house on 11 July. We told him that we were satisfied that he was responsible for taking a Ford Cortina car from Dunmore on the evening of 9 July, and that he had been seen on the roadway not far from where the Gardaí were searching for a man believed to have been involved in the bank robbery and the shooting of the two Gardaí. I outlined to him the seriousness of the case, and told him that if he was not involved in the bank robbery and the shooting, he should tell us where he was. His reply was, 'On my solicitor's advice, I am told not to account for where I was.'

At 2.55pm, Detective Garda Christie Reilly came into the office. He told Pringle that his detention was being extended for a further twenty-four hours, on the order of Chief Superintendent Green. A short time after that, Detective Sergeant Maurice Boyle and Detective Garda Seamus O'Neill, both from the Fingerprint Section at Garda Headquarters, came into the office and took Pringle's fingerprints and palm prints. Pat Culhane and I stayed with Pringle up to 7.05pm, and continued to try to get him to account for where he was from 7 July until 11 July. He declined to do so. Detective Garda Roche and Murphy then came into the office to speak with Pringle, and we left.

As well as Peadar Shevlin being in the Garda Station, Peter Pringle's girl-friend was also there. She spoke to the Gardaí and was cooperative, as was Shevlin. At 9.50pm, Detective Sergeant Touhy and Detective Sergeant Tom Dunne saw Peter Pringle in the presence of his girlfriend. Neither myself nor Pat Culhane was there. Pringle acknowledged that he knew her, and she stated in the presence of Pringle and in his hearing, that she had met both Pat McCann and Colm O'Shea in the Green restaurant in Galway in June. She said she went there with Pringle, and Pringle introduced her to them. She stayed on 4, 5 and 6 July at Cloonabinna House hotel in Moycullen. Pat McCann was there, and she met him one night, and Peter Pringle was talking to him in the hotel towards the end of the night.

She said Pringle stayed in her house on the night of 6 July, the night before the bank robbery and the murders. He was still there on the morning of 7 July when she was leaving for work. Significantly, she said he had a maroon-coloured jumper, and he was wearing it leading up to 7 July, and when she came back to the house after work on 7 July, Peter Pringle was gone and so was the jumper. When she last saw him in the bedroom that morning, he still had his long hair and beard.

She said that she met Peadar Shevlin in Garvan's pub in Galway on the pre-vious Tuesday or Wednesday – that would be 14 or 15 July. Pringle had nothing to say in relation to what she said.

Immediately after that interview, I saw Pringle in the Garda Station. I was accompanied by Superintendent Tom Maher, who outlined to Pringle the details of the bank robbery, the shooting of the Gardaí, the vehicles involved, where they had been seen, and especially the observations of the two Cortina cars and their occupants by the three Council workers at 1.20pm on the day of the raid. He outlined to Pringle the findings of the forensic scientists upon examination of materials from three of the cars – the white Cortina, the red

Volkswagen and the white Volkswagen. He told him that fibres identical to fibres from his jumper were found on the rear seat of the white Cortina and on the driver's seats of each of the two Volkswagens. He also told him that firearms residue had been found on his jeans.

I outlined to him the various observations of himself, McCann and O'Shea at Cloonabinna House hotel. He was asked if he had ever been in any of the three cars, or if he had any explanation to offer about the maroon-coloured fibres in the cars, or the firearms residue on his jeans. Superintendent Maher and I urged him to tell us the truth about the matter. He put his head in his hands, put his head down between his knees and said, 'I have nothing to say at this time; I am speechless.'

Now we come to another crucial issue, which was made much of later. Coming up to midnight or thereabouts, Peter Pringle got a slight nosebleed. He wiped the blood away with the back of his hand, and I could see there were slight traces of blood on his hand. He wiped his nose with a tissue, and I saw slight bloodstains on it. He handed the tissue over to me on request. Now, I was aware that some blood had been found on the seat of the red Volkswagen car. I was also aware that Pringle had refused to give a blood sample a short time before. I had some expectation that there may have been sufficient blood on the tissue for analysis.

On getting the tissue from Pringle, I left the office with it and went to another office. I put it into an envelope and wrote a note on the outside of the envelope, identifying its contents. I met Detective Sergeant Pat Ennis, and handed the envelope over to him for analysis. I had already given Pringle's clothes, and cigarette ends from cigarettes that Pringle had smoked, to Pat Ennis. Having given the tissue to Pat Ennis, I took out my notebook and I wrote in it: 'Pringle in upstairs office, Superintendent Tom Maher, nosebleed, tissue to Pat Ennis.'

I returned to where Pringle was, and Superintendent Maher was just about to leave. I made notes regarding the interview Tom Maher and I had had with Pringle when I went in, so my notes on the interview followed the note I made in relation to the tissue. This, again, would become significant later.

Pat Culhane came into the office at about 12.20am, and both of us left at 12.30am, when Detective Sergeant Touhy and Detective Sergeant Tom Dunne came in to speak to Peter Pringle. I am going to deal with that interview now, and the evidence the two members gave in relation to it before the Special Criminal Court. During that interview, Pringle told them that he was concerned about getting his girlfriend involved. At about 1am, he requested that they contact his solicitor, because he wanted to talk to him about this. The solicitor was contacted, and he arrived to have his consultation with Pringle. That consultation took place roughly between 1.30am and 2.30am.

All visitors and the times of their visits are recorded at the Garda Station, and these visits were outlined in the Court of Criminal Appeal. Peter Pringle's solicitor visited a total of six times while he was in custody, and this consultation, at 1.30am that morning, was the last time his solicitor visited him.

When the solicitor left, Pringle told the two Detective Sergeants that he had made up his mind, and that his girlfriend would not have to give evidence. He said he was worried about her, but that there was nothing he could do about it. She couldn't be made to give evidence, he told the two Detective Sergeants, and he said that his solicitor had told him that. Whatever his solicitor may or may not have told him, Peter Pringle's girlfriend was in fact a compellable witness. The privilege of not being a compellable witness would only have applied to Pringle's spouse, who was endeavouring to rear his family in Donegal. It would not apply to a girlfriend or partner.

The next interview I had with Peter Pringle was along with Pat Culhane. We went to the cell at 8.25am on Monday, 21 July, and brought Pringle out into an office in the Garda Station. We began by asking him where he was on 7 July, and he declined to answer. I asked if he had given any consideration to what Superintendent Maher and I had said to him the previous night, when we outlined the body of evidence against him. He said he had thought a lot about it, and that he was concerned about bringing his girlfriend into it. He said he wanted to tell the truth, and not get her involved, but that he had got his solicitor to discuss the matter with him again, and he was again advised not to say anything.

At 9.10am, Detective Sergeant John Tharpy and Detective Garda Brendan Moran of Galway entered the office, along with Peadar Shevlin. Detective Garda Moran put a number of questions to Peadar Shevlin, in Pringle's presence and hearing, and there was no doubt he could hear what was being said. Shevlin repeated all the information that he had already given to the Gardaí. He went through everything in Pringle's presence. When Shevlin had finished, I gave Peter Pringle an opportunity to contradict what Shevlin had said in his presence. I asked if he had anything to say in relation to it, and he said, 'I have nothing to say.' The two members and Shevlin then left.

I told Pringle that he could now see for himself that the one friend he had, whose house he had sought refuge in for a number of days, was telling the truth. Also that I understood that his girlfriend had outlined what she knew in his presence the previous night, and that she had told the truth. He could now see the position he was in. We again outlined to him the forensic evidence, and all the other evidence that had been accumulated against him. We went through everything with him, and he said, 'I know that you know that I was involved, but on the advice of my solicitor I am saying nothing, and you will have to prove it all the way.'

Immediately in his presence I wrote down the words that Pringle had spoken in my notebook. I read it over to him, and asked him if it was correct.

He replied, 'On the advice of my solicitor, I am saying nothing.' I asked if he wished to sign the notes that I had made of what he said, and he declined. I noted the time in my notebook: 9.28am. We continued to question him. When we mentioned about getting others involved, and asked him to tell the whole truth, he said, 'I am doing what my solicitor told me to do.'

Many times, Pringle declined to answer questions, but any replies he did make to questions were recorded by me in my notebook. I have notes of them, and produced them to the Special Criminal Court.

At 9.55am, Detective Inspector Joe Madigan came into the office, and Pat Culhane left. I produced my notebook, and told Detective Inspector Madigan what Pringle had told us. Detective Inspector Madigan asked Pringle if he was going to tell the whole lot, and Pringle said, 'I had said that, and I am saying no more.' I then left the office, as Detective Garda Murphy entered.

At 11.10am, I went back to Peter Pringle, and Detective Garda Cunningham was there. I asked Pringle to elaborate on what he had said about being involved. I tried to get him to tell the whole story, but he said, 'I am doing what my solicitor told me to do.'

On that same morning, 21 July, I met Detective Sergeant Pat Ennis in the Garda Station. He had come looking for me. He told me he had examined the tissue I gave him the previous night, and determined that there was insufficient blood on it for analysis. He now removed it from the envelope, and both of us examined it. There was only very slight staining on it – a dot the size of a pin-head and a little streak – and I agreed with him that there was insufficient blood for analysis. He then disposed of the tissue. This tissue, and the handling of it, was later to have great ramifications. Pat Ennis had not, when I gave him the tissue, recorded the fact that he had received it. At the trial, no questions were asked of anyone about the nosebleed.

Later in the morning, Pringle was escorted to Dublin, and in the afternoon he appeared before a sitting of the Special Criminal Court, where he was charged with the capital murder of Garda Henry Byrne, and robbery at the Bank of Ireland in Ballaghaderreen on 7 July. He was then remanded in custody in Portlaoise Prison, where McCann and O'Shea also were.

The Forensic Science Laboratory was still meticulously examining the clothing of the accused, and materials from the cars. We needed to get as much evidence as possible, to comprehensively prove the identity of the bearded man – the man seen in Cloonabinna House hotel with McCann and O'Shea on a number of occasions; the man seen by the Council workers at Kilgarriff on the day of the crimes; and the man seen around Dunmore in the days following.

It was decided to compile two albums of photographs, Album A and Album B, with thirty-four photographs in each. We would show the albums to certain people, and see who they would identify from the photographs. Pringle had now shaved off his beard and his hair had been dyed reddish and cut short, but we had a photograph of him taken when he was in custody in Galway Garda Station in November 1979, seven months before the crime. At that time he had long hair and a long beard.

I set out with the albums, to three locations: Cloonabinna House hotel; Kilgarriff, to talk to the three Council workers; and in and around Dunmore. First of all I went to Cloonabinna House hotel, and I showed the photographs to four persons there, two from the management and two from the staff, who had already spoken to us in relation to the bearded man. I produced the two albums to each individual on their own, out of sight and out of hearing of anybody else. Each one examined the two albums. They all identified the photograph of Pringle as being the man socialising in the hotel with McCann and O'Shea between 2 and 5 July.

I met each of the Council workers individually, again out of sight and out of hearing of anybody else. The three of them had made statements, and each had described the driver of the car roughly the same. The first man that viewed the photographs had made a statement, but, as was his privilege, he had not signed the statement. At the time, the Gardaí were delighted that he had at least spoken to them, and his description of the man he saw was of great assistance. He spent some time looking at the photographs in Album A, but did not pick out anybody from them. The second man who was at the roadblock examined all of the photographs in the albums. He picked out the photograph of Peter Pringle as being the driver of the blue Cortina. He picked out a photograph of Colm O'Shea as being like the man who drove the white Cortina behind the blue Cortina. The third worker examined all of the photographs, and he picked out the photograph of Peter Pringle as being the driver of the blue Cortina. He also picked out the photograph of Colm O'Shea as being the driver of the white Cortina.

Then I went to Dunmore, and I went to ten people in all. Again, I spoke to these people individually, out of sight or hearing of anybody else. I asked them to look at all of the photographs, and then asked them if they could identify anybody in the albums. In Album A, of the ten people, eight picked out the photograph of Peter Pringle as the man they had seen in Dunmore on the evening of 9 July. The other two did not pick out anyone from the albums. The people that picked out Peter Pringle from the photographs included: the lady, and the father and son who saw him at Knockatee, before he entered Dunmore village; the shop assistant, and the Garda's wife who was in the shop; the Garda who stopped the truck and saw the passenger jump out; and the truck driver who had given Pringle a lift.

Shortly after 22 July, I was asked to give a written summary of the evidence that I could give against Pringle, McCann and O'Shea. In that summary, I included Pringle's nosebleed on the night of 20 July, and my handing over of the tissue with a very slight blood stain to Detective Sergeant Pat Ennis later that night, in the hope that it could be analysed.

At a later date, when I was making my final statement of evidence for the book of evidence, I did not include this matter about the nosebleed or the tissue. I was of the view that, as the tissue did not have sufficient blood on it for analysis, as agreed by Detective Sergeant Ennis and myself, there was no evidential value in it. I was conscious that an issue could arise during the trial, that Pringle had had a nosebleed during the time that he was being interrogated. However, if it did arise, I had a record in my notebook of all that had happened.

I am going to deal with some of the evidence arising out of the examination of the cars. First, there was an item of clothing the girlfriend said Pringle was wearing in the days leading up to 7 July – the maroon-coloured jumper. When she came home after work that evening, Pringle was no longer there and the jumper was gone as well. Pringle's own car, XZM 311, was examined, and a number of wine-coloured wool fibres were found on the driver's seat. There was also a newspaper, *The Irish Times*, dated 2 July, with Colm O'Shea's fingermarks on it. The blue Cortina used at the bank was burned out, and nothing of evidential value was found in it. Six wine-coloured wool fibres were found on the rear seat of VZM 208, the white Cortina the raiders were in when they crashed into the Garda car. Flakes of red gloss paint were also found in the rear seat of this car, and exactly the same paint was found on the clothing of Colm O'Shea and Pat McCann, and in the rear pocket of Peter Pringle's jeans. Three wine-coloured wool fibres were found on the front seat of YAI 895, the red Volkswagen taken at the scene. Blood was also found on the seats, and it was not O'Shea's blood. Fifteen wine-coloured wool fibres were found in 9682 IZ, the white Volkswagen taken from the lady shortly after they crashed the red Volkswagen. Sixteen wine-coloured wool fibres were found on the driver's seat of the car that was stolen in Dunmore, that Pringle was seen driving into Galway.

The owners of those cars were spoken to, and the Gardaí examined any garment that they wore with wine-coloured fibres, but they could not associate the wine-coloured fibres with the vehicles' owners. Forensic scientist Dr Jim Donovan, Director of the Forensic Science Laboratory at the time, examined the maroon-coloured jumper Pringle handed to me, and this is what he said about it:

I examined the wine-coloured jumper of Pringle, and found eleven pieces of plant material embedded deep within the weave of the jumper. The jumper itself was cleaned and appeared to have been recently washed. The pieces of plant material were sufficiently tightly embedded to suggest that they had been obtained by forceful contact with such material, and also to survive a washing process. The material consisted of very small pieces of twig, hayseed, hay stalk and fern. The front pockets of the jeans were completely clean, the back pockets contained dust, grit, pine needles, hayseed and pieces of straw. The jeans themselves appear to have been recently washed. In the left rear pocket of the jeans were three fragments of red paint. I found this paint to be the same as three fragments of dark hard gloss paint I found on a cellophane lift [a forensic technique] from the rear of the white Cortina VZM 208. It was also the same in all respects as the red paint from the shirt of O'Shea and the pocket of McCann's jacket. Head hairs that were found in the car were similar to head hair taken from the maroon-coloured jumper of Peter Pringle.

We now have a solid trail of evidence from Peter Pringle's jumper, the whole way along from the morning of the crime – in his own car, the white Cortina, the red Volkswagen and the white Volkswagen. The lorry driver said that he was wearing a maroon-coloured jumper in the lorry, the same colour as the Galway flag. Then there was the brown Cortina stolen near Dunmore, found to have fifteen or sixteen wine-coloured wool fibres on the driver's seat.

The forensic scientists reported that all the wool fibres found in the cars were exactly the same as fibres from Pringle's jumper. They outlined in evidence the processes they went through to establish that fact in the Forensic Science Laboratory. They also found that the red, hard gloss paint found on McCann, O'Shea and Pringle was exactly the same paint.

The Gardaí compiled the file on this case in a comparatively quick time, considering the volume of work that went into it. It was sent to the State Solicitor and the DPP, and the DPP selected two Counsel from the panel of Counsel that do prosecution work for the State: Mr McDonald and Mr Barr, with Mr McDonald as leading Counsel. As this was a capital murder charge, each of the three accused were entitled, on free legal aid, to two Senior Counsel, a Junior Counsel and their solicitor.

Now, when prosecution Counsel get a file for prosecution, it is their job, of course, to prove the case beyond reasonable doubt. Upon close examination of the file, it is a matter entirely for Counsel to select what witnesses they require to support the charges. The Gardaí have no say whatsoever in who is to be called, or in what order. In the Pringle case, Peadar Shevlin and Pringle's girlfriend were not called by the State to give evidence. I do not know for what reason, because it seemed to me that they were important witnesses. Shevlin could have given evidence on what Pringle may or may not have told him when he arrived at the house. The girlfriend could have given evidence of association with O'Shea and McCann, and that Pringle was wearing the maroon-coloured jumper up until 7 July. I am sure Counsel had a good reason for not calling them – perhaps he wanted to leave the defence Counsel to call them, so that he could then cross-examine them, because you cannot cross-examine your own witness.

The trial of the three raiders commenced at the Special Criminal Court on 6 October 1980, just three months after the crime was committed. Mr Seamus Egan, later a High Court Judge, was the leading Senior Counsel for Peter Pringle. Mr Eoin Fitzsimons, who later became the Attorney General, was his other Senior Counsel, and there was a Junior Counsel.

Dr Jim Donovan gave his evidence. One of O'Shea's shoes, that he was wearing when he was found in the wood, was the shoe that made the impression on the bank counter, said Dr Donovan. He had no doubt that no other shoe made the mark, and identified numerous characteristics found both on the shoe and on the impression from the counter. There was plenty of other evidence against O'Shea – he could be connected with the white Cortina, the red Volkswagen and the white Volkswagen. Head hair and fibres from his clothes were found in these cars, and the red paint from the back of the white Cortina was also found on his shirt. He had also been shot, and was found sitting on a wall very close to where Andy Gallagher's white Volkswagen was found.

Evidence against Pat McCann included the admissions that he made of his involvement, and his fingermarks, found on a road map that was sitting open on the front passenger seat of the white Cortina. A balaclava was found at the scene, and the Forensic Science Laboratory found head hairs in it, which were exactly the same as Pat McCann's head hair. Fibres identical to McCann's clothing were found on the seat of the white Cortina, and the red paint found in the back of the car was also found on his jacket.

Counsel for O'Shea and McCann did not dispute any of the evidence. Neither of them gave evidence themselves, and there were no allegations that they were ill-treated or abused in custody in any way.

At the trial, a great many Garda witnesses gave evidence, particularly Gardaí that had had dealings with Peter Pringle from the time he was arrested, until the time he left Galway Station to go to the Special Criminal Court. Pat Culhane and I gave our evidence to the Court, in accordance with the statement of evidence that had been submitted for the book of evidence, and which was served on the accused. We were cross-examined by Mr Egan, Pringle's Senior Counsel, and during that cross-examination no question was put to either of us regarding the maroon-coloured jumper and the jeans that Pringle was wearing on the day of his arrest. Not alone that, but the question that Pringle may not have been wearing these garments on 7 July never arose at any stage during the trial. The jumper formed a very crucial part of the evidence against Pringle, and the defence clearly accepted at trial that he was wearing the jumper on 7 July.

The only part of our evidence to be really questioned by Mr Egan related to the interview of Peter Pringle on the morning of 21 July, when Pringle made the admission. We were subjected to intense cross-examination, as we would expect, as to what exactly Pringle said. The defence at no stage suggested to us that Pringle merely focused on a spot on the wall, and refused to answer any of our questions, as Pringle later asserted in his book. They clearly accepted that he did say something to us, as Counsel continued to maintain that what he said was, 'I know that you think I was involved.'

The forensic scientists were also subjected to intense questioning, regarding the scientific procedures that they followed when examining the fibres from the jumper and other clothing, as well as the paint, the hair samples and the firearms residue.

Mr Egan did not call any witnesses for the defence. Pringle gave evidence at some stage during the trial, alleging that he was subjected to ill treatment by Gardaí. Along with the other defence Counsel, Mr Egan submitted on behalf of his client that the prosecution had not proved their case beyond a reasonable doubt.

All three defence teams during the trial tried to break down the State's case, to find some crack or flaw in evidence or procedure. When the prosecution's case had finished, they applied to the Court for direction to have their clients acquitted, because they said the State had not proved their case beyond a reasonable doubt. It was the only card the defence had to play. The Court refused to acquit. The defence didn't call any witnesses.

In his judgement, Mr Justice Liam Hamilton said that the Court was satisfied beyond all reasonable doubt that the words 'I know that you know I was involved,' were spoken by the accused Peter Pringle, and that it was a voluntary statement. He also referred to the forensic evidence regarding the wine-coloured wool fibres, the fragments of red paint, the firearms residue, and all the rest of it.

The three men were convicted, and sentenced to the mandatory sentence: execution. They were sent to Portlaoise Prison to await execution. All three applied to the Court of Criminal Appeal for leave to appeal. That hearing commenced before the Court of Criminal Appeal in April 1981.

The following month, on 22 May, the Court gave its decision, refusing leave to appeal by all three. They set the date for the execution of Peter Pringle as 8 June 1981. Before that date arrived, however, the president, acting on the advice of the government, commuted all three sentences to forty years' imprisonment without remission. They commenced to serve that in Portlaoise Prison.

Now we move on from 1981 to 1992. Between these years, I had left Garda Headquarters, gone to Store Street, then back to Garda Headquarters, to Tallaght and then Dundalk. In 1992, Peter Pringle took a civil action against the State, claiming a breach of his constitutional rights and other matters. He was in correspondence with the Chief State Solicitor's office regularly in relation to his case, and in relation particularly to an order that the High Court had made for the State to hand over all documentation in their possession relating to his case.

Pringle eventually got copies of all the documentation, which I have no doubt was a huge amount of paper, and included in this were three documents of mine. One was my notebook, which documented all the interviews I had with Pringle. I handed it in to the Special Criminal Court, and the next time I saw it was fifteen years later, in the Court of Criminal Appeal in 1995.

Pringle also got a copy of my original summary of evidence that I gave early in the investigation, and a copy of my original statement of evidence, which I made for the book of evidence.

When he examined my notebook, he saw my entry in relation to his nosebleed. I had taken the tissue from him and handed it over to Detective Sergeant Pat Ennis. Pringle corresponded with the Chief State Solicitor's office, and he asked them, what was the result of the analysis of the bloodstained tissue? The Chief State Solicitor's office communicated with the administration office at Garda Headquarters, and I was sent a memo from the administration office, dated 19 January 1993, asking, what was the result of the analysis of the bloodstained tissue? I answered that memo in writing on 5 February 1993, answering that I handed the tissue to Detective Sergeant Pat Ennis of the Ballistics Section at Garda Headquarters, and that I understood that no analysis was carried out on it, due to the insufficient amount of blood available on the tissue.

The administration office communicated with the State Solicitor's office, and the Chief State Solicitor's office wrote to Peter Pringle. This is their reply to his question: 'I understand that Detective Sergeant Connolly did send the tissue for analysis, but there was insufficient blood on the tissue to do the analysis. He does not recall whether the tissue was ever retained.' Now, I never said, verbally or otherwise, that I sent the tissue for analysis. Of course, the purpose of giving it to Detective Sergeant Pat Ennis *was* to have it analysed.

A new piece of legislation came into being on 29 December 1993 – the Criminal Procedure Act. That Act entitles convicted persons who have discovered new evidence to come back before the Court of Criminal Appeal and have another appeal heard. Peter Pringle now changed direction. Leaving his High Court action aside, he applied in January 1994, under Section 2 of the Criminal Procedure Act, for an order quashing the orders of conviction and sentence of the Special Criminal Court on 27 November 1980. He asked the

Court to consider whether there was either confusion, or deliberate suppression of evidence, in the State Forensic Science Laboratory during the examination of evidence in his case. Pringle had been in contact with the Forensic Science Laboratory, seeking the results of the analysis of the bloodstained tissue. He was told that the tissue was never sent to the Forensic Science Laboratory, which is correct.

Another ground of appeal centred around the fact that the Special Criminal Court did not hear any evidence on Pringle's nosebleed, or on the tissue used to wipe his nose. I retired from the Force in June of 1994, some months prior to the hearing of Pringle's appeal before the Court of Criminal Appeal. Myself and a number of other Garda witnesses, including Detective Sergeant Pat Ennis, attended a conference with Senior Counsel for the State. At that conference, I drew the attention of the Senior Counsel to the conflict of evidence between Pat Ennis and I in relation to the tissue. In a statement, Pat Ennis had said, 'I am convinced that no such tissue was ever given to me by Detective Superintendent Connolly, and it equally follows that I never passed on any such tissue for scientific analysis.'

The judgement of the Court of Criminal Appeal says:

… during the course of his questioning, the applicant suffered a nose bleed on the night of 20 July, and that a tissue was used to clean blood from his nose; that tissue must have been passed to the State Scientific Laboratory for analysis, but it is alleged the results of this analysis were either suppressed or lost. Since the applicant has declined to give a blood sample, and since the State was anxious to discover whether the applicant's blood matched the bloodstains found in the red Volkswagen car which was used by two of the raiders to make their escape, it is beyond belief that such a vital piece of evidence was not passed to the State Laboratory. That in the circumstances, the Court of Trial should have had available to it the results of this analysis, which might have been of assistance in establishing the innocence of the accused.

... It is submitted that while the applicant was aware of the existence of the tissue since he had used it to clean his nose after a nosebleed, he had no knowledge of what happened to it after it passed into the possession of Sergeant Connolly. Counsel also said, that at that time when the tissue bearing the applicant's blood sample was in the possession of Sergeant Connolly, such a sample was a matter of prime importance in the investigation of this offence, as it provided a possible link between the applicant and bloodstains found in the car. However, Sergeant Connolly never forwarded this sample to the Forensics Science Laboratory for analysis. ... and at all times existed a fundamental dispute between Sergeant Connolly and Sergeant Ennis as to what happened to this tissue. Sergeant Connolly has at all times stated that he passed the tissue to Detective Sergeant Ennis. Detective Sergeant Ennis denied that he received it, and Counsel submitted that fair procedures would have required that the prosecution should have disclosed the foregoing matters to the defence. He said that the defence should have been made aware of the fact that the tissue had not been passed to the Forensic Science Laboratory, notwithstanding its importance as an exhibit, and that no analysis was made on the blood. It further stated that the existence of the dispute between Detective Sergeant Connolly and Detective Sergeant Ennis, as to what became of the tissue, should also have been disclosed to the defence. It is accordingly submitted that this newly discovered fact renders the conviction of the applicant unsatisfactory and unsafe.

This Court of Criminal Appeal was presided over by a Supreme Court Judge, Judge Hugh O'Flaherty, along with two High Court Judges, Judge Lavin and Judge Morris. I attended the Court for the first two or three days, but on a day

I missed, a matter arose over this famous tissue. Pringle had received a letter from the State Solicitor, stating that the tissue had been sent for analysis, and the Forensic Science Laboratory said they had no record of having received it. The Court adjourned for some days, so that a search could be made through the records at the Forensic Science Laboratory, to ascertain what had happened to the tissue. The following day, one of the daily newspapers carried a report on the Court proceedings. It mentioned the adjournment, and the reason for it. I read the report, and immediately telephoned the State Solicitor's office. I told them that the tissue was never sent to the Forensic Science Laboratory, and that I had never said that it was.

When the Court resumed, I gave evidence. I had never been asked up to then what had happened to the tissue. I told the Court that on the morning of 21 July, Pat Ennis came to me and told me he had examined the tissue, and there was insufficient blood on it for analysis. I looked at it myself and I agreed with him, and the tissue was then disposed of by Sergeant Ennis, as it was of no evidential value.

The Court's judgement on this issue stated: 'The Court is satisfied beyond any doubt, that no scientific examination was carried out on the tissue, and it was never forwarded to the Forensic Science Lab.'

Another issue that came up for a decision by the Court of Criminal Appeal was that certain entries in my notebook were not in chronological order. In about May of 1994, a short time before the appeal hearing, Gregory O'Neill, solicitor for Pringle, wrote to the State Solicitor and requested that my notebook be examined by an independent forensic document examiner. The notebook was brought to Garda Headquarters, and Dr David Baxendale, formerly of the British Home Office Forensic Science Laboratory, carried out an electrostatic document analysis, to establish in what order the entries had been put in the notebook by me. Dr Baxendale was satisfied, having examined my notebook, that the entries were made exactly as I had said they were made. In relation to the notebook entries, the Court said:

> To dispose of this latter point, and that point is about the order the entries were made, the Court is of the view that nothing turns on it. It is simply the case that the Sergeant entered the admission that he regarded as critical at the time that it was made, and later entered the account of matters that had taken place prior to this admission. That he gives as his reason for the fact that the entries are out of sequence, and the Court accepts that explanation.

The Court's judgement stated:

> When Detective Sergeant Connolly compiled his notes on 21 July 1980, he stated, 'I then took the tissue from him and I handed it over to Detective Sergeant Ennis.' This statement is in accordance with what is in his notebook, which reads, 'nosebleed, tissue to Pat Ennis'. Counsel for the applicant submits this information should have been, but was not, contained in the statement of evidence which was required to be served on the accused prior to trial. He submits that if Counsel for the accused at the trial had been aware of the existence of the tissue, and the fact that it was said to have been passed to Sergeant Ennis, he would have undoubtedly drawn the attention of the Court to the fact that this tissue was not referred to in any of the scientific evidence, and would have invited the Court to draw the conclusion that, had the analysis of the blood on the tissue been available at the hearing, it would have been of assistance in establishing the innocence of the accused. It would moreover have been possible for Counsel for the accused to criticise the investigating Gardaí for their failure to send the tissue for scientific examination.
>
> If that were the case, an opportunity would have been available to the defence to question the reliability of Detective Sergeant Connolly,

in relation to this tissue, if, as would appear to have been the case, his statement was contradicted by Sergeant Ennis. It is submitted that such a challenge to Detective Sergeant Connolly, if successful, must have raised a significant doubt in the mind of the Court as to the extent they should rely on Detective Sergeant Connolly's evidence, in relation to the words alleged to have been spoken by the accused in his admission.

If Sergeant Ennis is correct, then why did Sergeant Connolly fail to pass on this potential important piece of evidence to Sergeant Ennis, for further transmission to the State Laboratory, and why does the notebook entry say that he did?

We are not required to resolve this contradiction at this hearing. However, the significance of this new evidence is this: Sergeant Ennis is very clear that if he got the tissue, he would have passed it on to the State Laboratory. If Sergeant Connolly did not hand it over to Sergeant Ennis, why does his notebook entry say that he did? If the notebook entry is unreliable in that regard, it is unreliable with regard to the entry of the admission of [Pringle's] involvement in the crimes being investigated.

It has to be emphasised, that the matter of the blood on the tissue would not have advanced either the prosecution or defence at trial, since we now know that the accused's blood type is similar to the bloodstains found in the red Volkswagen car, and therefore naturally that bloodstains in the red Volkswagen car would have corresponded to the bloodstains on the tissue, had it been analysed. But because this is a common blood type – it is common to about twelve percent of the population – it does not prove anything.

The judgement continues that the Criminal Procedure Act 1993,

> … is intended to afford relief to those who could point to materials which, if they had been available at the trial, might – not necessarily would

– have raised a reasonable doubt in the mind of the Court. Applying that test, this Court is left in no doubt that if Counsel for the accused at the hearing had had available to him the knowledge that Detective Sergeant Connolly would say that he handed the bloodstained tissue to Detective Sergeant Ennis, and that Sergeant Ennis would say that he did not receive the tissue, then this conflict as to the credibility of Detective Sergeant Connolly might have raised a reasonable doubt in the mind of the Special Criminal Court, resulting in rejection of the disputed statement by the Court. Accordingly, the Court finds that a newly discovered fact exists in the case, which renders the conviction of the applicant unsafe and unsatisfactory. The court wishes to emphasise that in its view, on the evidence which was then available to the Special Criminal Court, and to the Court of Criminal Appeal, who sat to consider the applicant's application for leave to appeal, the decision of each of these Courts was correct, and the only basis for reaching the conclusion that the conviction was unsafe and unsatisfactory was the consideration of the newly discovered facts to which reference is made in this judgement.

Counsel for the Director of Public Prosecutions submitted that if the conviction should be quashed, then the Court should order a retrial. Counsel for Pringle made no contrary submission, and the Court quashed the conviction, and ordered a retrial.

After the judgement, Peter Pringle remained in custody, and the Court sat again about a week later. In the meantime, the State reviewed the file, to see if all the witnesses were available for the retrial. The case at this stage was fourteen years old, and it was discovered that an essential witness in the case, Chief Superintendent Green, had died. He was a member of the Garda who extended Pringle's detention for the further period of twenty-four hours. During that second twenty-four hours, essential evidence was obtained, including the admission, 'I know that you know I was involved.' The State had to justify the extension of Pringle's detention, and that evidence could not be given by any other person. Without the Chief Superintendent's evidence, the bottom fell out of the State's case. They could not proceed.

When the Court sat for the second time, Counsel for the State entered a *nolle prosequi*, a decision not to proceed, in the case. A *nolle prosequi* does not prevent a case from being brought again before the Court, but when the State said they were not going to proceed, Peter Pringle was a free man. He walked out of the Court, entitled to a full presumption of innocence.

It was hard to accept the decision of the Court of Criminal Appeal, but I did accept it, because the Court in my mind had dealt with it in a scrupulously impartial way. I was very disappointed that my credibility had been questioned, but I felt that the Court could not have come to any other decision, because of the clear conflict between Sergeant Ennis and I. Of course we will never know what would have happened had these questions arisen at the Court of Trial, three months after the crime had happened, instead of fourteen years later.

On 30 May 1995, two weeks after Pringle's conviction was quashed, a solicitor on his behalf wrote to the Minister for Justice of the time, Nora Owen TD:

> … Mr Pringle now finds himself an innocent man, who while he has always protested his innocence, now stands in the eyes of the law an innocent man, who has spent all of fourteen years in prison, and against whom there is no conviction and charge. When Mr Pringle was convicted and sentenced to death in 1980, he was forty-one years of age; he is now fifty-six. As a result of his long imprisonment, he has lost all hope of any career, and has been separated from his family and friends, he has prematurely aged, and is now without occupation or any prospect of employment. The effect of his prolonged and wrongful imprisonment has been devastating.

... I am instructed to write to you, Minister, to request that you would, if necessary following consultation with the Government, provide some immediate *ex gratia* payment to Mr Pringle in the way of some interim compensation lump sum payment, so as to assist him to rebuild his life in the short to medium term. The exercise by the Government to make an administrative decision to pay funds out of the public purse, to discharged prisoners for the purpose of relieving hardship, has, we understand, precedent in Irish Governmental practice.

In the United Kingdom in celebrated cases of miscarriages of justice, the Home Secretary has seen fit to make very early interim payments of compensation, by way of substantial lump sum grants or allowances, for victims of such miscarriages of justice. We understand that in the case of the Birmingham Six, where the individuals involved had spent comparable periods in prison, that the payments made to each of the men was in the region of £50,000.

... In these circumstances, it is clear that Mr Pringle's case comes within the realm of cases where miscarriages of justice have been suffered due to a default on the part of an employee or organ of the State.

Our client is aware of his rights to apply to the Court of Criminal Appeal pursuant to Section 9 of the Criminal Procedure Act, 1992. Mr Pringle is also aware of his right to bring a claim in the High Court against Ireland and the Attorney General, seeking damages for violation of his constitutional rights. Our client reserves his right to take either of the above-mentioned steps, to obtain some monetary compensation for the grievous wrongs suffered by him. However, it is likely that the processing of such matters may take several months, if not years.

In the meantime, Mr Pringle is effectively destitute, he has no home of his own, he is dependent upon the charity of his loved ones, family and friends to provide him with shelter, and to supplement his meagre income from the State to obtain life's necessities. Given Mr Pringle's dire circumstances, and his entitlement to start rebuilding his life at the earliest date, we would respectfully request to the Government to make an allocation to Mr Pringle, by way of an interim *ex gratia* payment of compensation, having regard to the extraordinary circumstances of his case.

Such a payment could be made without any prejudice to the position of the State, in the event of any civil litigation. By corollary, such a payment would not be accepted by Mr Pringle as in any way compromising his legal and constitutional rights. However, any payments made by the State could be taken into account in the event of the final reward or settlement of compensation.

I would urge the Government to give immediate and generous consideration to this request, having regard to the duty of the State to vindicate the personal rights of a citizen, particularly in cases of injustices done pursuant to Article 40 of the Constitution. ...

The government considered the matter, but did not accede to the request made in this impassioned solicitor's letter. This is because the Courts have never declared that Pringle suffered a miscarriage of justice such as that suffered by the Birmingham Six.

Pringle had refused to give a blood sample when he was in custody in Galway, but during his appeal in the Court of Criminal Appeal, he did give a blood sample, and it was indeed the same blood group as the blood found in the red Volkswagen.

Some time after the government had refused the compensation request, samples from the white Cortina car that had crashed into the Garda car were sent to an independent forensic science laboratory in the UK, together with blood and head-hair samples of Peter Pringle. These underwent DNA analysis, using a technique known as low copy number, which has been in use since 1999 in some countries. The analysis and comparisons showed indications that the samples from the car came from the donor of the blood sample, and that the DNA found came from the maternal side of the donor's family. However, the reports stated that further DNA analysis would be required to establish an absolutely definitive finding.

Around the summer of 2013, a man came before the Court who had been convicted of capital murder, that of Sergeant Morrissey, in Ardee in County Louth. The man had been convicted and sentenced to death, which had then been commuted to forty years' imprisonment without remission. After some years he went before the Court, claiming that he should be entitled to remission. The case eventually reached the Supreme Court, and their eventual judgement was that a person convicted of capital murder should be entitled to the same remission as any other prisoner. That remission would be twenty-five percent of the sentence. In other words, you get forty years and you serve thirty years. When that judgement was announced, Pat McCann and Colm O'Shea had been in prison for thirty-three years, so they were immediately released.

There are several incorrect accounts of this case in the public domain – on various websites, on radio and television, in newspaper articles, and so on – stating that evidence was concocted by Gardaí, that Pringle was ill-treated by Gardaí, and that Gardaí lied in the witness box.

At no time was Pringle ill-treated or abused by me, or by anybody in my presence, or to my knowledge, in any way. He did not complain to me, or anybody in my presence, of being ill-treated or abused. All our interviews were forthright and to the point, and there was not a harsh word spoken to or by Peter Pringle. I am not aware of any complaints of assault or abuse having been made by Pat McCann or Colm O'Shea during their time of detention and questioning either.

I also want to completely and utterly deny, in the strongest possible terms, that I ever concocted any piece of evidence. I gave a truthful account of everything that happened. I believe that my record of thirty-nine years' service in the Garda Síochána, and all of the cases outlined in this book, go to show my integrity as a police officer.

I mentioned that in my earlier days in the Garda Síochána, I got a good roasting in the witness box from a Judge in the Circuit Court. In that case I was being completely impartial, and not swayed by evidence from other sources. That has been my attitude throughout my career when giving evidence. I think my attitude is shown in my review of the Livingstone murder case, examined in a later chapter. Again, I was not swayed by my colleagues. I have, like many other members of the Garda Síochána down through the years, been commended by Judges in the District Court, Circuit Court, Central Criminal Court and Special Criminal Court. On some occasions, I have been complimented by Counsel for the accused, for the impartial manner in which I give evidence.

Peter Pringle told me, during our first interview, that he would not be able to produce a witness at any time to say where he was on 7 July. He has been true to his word. No person has come forward on his behalf in the intervening years, to vouch for his whereabouts on that day.

Now, I can be an emotional and sentimental person, and some things just get lodged in my mind. For instance, the poems 'The Old Woman of the Roads', a very sentimental poem, and also 'Caoch O'Leary', about the blind piper. Every time I hear or recite those poems, I see myself walking in their footsteps, and I feel a part of their sadness and loneliness. This crime has been one of the ones that has left the deepest impression on my mind. The sadness of it, the tragedy of the two deaths, the investigation, the interrogation of McCann and Pringle, the time at the Special Criminal Court, the Court of

Criminal Appeal that quashed the conviction years later, and of course the false allegations that I fabricated evidence on oath before the Court of Criminal Appeal.

I will not forget John Morley and Henry Byrne, and to be true to my emotional and sentimental self, I will end with an amended version of the last verse of 'Caoch O'Leary'.

> The neighbours came and dug their graves
> Very close together,
> And there they sleep their last sweet sleep,
> God rest you John and Henry.

MURDER OF ELIZABETH TUITE, DELVIN, 1981

In my opinion, the greatest obstacle to the successful investigation of crime, from the foundation of the State up to 1987, was the lack of power of the Gardaí to detain suspects for the purpose of investigation of crime. That includes the power to detain persons for the purpose of questioning. We know from the Shaw and Evans case, what the situation was in 1976. Up to 1987, suspects were invited to the Station to be interviewed. This was, and still is, the best place to interview a suspect. Interviewing a suspect at home, in front of his family, or at work, or in a car, or any other such place, is not in the best interests of any investigation. The use of cajolery and persuasion to get a suspect to come to a Garda Station for questioning was a very important element in the successful investigation of crimes.

However, on many occasions, the Court has found that suspects invited to a Garda Station for questioning were in unlawful custody when they made statements admitting to crimes. Many cases dealing with serious crimes have faced difficulties in Court, due to the accused being found to have been in unlawful custody, and a statement therefore not being admitted into evidence. Over the years, no doubt, some members have been reckless as to whether a suspect had agreed to come to a Garda Station, and was brought there nevertheless. I cannot exclude myself in this, and accept that I may have been reckless on occasion. Many suspects of course have refused to come to the Station for interview, and I have no doubt that a great many crimes have gone unsolved as a result.

Members, I feel, have always felt morally bound to do their best to solve crimes. However, the law of the land supersedes all moral feelings, and of course must be obeyed and accepted. I do not know if any particular case was responsible for the enactment of the 1984 Criminal Justice Act, which gave the Gardaí powers to detain persons for questioning.

Miss Elizabeth Tuite, sixty-five, from Delvin in County Westmeath, lived alone, and suffered from Parkinson's disease. She was paranoid, according to her doctor, believing that people were always against her. The local Postman, Peter Cook, called to Miss Tuite's house on Friday, 13 March 1981. Her front gate was open, and her front door was partially open, and when he looked into the house he saw what appeared to be a body lying on the floor. He went to Delvin Garda Station, and informed Gardaí there. Then he went to the parochial house, and told Reverend Father Troy what he had discovered. Cook accompanied Garda Thomas Moran of Delvin back to Miss Tuite's house. Father Troy was there before them. They went in, and saw an open handbag lying on an unmade bed in the house, and Elizabeth Tuite's dead body lying on the floor.

The body was removed to Mullingar Hospital for post mortem examination by Dr John Harbison. He established that the deceased had died from a fractured skull, and a murder investigation was commenced. During the investigation, a suspect was sought for interview.

Exactly a week afterwards, on 19 March, this suspect was arrested about seven or eight o'clock in the evening. Drunk and incapable, he was brought to Mullingar Garda Station, and detained there for his own safety. He was subsequently charged with the murder. Assistance was sought from Crime Branch to interview him. I went to Mullingar that night, with a number of other members from the Investigation Section, including Detective Sergeant Pat Lynagh and Tim Mulvey. Pat Lynagh and I interviewed him at about 3am, when we were satisfied that he was sober. He made a statement to us, making various admissions.

He appeared on trial before the Central Criminal Court in Dublin on 27 October. Dr Harbison told the Court in evidence that the injuries to the deceased's skull were caused by a blunt instrument, which left her skull looking like crazy paving. He said considerable force was used to inflict the injuries, and she died from a laceration to the brain.

The trial came to the stage where the prosecution were going to give evidence of interviews with the accused. Martin Kennedy, Senior Counsel for the accused, objected to the admission into evidence of any statement that his client made to the Gardaí. Legal arguments followed, in the absence of the jury. Mr Kennedy told the Court that his client was arrested for being drunk, and when sober was interviewed by the Gardaí. He submitted that his client should have been released when he became sober, and that the Gardaí had no authority to detain him any further for the purpose of questioning him in relation to the death of Elizabeth Tuite.

The presiding Judge decided that the accused was indeed in unlawful custody when he made his statement, and did not allow it into evidence. The Judge brought back the jury, and directed them to find the accused not guilty of the murder. The accused was discharged. Another case affected by having no power to detain a person for the purpose of questioning.

MURDER OF MARGO KELLY, ATHBOY, 1981

Affairs of the heart have been known to raise the feelings of young couples to the pinnacle of happiness, and from there plunge them to the depths of despair. When lovers fall out and engagements are broken, it has on occasion ended in tragedy. At times one of the parties is driven to suicide, or one of the parties kills the other in an obsessive rage, and then themselves.

These explosive circumstances unfortunately entered the lives of two young lovers in County Westmeath, in March 1981. The couple's engagement had been broken off about six months prior to the murder of one of them. Margo Kelly, twenty-one years of age, from Girley, Fordstown, Navan in County Meath, got engaged to Frank Higgins, twenty-three, unemployed, of Kilrush, Clonmell in County Westmeath, in about September 1980. Margo worked in a shop in Athboy, County Meath. After the engagement was called off, Frank Higgins would telephone her on occasion, and they met a few times. He wanted to resume the relationship.

On 27 March 1981, Margo told her friend, Bernadette Larkin of Ballivor, County Meath, that Higgins was to meet her in Athboy at 8pm that night, outside Cregan's shop. She met Bernadette at 8.10pm, and told her that Higgins had not arrived. Later that night, Higgins was seen with Margo in Athboy. He was driving a car. Margo did not return home that night. At 10am the following morning, her father went to the Garda Station, and reported her missing to Sergeant Joseph McGlynn. Sergeant McGlynn went to Margo's house at about noon that day, and Margo had not been found.

Margo's brother Tony went to see Frank Higgins that same morning. He told Higgins that Margo had not returned home last night, and that he and his father had searched for her, without success. He asked Higgins if he had met Margo the previous night in Athboy. Higgins said that he had – he had picked her up outside a shop in Athboy at 8.05pm, and left her out of the car at 8.40pm. Higgins seemed very concerned about Margo's disappearance, and asked Tony to ring him at Callaghan's pub if he had any news. Tony went to the Sergeant's house in the early afternoon, when Margo's body had been found, and told Sergeant McGlynn what he knew of Higgins's movements.

On the same day, 28 March, a farmer named John Carr, who lives in Athboy, went out foddering cattle and sheep. He was returning home by the back gates to Killua Castle, when he saw an open red-and-white umbrella on the ground, in the grass margin. Then he saw a body, lying face-down. He immediately rushed off to a neighbour's house, and they contacted the Gardaí. The Gardaí went to the scene, as did Dr James O'Neill, who examined the body. He reported severe lacerations to the girl's head, and her brain was visible. Her body was removed to Mullingar Hospital, where Dr John Harbison carried out a post mortem.

Due to the serious injuries to Margo Kelly's head, murder was immediately suspected, and an investigation was commenced. Frank Higgins became a suspect early in the investigation, due to the fact that he was seen in Margo's company after 8pm on 27 March, and also because he had been engaged to her, and the engagement had been broken off. A few days after the finding of the body, Frank Higgins was invited to Mullingar Garda Station for interview. Gardaí were well aware that when inviting people to the Garda Station, we had no power to detain them for questioning.

On Frank Higgins's arrival at the Garda Station, I met him, accompanied by Detective Sergeant Pat Lynagh. In reply to the first question I put to him, he said, 'I was asked by a Sergeant to come to Mullingar Garda Station this evening, to assist in investigations into the death of Margo Kelly. I agreed to come, I am willing to stay in the Garda Station as long as the Gardaí want me to help in their enquiries. I have been told by Detective Sergeant T. Connolly that I can leave the Garda Station any time I want to.' The time was 8.55pm. I recorded in my notebook exactly what he said, then I read it over to him and he signed it, witnessed by Pat Lynagh and myself. This was in case at a trial an issue arose about custody, about whether he had consented to come to, and stay in, the Garda Station.

Pat Lynagh and I interviewed him about his relationship with Margo Kelly, and the last time he had seen her. He said he met Margo in Athboy, on Friday night, 27 March, at 8pm. He was very specific about the time – apparently he was rushing to be there on time. He got into the car at 7.50pm; at 7.58pm, he was going into Athboy, and he said he had one mile to go. He parked at 8.05pm, and met Margo at 8.10pm. She sat into the car for a few minutes, and then came with him to Tommy Mahon's shop. He brought her back again, and dropped her off outside Faulkner's shop at 8.40pm. He then went to his sister's house at Beech Park. She was not there, so he drove home, and was at home at 9.25pm. That was his story. He said that Margo was to go home with John Bradley. He said one Wiggy Geraghty passed when Margo and himself were in the car on the Main Street.

It was 9.35pm, and I was taking notes of this conversation, when Frank Higgins said, 'I done it.' He outlined what he had done to Margo, and agreed to make a statement, which I wrote down.

Higgins told us about the broken engagement, and that he had wanted to resume the relationship, and that Margo had been seeing somebody else. On the afternoon of 27 March, he was chopping timber at home with a hatchet. The thought occurred to him that if Margo refused to resume their relationship, he would kill her with the hatchet. He had an appointment to see her in Athboy at 8pm. He put the hatchet into the car, drove to Athboy and met Margo. He brought her to Killua Castle, a well-known courting spot, and asked her to resume the relationship. She said she would have to continue going out with the other man for a while.

She got out of the car to go to the toilet. He got out and took the hatchet out of the car, came up behind her and hit her a few times on the head with it. She fell to the ground and he left her there. Higgins then drove home, washed the hatchet in a barrel of water, and hid it behind a press in the outhouse. The hatchet was found in a search, exactly where he said he had put it. He identified the hatchet he used, the clothing he was wearing on the night of the murder, and also Margo's shoulder bag, and he said he had thrown it in the gripe. He identified a slip in a paper bag and said, 'That's what she showed me all right, I threw that in the gripe as well.'

Higgins was charged with Margo's murder. The trial commenced in the Central Criminal Court in Dublin on 14 July 1982, and ended the following day. The presiding Judge was Mr Declan Costello. Senior Counsel for the DPP was Mr Erwan Mill-Arden, and he outlined the case for the prosecution. Dr James O'Neill, who examined the body on the roadside, said that he noticed large lacerations on the girl's head, and her brain was visible. State Pathologist Dr John Harbison said that severe head wounds were the cause of the girl's death. Her skull was fractured like crazy paving. There were five wounds to the head, consistent with being struck with a hatchet. Considerable force had been used in the blows. The injuries had been inflicted at the scene where the body was found. There were no injuries on the arms, and he formed an impression that the girl had been surprised, and did not put up a struggle. There was no evidence of sexual assault.

Frank Higgins also gave evidence. He said he met Margo on 27 March in Athboy. They discussed their relationship, and drove out to Killua Castle. He asked her to resume their relationship, and she told him she would have to go out with another man for a while. Higgins told the jury that they were hugging and kissing at Killua Castle. Margo asked him to drive her home, but he asked her to stay for a while. Margo got out of the car. He picked up the hatchet, and he hit her. She staggered around and fell. He dropped the hatchet and went over to her, and he put his hand on her head, lifted her up and started talking to her. He asked if she was okay. When she didn't answer, he thought she was messing. He then removed his hand, and it was covered in blood. A dog barked and it panicked him. He hit her three more times and then left her down, and hit her one more time. Under cross-examination for the State, Higgins said that when Margo didn't give him the right answer, he decided to kill her.

The jury deliberated for an hour and a half. They found Frank Higgins guilty of the murder of Margo Kelly. The Judge imposed the mandatory sentence for murder, life imprisonment.

This was a senseless, savage, callous, inhuman murder, and all because Margo Kelly had decided, as she was quite entitled to do, that Frank Higgins was not the man she wished to spend her life with.

MURDER OF WILLIAM MANNION, NEWBRIDGE, 1981

William Mannion, seventy-one years old, was a bachelor farmer. He resided alone on his thirty-acre farm at Ballynacorra, Newbridge in County Galway. He had the land let to another farmer, Thomas Dowd of Creggs in County Galway. William was last seen alive at his home on the evening of 19 July 1981, between 7.30pm and 7.45pm, by his neighbour Martin Kelly. William used to visit another neighbour, Bob Cunningham, every Sunday at 9pm, to watch television. He did not visit on the night of 19 July. Peter Dowd, a relation of Thomas's, spoke to William Mannion at Mannion's home at 6pm that day, and he accompanied William down the field to look at a sick cow. At 6.20pm, Mannion looked at his watch and told Peter the time, then Mannion left and walked into his house.

Martin Kelly called to the Gardaí at Ballygar, County Galway, at 10.55pm the following day. He said that William Mannion had not been seen that day; the lights were on in his house, but he hadn't seen him. Gardaí Muldoon, Kane and McDonald immediately went to Mannion's house. They got into the house somehow at 11pm, and found William Mannion dead in his kitchen. He had a number of wounds to his face and neck, and it was quite obvious that he had been murdered.

The usual crime scene preservation measures were put into place. The local doctor was called, and he pronounced death. A murder investigation was commenced, and an incident room was set up in Roscommon Garda Station, six or seven miles from Ballygar. William Mannion's body was moved to a local hospital, where State Pathologist Dr John Harbison performed a post mortem. He confirmed that Mannion had died as a result of multiple stab wounds to the neck and face. He also had stab wounds in his hands. Dr Harbison stated that he believed the knife had a four- or five-inch blade, the top of it tapered about an inch and a half down the blade.

On 21 July, I travelled to Ballygar to assist in the investigation, with six or seven other members of the Investigation Section. Detective Inspector Christy McCaffrey was leading the investigation. A number of local suspects had been nominated by local Gardaí, and were being systematically checked out and eliminated. One such suspect was a young chap called Thomas Murray, of Cloonlyon, Ballygar, an eighteen-year-old youth.

Detective Sergeant Pat Prior of Roscommon was nominated to interview Thomas Murray. He made contact with Murray somehow, and Murray volunteered to come to Ballygar Garda Station to see him. He came to the Station on 28 July, and was questioned by Detective Sergeant Prior about his movements on Sunday evening, the night of the murder. Pat Prior took a statement from him, outlining his movements.

According to his statement, on Sunday, 19 July, at 11.30am, Thomas Murray went to Mass in Ballygar on his bicycle. He saw William Mannion cycling away from the church. He went home, had dinner and was listening to the match – Cork vs Kerry. He cycled to Ballygar, as he thought there was a pony show on there. That was at 5.15pm. Then he went to the home of his uncle James Mulvey, in Cloonlyon, not too far from his home place. He was there until 7.30pm. He was home by 7.45pm, watched television and saw the nine o'clock news.

He was asked what clothing he wore when he was at his uncle's. He said he wore a black-and-brown-striped shirt, blue trousers and a black pullover with the emblem of a deer on the front of it. He said he then went to a carnival. At the carnival he said he was wearing a green shirt, a brown pullover and the same blue trousers he had on during the day. At 10.30pm, he cycled from home to Ballinamore Bridge via Cloonlyon and Corcoran's caravans. He said his father was going to Fleming's pub in Mountbellew.

He arrived at the carnival at about 10.50pm, put the bicycle against a house, and there were two men standing near the wire. He didn't know who they were. He stayed there until 11.10pm, looked at his watch and went home again by the same route, arriving at 11.30pm. He stayed at home for ten or fifteen minutes, then returned to Ballinamore Bridge via the same route, arriving at 11.45pm. His father was not home at this stage. He said he met Seamus Smith, his first cousin, near Cunningham's and Colemen's, on the Cloonlyon Road. He arrived there shortly after midnight. He was home at 2.35am, and his mother got up to make coffee.

Having made his statement, he left the Station with Sergeant Prior, who was not one bit happy with him. On that same night, 28 July, Thomas Murray took an overdose of tablets at home. He was removed to Roscommon hospital for treatment. Dr Patrick McHugh spoke to Murray in the hospital, found him in a drowsy condition and suspected that he had taken an overdose of drugs. The following day, he spoke to Murray again, and Murray told him he had taken one hundred of his brother's epilepsy tablets. He told him that Gardaí were asking him about a murder in Newbridge.

While he was in the hospital, one of the nurses spoke to him, and someone took a note of what was said. She said, 'How are you feeling?' He said, 'All right.' She asked, 'What did you take?' He replied, 'I took tablets.' She asked, 'Where did you get them?' He replied, 'They belonged to my brother.' She asked, 'Why did you take them?' He replied, 'I was in trouble.' She asked, 'What kind of trouble?' He replied, 'I killed a man.' She asked, 'How did you kill him?' He replied, 'With a knife.' She asked, 'What did you do with the knife?' He replied, 'I dumped it.' She asked, 'Where did you dump it?' He replied, 'You wouldn't know the place.' That nurse's name was Pauline Mahon, and I think she should have been in the Gardaí.

That conversation was of course related to the investigating Gardaí, and Murray now became the prime suspect for the murder of William Mannion. A Garda took up duty at the hospital, keeping Murray under observation. On release from hospital, Thomas Murray was sent home to his parents. He remained at home, and was not seen out until the end of August. Surveillance of sorts was placed on Murray's home, to monitor his movements. Myself and other members of the Investigation Section went on holidays with our families, as our holidays had been booked months in advance. There was nothing happening in the investigation, because Murray was recovering from his overdose, and would not be available for interview for quite a while. I returned to the investigation at the end of August.

Thomas Murray used to leave home early some mornings, and go to a nearby bog with a donkey and cart for turf. It was believed that Thomas's father and mother were very protective of him. It was decided that Detective Garda Tom Byrne and I would go to the bog on the morning of 2 September, and interview

Thomas Murray about Mr Mannion's murder, if we could locate him there. We went to the laneway leading to the bog early that morning. I remember we had a flask of tea and sandwiches, expecting a long day there. We came across an old unoccupied house, and we went into it. We had a great view of the bog and laneway from there. I remember I brought some Law books with me, as I was studying for the Inspector examination at the time. Tom Byrne brought a pack of cards, and he played patience.

After some hours, we heard a cart coming along the laneway. It was Thomas Murray, coming from the bog with a load of turf, with the donkey and cart. He was walking directly behind the cart and didn't see us until the cart had passed us. We stopped him, told him what we were investigating, and asked if he would sit into the car with us. He did, and agreed to go anywhere to have a conversation. We drove to near Newbridge village, and stopped on the roadside.

We asked him to tell the truth about William Mannion. He said, 'I told you the truth about where I was on the forms that were filled out.' We went over the movements again. I asked him to tell the truth, that we believed he was some way involved. He said, 'All right, I stabbed William Mannion, that's the truth, now you have it.' He was cautioned, and he said, 'I am in trouble now.' Detective Garda Byrne drove the car as we spoke. Murray told us, 'I cycled to Mannion's, and he let me in. We had a chat and I drew the knife. I stabbed him a good few times in the neck and face. I left him sitting in a corner; he was all blood. I cycled home, threw the knife away down the bog road.'

By now, we were in Ballinasloe Garda Station yard. Murray didn't want to go in. He said, 'Can we not talk here?' We continued our conversation there in the car. He repeated that he had stabbed William Mannion; he got the knife from James Mulvey's and he sharpened it. James Mulvey turned out to be his uncle. Mannion shouted at him to get out, and he left him sitting in a corner all covered in blood. He took up a hatchet and left it in the same place again.

He didn't hit him with the hatchet. He threw away the knife on the way home, and washed his hands at home as they were all blood. He got home at 11.30pm, and then he went to the dance. He said, 'I don't know why I did it. I am not sorry over it.'

When asked to make a statement, he said, 'I suppose I might as well now.' We went into the Station at 2.20pm. The notes were read over to him, and he signed them. Also in the Station, he drew a sketch of where he threw the knife, and he said, 'I'm not too sure.' On a sketch of Mannion's kitchen, he marked the location of a clock, table, chairs, the cooker and the corner where he left the hatchet. He agreed to give samples of blood and head hair. A doctor came in and took the samples, and his fingerprints were also taken.

On the night of 3 September, Thomas Murray was charged before a special sitting of Ballinasloe District Court, presided over by Mr Justice Macklin. He was remanded in custody, to appear at the next sitting of Loughrea District Court. Earlier that day, Murray had brought Detective Sergeant Prior to the area where he said he threw away the knife. A search of the area was carried out, and a knife was found by Garda John Durkin. Blood on it was found to be the same blood group as the deceased.

The trial of Thomas Murray took place at the Central Criminal Court in Dublin, before Mr Justice Gannon. Murray pleaded not guilty. The question of the accused being in unlawful custody at the time he made a statement raised its head again in this case. Counsel for Murray objected to the admissibility of the statement of admission made by Murray in Ballinasloe Garda Station to Detective Garda Byrne and I.

There was the usual trial within a trial. Detective Garda Byrne and I described meeting Murray in the bog, our conversation with him and his agreement to come with us, 'any place you like', to be interviewed. I outlined the notes that I had taken. Both Counsels made their submissions to the Court.

Having considered the matter, the Judge decided that Murray was in unlawful custody once he entered Ballinasloe Garda Station. Therefore the statement was not admissible. I had recorded in my notes that Murray said he didn't want to go into the Garda Station. In spite of that, the Judge said, he was brought into the Garda Station. Therefore he had not consented to go in.

However, all was not lost. The Judge allowed in evidence all the admissions made and recorded in my notebook before we entered the Garda Station. They had been read over to Thomas Murray, and he had signed them as being correct. The notes contained an admission to committing the crime.

There was also plenty of corroboration. There was the admission to Nurse Mahon. There was a thumb mark on the door latch of William Mannion's front door – this was made in blood by one of Murray's thumbs. The blood was the same group as William Mannion's. There was also the finding of the knife in the spot indicated by Murray. Murray was found guilty, and received the mandatory sentence of life imprisonment.

That was not the last that was heard of Thomas Murray. Eighteen years later, on 14 February 2000, he was involved in another murder. Nancy Nolan, eighty years of age, had five daughters and one son, all living in different parts of the country. Her husband had died five years previously.

On 15 July 1998, Thomas Murray was still a guest of the State. On temporary release, residing in sheltered accommodation in Galway, he indecently exposed himself to a group of children in Galway city, at a place called Fisher's Field, along the banks of the Corrib. A lady nearby started to shout at him. A number of teenagers in the vicinity ran over. They saw what Murray was doing, and they shouted at him. He ran away, followed by the teenagers. The Gardaí were informed, and soon Garda Patrick Brick of Galway arrived at the scene. The teenagers pointed out Murray, saying, 'That is the man we saw exposing himself.'

Garda Brick brought Murray to the Garda Station. Murray gave his name, and asked if he could make a phone call, to his father. During that conversation, a Garda heard Murray say to his father, 'They have me again.' The Garda made enquiries into Murray's background, and discovered that he was on temporary release from Castlerea Prison, and had a conviction for murder. He was returned to Castlerea Prison that evening.

On Monday, 14 February 2000, Nancy Nolan drove into Ballygar and spent a few hours around the village, doing some shopping. She met a number of people, and went home that evening. She normally put her car into a garage at nighttime, but she didn't put it into the garage on this night. The next day, a neighbour of Nancy's contacted Roscommon Garda Station, and said she was concerned about her neighbour Nancy. She was not answering the phone to her family, and her family had telephoned this neighbour to see if Nancy was all right. She had not seen Nancy all the previous day, and the car was on the roadway outside, instead of in the garage.

At 1pm, Sergeant Damian Lawler, Garda Eoin Creegan and Garda Colm Corcoran arrived at Nancy's house. They were given a key by a neighbour and went into the house. They found Nancy's body lying on the floor in the hallway. From the very severe head injuries the unfortunate woman had suffered, it was clear to the Gardaí that she had been murdered. The usual crime scene measures were put in place. The local doctor was called, and he pronounced death. A murder investigation was commenced, an incident room was set up, the State Pathologist was informed, and a post mortem was carried out.

Thomas Murray was the number one suspect. It emerged at a very early stage that Murray was out on temporary release from Castlerea Prison on the day of Nancy Nolan's murder. He had been seen in Ballygar that day, and had returned to Castlerea Prison that night, at the end of a twelve-hour release. Every Monday for quite some time prior to that, he was allowed out on temporary release during the day. His father would collect him and bring him home, and he would either drive him back or he would get a lift back.

On Wednesday, 16 February, Inspector William Gallagher received two search warrants from the local District Justice. The first was for the home and lands at Ballygar where Murray's father resided, and where Murray was on the day of the murder. The other warrant was to search the accommodation occupied by Murray at Castlerea Prison, and his property at the prison. The house, lands and property were searched by a number of Gardaí. A Garda spoke to Murray at the prison, and he took possession of two items of his clothing – a black, knitted jumper and a beige-coloured jacket.

On 20 March 2000, Gardaí went to Castlerea Prison and arrested Murray on suspicion of the murder of Nancy Nolan. He was taken to a local Garda Station and interrogated for quite some time. He denied any involvement, saying that the last time he saw Mrs Nolan had been about two weeks before her death. He had seen her in and around Ballygar. He was returned to Castlerea Prison. Murray's clothing, taken from Castlerea Prison, was sent to the Forensic Science Laboratory. It was examined by forensic scientist Dr Thornton, who discovered fibres similar to Murray's clothing on Nancy Nolan's clothing. Fibres similar to Nancy Nolan's clothing were also found on Murray's clothing.

On 24 April 2000, Murray told the prison authorities that he wanted to speak to Detective Garda Basil Johnson again. Detective Garda Johnson and Detective Garda Fitzmaurice travelled to Castlerea Prison and spoke to him. He said he had something important to tell them. He wanted to tell all, and give the whole thing up. He made a statement to the members, admitting that he had killed Nancy Nolan, and said that he was sorry. He said, 'It's an awful thing to do, to kill a woman like Mrs Nolan.'

Murray had gone to Mrs Nolan's house on 14 February 2000, and attacked her with a lump hammer he had brought with him. He hit her on the head several times, and he took her spectacles when he was leaving. He described the location where he had thrown away the spectacles and disposed of the lump hammer.

On 25 April, Gardaí Ciaran Doyle and David Finn searched the area nominated by Thomas Murray. Using a metal detector, they found a lump hammer in a bog hole at Cloonlyon Bog, close to Murray's home. About 100 yards from the bog hole, they found a pair of spectacles, which were identified as Nancy Nolan's.

Murray was charged with the murder of Nancy Nolan, and the trial took place at the Central Criminal Court in Dublin in December 2000. Murray pleaded guilty.

There was a lot of media criticism about the fact that Murray had been allowed out unsupervised on temporary release, and given the opportunity to kill another innocent person. He had for years been let out on temporary release, and on some occasions his behaviour was suspect. After his arrest for William Mannion's murder, he had spent some time in the mental hospital in Dundrum.

During a prisoner's detention, efforts are made to rehabilitate them, and to prepare them to re-enter the community again. Psychiatrists unfortunately cannot attach monitors to patients and take readings that will tell them what goes on in a patient's mind, or what they are likely to do. Medical professionals are consulted before a decision is made to grant prisoners like Thomas Murray temporary release. This decision is given very careful consideration, considering both the prisoner's welfare and the safety of the public at large. I do not think for one moment that a prisoner would be released, if there were a question in the mind of a psychiatrist that the public would be in danger as a result. Everybody can make mistakes, and professional medical opinion can be wrong sometimes, though it is made in good faith. I can see how this can happen, but who am I to criticise them?

MANSLAUGHTER OF MARIAN ANN CULLEN, WATERFORD, 1981

The village of Kilmacow is about five or six miles from Waterford city. It was plunged into horror and shock at the discovery of the brutally murdered body of a twelve-year-old girl in an old building near her home, on the evening of 23 October 1981. The girl was identified as Marian Ann Cullen, and the whole community poured out their deepest sympathy for her parents, and her brothers and sisters. Marian at the time was one month short of her thirteenth birthday.

Initial reports were that Marian and her brother, Sean Jr, were walking in fields five or six hundred yards from their home, when they were approached by a man. Both children ran away, in different directions. Sean Jr came home some time later, but there was no sign of Marian. Sean related the story of the incident in the field, and a search for Marian was commenced immediately.

Marian's father Sean Sr and Marian's brother Patrick ran immediately to the area indicated by Sean Jr. They entered a disused house or shed of some sort at about 6.30pm, and found the body of Marian. She had head injuries, and blood around her head. Patrick felt for a pulse, and came to the conclusion that she was dead. Gardaí were notified, and the usual crime scene preservation was put into place. A doctor visited the scene, and confirmed that Marian was dead. A murder investigation was commenced, and an incident room was set up in Waterford Garda Station.

That same night, Detective Sergeant Jim Hurley called to the Cullen home. He sympathised with the parents and the rest of the family. He spoke to Sean Jr, and Sean related to him the story about the man in the field. He gave a description of the man to Sergeant Hurley. Jim Hurley requested the clothing that Sean Jr had been wearing on his walk in the fields with Marian, and this was handed over.

Marian's body was removed to Ardkeen Hospital in Waterford. State Pathologist Dr John Harbison performed a post mortem. He established that Marian had severe head and facial injuries, and both hands were severely wounded. She was not sexually assaulted. The cause of death was multiple head injuries.

A special search was made for the man alleged to have been in the field. Despite numerous enquiries among the local community, nobody reported seeing a man who fitted the description given by Sean Jr. At a conference some days after the murder, Jim Hurley said that he thought Sean Jr may have wiped his eyes the night he handed over his clothing. Detective Sergeant Hurley said that he had accompanied Sean Jr to the bedroom, where Sean commenced to strip. When he came to the underpants, Sean stood in front of a wardrobe, opened one door wide, and stood in behind the door. He was then out of view of the Sergeant. He handed the Sergeant a pair of underpants around the open door. But the Sergeant did not see him remove them from his body. Sergeant Hurley said that for a split second, he got the feeling that the underpants lacked body heat. The clothing of Sean Jr had been sent to the Forensic Science Laboratory for examination, with negative results so far. The underpants were reported to be spotless, and very recently washed. For this reason, and when no other sightings of the man in the field were reported, focus was placed on Sean Jr. At the time, Sean Jr was fifteen years old.

On 25 October, Marian's remains left Ardkeen Hospital, Waterford, and were taken to a packed parish church, St Senan's in Kilmacow. Marian had enrolled at the Mercy Convent School in September, and friends and companions from there formed a guard of honour as her remains left the hospital. Teammates from St Senan's camogie club in Kilmacow, of which she was a leading member, provided a guard of honour at the church. Reverend Father Tom McGree celebrated the funeral Mass the next morning. He spoke in glowing terms of Marian, recommending that the young people of the parish should take a leaf from her book, and be as kind and obedient as she was. He reminded the congregation that Marian had stood so many times at the altar in the church, giving the readings at Sunday Mass. Marian's coffin was draped with her camogie uniform. She had been awarded a special cup by the camogie club in 1980, for being their most dedicated player.

After Marian's funeral, Marian's parents were anxious to have Sean Jr's clothing returned. Detective Inspector Christie McCaffrey and Detective Garda Tom Byrne, both from the Investigation Section of the Garda Technical Bureau, went to their home and spoke to them. It was agreed that Sean Sr would bring his son to Waterford Garda Station the following day, where he would be measured and new clothing provided to him. His clothing was still at the Forensic Science Laboratory, and not yet available for return.

Sean Sr brought his son to the Garda Station as arranged, and was spoken to by Detective Inspector McCaffrey. The Inspector asked Sean Sr if he would allow his son to be asked some questions about Marian's death. The Inspector explained that he felt that his son may have some further information that he might not want to talk about in the presence of the family. His father agreed.

Sean Jr was interviewed by Detective Garda Tom Byrne and I. We spoke for five or ten minutes about school and other matters unrelated to our enquiry. Then I put it to him that he did not give Detective Sergeant Jim Hurley the underpants he had been wearing on the night that Marian died. He was somewhat taken aback, and he said, 'How do you know that?' We told him that was not all we knew about what happened in the field. We asked him to tell us the correct story. He then admitted to us that there was no man in the field.

He said that when Marian and himself were out walking, they came to an old building. They went in, and he started to mess around with Marian. He started to sexually molest her. She resisted, but he continued. She said she would tell

Mammy and Daddy about him. He took up a stone and started to hit her with it on the head. She was on the ground and he left her there, and went home.

His father was brought into the office, and the son related to his father what he had told us. Sean Jr made a complete statement of admission in the presence of his father, outlining all he had done to his sister. He was later charged with the murder of Marian Ann Cullen, before a special sitting of Waterford District Court. He was remanded in custody at St Michael's institution in Finglas, to appear at Waterford District Court the following Tuesday.

There is no doubt that the death of Marian in such a violent manner must have had shockingly traumatic consequences for the whole family. But to discover that the next youngest of the family was responsible must have exacerbated this greatly. I asked Sean Jr, in Waterford Garda Station, where he had got these ideas of sexual behaviour at the age of fifteen. He told me that he got them from looking at English sex magazines.

Sean Jr was finally dealt with at the Central Criminal Court in Dublin. He pleaded not guilty to the murder of Marian. Having heard all the evidence and submissions from both sides, the jury retired to consider their verdict. They found that this young boy, Sean Cullen, was not guilty of murder, but guilty of manslaughter.

Senior Counsel for the DPP, Michael Moriarty, told the Court that the Department of Justice had not seen fit to send a senior person to advise the Court on a suitable place of detention for the boy. Paddy McEntee, Senior Counsel for the defence, submitted that the Judge should not decide on the place, or the duration of sentence, until he knew what therapeutic care and intervention the State could provide. He said that the boy had a constitutional right to have therapeutic intervention. The Judge directed that the Department of Justice provide a senior official to advise the Court of a suitable institution for the detention of the boy.

Inspector PJ Hayes told the Court that the boy was the third-youngest of a family of five, that he was a bright boy, and rated above average at school. He was continuing his studies for the Leaving Certificate while in custody. Sean Jr was remanded in custody to allow time for a full psychiatric examination and the attendance of a Department of Justice official.

Sean Jr appeared again before Mr Justice Barron on 13 July 1982. Psychiatrist Dr Paul McQuaid told the Court that, without treatment, the boy would be liable to further outbursts. He said St Patrick's institution would not be the ideal institution for him. The Judge said, 'I have no jurisdiction in saying where he should be detained, but I am making a recommendation that the Minister for Justice pay attention to the submissions of the psychiatrist.' Sean Jr was sentenced to a period of four years' imprisonment, in whatever place of detention the Department of Justice decided on. This was a very, very sad case.

MURDER OF MICHAEL CASEY, DRIMOLEAGUE, 1981

In November 1981, I was Detective Sergeant in the Investigation Section at Crime Branch. I became involved in the investigation of a murder in the Skibbereen–Drimoleague area of West Cork, an area well known to me. This case clearly illustrates the lack of respect some people have for human life. Two men considered the success of an intended robbery more important than the life of a man they decided to rob.

Drimoleague is on the road from Dunmanway to Bantry, about an equal distance from Bantry or Skibbereen, and that would be about eight miles. A local farmer who resided alone had been found dead in his home, on Wednesday, 18 November 1981. A post mortem established that he had been asphyxiated. Assistance in the investigation of the crime was sought by Superintendent

Farrelly of Bantry. That is how I became involved, along with other members from the Investigation Section.

The previous Sunday night, 15 November, two men were drinking in a pub in Skibbereen. These two men both had convictions in Skibbereen, including breaking into a sports club, stealing alcohol and a few other bits and pieces. They were known to the Gardaí. They were low on funds to support their drinking habits, and they considered their options for where they could get some money. Working was clearly not one of their preferred options. They decided to go to the home of a farmer known to one of them, six miles or so outside of Skibbereen. They decided in the pub that they would have to kill him before they robbed him, because he would know one of them. The possibility of wearing gloves, and perhaps putting some sort of material over their heads to prevent identification, was not considered. They just decided to kill him.

Michael Casey, a bachelor of about sixty-eight, lived alone in a farmhouse in an isolated part of Tooreen, Skibbereen. Michael's house was situated at the end of a laneway, inside a gateway with two big stone pillars.

On 18 November, Sergeant Brendan Conway was contacted by a neighbour of Michael Casey's. The neighbour said he had not seen Casey for a number of days, and the electric light was continuously on in his house. Sergeant Conway went to Michael Casey's house, and got no response to repeated knocking at the door. There was a window open in one of the upstairs rooms, so the Sergeant got a ladder, and climbed up and in through the window. He searched around, and found Michael lying on the floor at the bottom of the stairs. He was dead, and appeared to have been dead for quite some time.

The Sergeant had a look around. Downstairs there were broken bottles, a broken vase and an upturned chair, and papers and books were scattered around the floor. Not far from the body was a broken belt. Sergeant Conway notified a priest and a doctor, and the scene was preserved. The priest arrived and administered the last rites to Michael Casey. The Sergeant also noticed that the deceased's Ford Escort car had crashed into one of the gate pillars. It was facing out of the yard, out into the lane, up against a pillar. A local doctor arrived and pronounced Michael dead, expressing the view that he may have died of a heart attack.

Superintendent Farrelly, in whose area this crime had been committed, came to the scene. He decided to request the services of the State Pathologist. Dr Harbison was not available, so Dr Charles Connolly, an assistant State Pathologist, travelled down to Skibbereen to perform a post mortem examination on Michael's body. Dr Connolly found extensive swelling and bruising on Michael's left ear. He had a black eye, and there was blood on his nose, face and scalp. He had faint abrasions on the left side of his neck, and there was pinpoint haemorrhaging in the eyes, which suggested that Michael had died from asphyxia. He did not find any haemorrhaging in the tissues of his neck. The enquiry into Michael's death became a murder enquiry.

A short time into the enquiry, I received a phone call in the incident room in Drimoleague. It was a male caller, who wanted to speak to somebody involved in the investigation of Michael Casey's murder. He spoke about two young men, and mentioned two different locations. I did not know the locations, or the men he was talking about. I asked him if he would speak to a local Garda and give him the information, and he agreed. I handed the phone to Garda Michael Malone. This good-spirited local citizen gave Michael very good information, which was instrumental in pointing us in the right direction. Two persons were named, both known already to the Gardaí.

It was decided to invite both of these men to Skibbereen Garda Station. I was in one group, and another group went out to the other person. The man that I was interested in was a chap called Joseph O'Mahoney, with a few addresses around Skibbereen and Drimoleague. The other chap was Dennis O'Callaghan, from Glenamagh in Skibbereen. We went in search of Joseph O'Mahoney, and found him in a particular licensed premises three or four miles outside Skibbereen. I stayed in the car, and the other member went into this premises. Within a short time, he arrived out with O'Mahoney. I got out of the car and spoke to O'Mahoney, telling him who I was and what I wanted, and asking him would he come to Skibbereen Garda Station to talk to us. He said he would.

This was 1981, when the Gardaí did not have authority to detain persons for the purposes of questioning. I was very conscious of this fact when talking to O'Mahoney, having learned from previous bad experiences, so we had to go gently.

Joseph O'Mahoney had a Honda 50 motorcycle with him, and I asked him would he follow us to Skibbereen Garda Station on it. He agreed and did follow us in. He came into the Station, and we sat down and started to talk.

Someone else had gone in search of O'Callaghan, and they arrived at Skibbereen Garda Station with him at some stage on the same date.

O'Mahoney was very talkative and friendly, in no way hostile whatsoever. He answered all the questions that were asked, initially denying any involvement in Michael Casey's death. After about thirty minutes, he put his hand in his pocket, took out a car key and handed it to me. He said, 'That's the key of his car; we done him in.' He went on to relate what had taken place in the pub in Skibbereen on the night of 15 November, and what took place later at the home of Michael Casey.

He said that he met Dennis O'Callaghan on Sunday night, 15 November, and they had a few drinks in a pub in Skibbereen. O'Callaghan asked if he knew any place that they could get money. O'Mahoney told him that a neighbour of his lived alone, and had plenty of money. They decided to go to his house that night, and rob him. They decided to put the strap from the motorcycle – one of those bungee straps with a metal hook at either end – around

Michael Casey's neck when they went in. They would knock on the door, and O'Mahoney would say his uncle was dead. They would kill Casey, and then search the house.

The two men left the pub on O'Mahoney's motorcycle, and drove out towards Casey's home. They got off the motorcycle somewhere short of the house, and left the motorcycle in the side of the ditch. O'Mahoney took the strap off the carrier of his motorcycle. He put it in his pocket and they went across the fields to Casey's house.

When they arrived at the house, O'Mahoney called out to Michael Casey, and knocked at the door. Casey put his head out the top window. O'Mahoney told him his uncle was dead, and O'Callaghan said that they wanted to get a priest. Casey said, hold on, I will be down. He came down and opened the door, and O'Callaghan rushed in past him. O'Mahoney told Casey that he wanted to be taken to Skibbereen to get a priest. O'Mahoney stood in the hallway speaking to Casey, and O'Callaghan went into the sitting room.

O'Callaghan came out and banged the front door. He put a belt around Casey's neck from behind, and came around the front then. O'Mahoney caught hold of Casey's hands, and held them behind his back. O'Callaghan started to squeeze the belt around Casey's neck, and Casey said, 'Leave me alone and I will give you money.' O'Callaghan kept squeezing the belt, and O'Mahoney kept his hands behind his back.

They struggled, and the two men fell on top of Casey on the ground. They struggled with him again on the floor. O'Callaghan still had the belt around his neck, Casey was lying on his back, and O'Mahoney had his hands held on his stomach. O'Callaghan had one knee on his chest, and he was working away on his neck with the belt, which was against the flesh of his neck. O'Callaghan said to O'Mahoney, 'I will open his shirt and bring the belt down further on his neck, for to squeeze him right.' O'Mahoney saw him open his shirt and bring the belt down further on his neck. The belt broke just as he was passing out. O'Mahoney took out the rubber strap, and O'Callaghan tied it around Casey's neck. He pulled the strap around Casey's neck a few times, and hooked the ends together.

The men searched Casey, and found a chequebook and £180 in an inside pocket. In the kitchen they made mugs of Bovril, drank them and washed up the mugs. They found a bottle of whiskey, and had a drink.

Before leaving the house, they removed the strap from around Casey's neck. They divided the money, took Casey's car and crashed into the pillar coming out the gate. They went back to O'Mahoney's motorcycle, and drove to Donal O'Donovan's house. O'Mahoney told O'Donovan that himself and O'Callaghan had murdered Casey. O'Mahoney stayed in O'Donovan's house that night.

Later that night, O'Mahoney and O'Callaghan were charged before a special sitting of a Court in the Garda Station in Skibbereen, presided over by a local Peace Commissioner. They were remanded in custody and appeared before Skibbereen District Court on 24 November. O'Callaghan had also made a full statement admitting what had happened, and his statement very much agreed with the events outlined by O'Mahoney.

The car key that O'Mahoney had given to me, after admitting he had killed Michael Casey, was brought to Slattery's Ford dealer in Bandon. Casey had purchased his car there, a year or two earlier. A representative from Ford in Cork identified the key from a number stamped on it, as one of the original keys that was supplied with the Ford Escort that Michael Casey had purchased from Slattery's. The chequebook of the deceased, taken by the two men during the murder and robbery, was located by Detective Sergeant Timothy O'Brien in the home of Patrick Collins, an uncle of O'Mahoney's. It was found in a bedroom in Collins's house that was occupied on and off by O'Mahoney.

The two accused appeared together before the District Court in custody on a number of occasions, until eventually they were returned for trial to the Central Criminal Court in Dublin. Each was given a separate trial. In July 1982, Joseph O'Mahoney went on trial before Mr Justice Costello. Joseph O'Mahoney pleaded not guilty. The trial lasted four days, before a jury of eleven men and one woman. O'Mahoney was found guilty, and received the mandatory sentence of life imprisonment.

O'Callaghan's trial took place in October 1982, presided over by Mr Justice Gannon. O'Callaghan also pleaded not guilty. After a few days of trial, Seamus Sorohan, Senior Counsel for the defence, told the Court that certain matters had been put to the accused for the first time and, as a result, O'Callaghan changed his plea to guilty. Mr Justice Gannon told O'Callaghan that he had pleaded guilty to an offence for which the mandatory sentence was life imprisonment. He had no discretion in the matter.

I look back on this case, and think of the torture and torment Michael Casey went through in the period leading up to his death. These two men left Mr Casey lying on the floor, wriggling in agony and terror, with an elasticated band with a metal hook at either end wound tightly around his neck. They ransacked his house and drank his whiskey, stepping over him several times as they went between the kitchen and the sitting room.

MANSLAUGHTER OF JOHN ROCHE, CORK, 1982

In September 1982, John Roche, twenty-nine years of age, was employed as night porter at the Munster Hotel, on Coburg Street, Cork city. John was unmarried, and resided with his father at Blarney Street, not far from the hotel. John Roche was last seen alive by John Coughlan, the owner of the hotel. That was at 4am on 8 September, when they had a conversation in the hotel. A guest in the hotel, who was making his way up to his bedroom, also saw him at the time.

A female receptionist, who resided in the hotel, got up that morning at 7.55am and walked down the corridor a short time afterwards. She saw that the door of room 26 was slightly open. Room 26 was under repair. It wasn't for guests, but the night porter was using it as a rest room as there was a bed in it. She looked into the room, and saw John Roche behind the door, partly on the floor and against a chair. She didn't try to speak to him, as she was busily getting ready to start work.

She came back a short time later, called him by name and tipped him on the head and the arm. She said she guessed that he was not alive. She telephoned the hotel owner, Mr Coughlan, and he went to room 26, arriving at 8.30am. He found Roche, half-sitting on an upturned chair, and saw that there was a tie wound loosely around his neck, the other end of which was loosely tied to the leg of the chair. He telephoned for an ambulance, but said he didn't think Roche was alive.

Dr Michael Ryan, from Ballincollig, went to the hotel and saw the body of John Roche. He was dressed only in underpants, with an obvious stab wound in his chest, made with a double-edged blade. Sergeant Christopher Halligan also arrived in the room, and noted spatters of blood around the room. A search was made, but there was no sign of a knife in the bedroom. It was obvious to the Gardaí that they had a murder on their hands.

The scene was preserved and examined, and the State Pathologist notified. Dr John Harbison performed the post mortem on the deceased. He concluded that Roche had died from one stab wound to the chest, which penetrated the heart.

The morning that Roche was found, Gardaí received a report that a knife had been seen on a wall at St Patrick's Place, not far from the hotel. The knife subsequently disappeared. After an appeal for information in relation to the murder, and in relation to the knife, a member of the public came forward and handed over a knife that he had found, somewhere around St Patrick's Place, on the morning of the murder. The knife turned out to be very important. Engraved into its blade were the words 'I cut my way'.

The local Superintendent sought assistance in the investigation, and Detective Superintendent John Courtney, Detective Sergeant Gerry O'Carroll, Detective Sergeant PJ Brown and I, and a number of others, went to Cork.

Two or three days after the murder, Superintendent John Casey received two telephone calls from an anonymous male caller, which were recorded. During one call, he told the Superintendent to look at the knife and he would see the words 'I cut my way' engraved on it. Of course, that was correct. He also told the Superintendent where to find some underclothing relevant to the case. Detective Sergeant Pat Casey searched the location mentioned, and nothing of interest was found there.

In the second call, the caller agreed to meet the Superintendent, and said he would meet outside Eason's in Patrick Street at a particular time. The caller did not keep his appointment with the Superintendent. The area around Eason's was videotaped, covering the arranged time. Later that evening, the video was shown to members of the local Detective Branch, and the recordings of the phone calls were also played to them.

Detective Sergeant Pat Casey expressed the view that the voice was very like that of one Michael O'Connor, from the St Luke's area of Cork. He stated that O'Connor had passed on two occasions when he was searching for the underclothing. Studying the video, he identified O'Connor moving around the area in front of Eason's. Many lines of enquiry in relation to this murder, checking up on prospective suspects, were being pursued at this time. All emphasis was now shifted in O'Connor's direction, and he became the main suspect.

In 1982, as I have mentioned, there was no power to detain a person for questioning regarding a crime. The decision was taken to invite Michael O'Connor to MacCurtain Street Station, to be asked questions about Roche's murder. I do not recall the circumstances of how he came to be at MacCurtain Street Station, but there was no issue later in relation to it. He was interviewed by a number of members while there. Detective Sergeant Gerry O'Carroll and I interviewed him, and he denied involvement for some time. Eventually, he admitted that he was involved, and outlined the full circumstances of it in a statement that he made to us.

He said he was chatted up by Roche on several occasions, and invited back to the hotel for a cup of tea. He had seen Roche hanging around with gay people, and he did not go to the hotel. The day before the killing, he met Roche, and agreed to go to the hotel that night. He then went off and bought a seven-inch knife, for £11.25. He had decided to kill Roche if he tried to make him gay. He went to the pictures that night, and then on to the hotel at about midnight. He said he didn't stay, but he told Roche that he would be back around 4am.

He returned about 4am, and was offered a cup of tea in a bedroom by Roche. He left the hotel and got the knife, and returned with it at about 5am. Up in the bedroom, Roche took off his clothes, lay on the bed and took down his underpants. O'Connor said he then stabbed Roche in the chest, telling him that his gay days were over. Roche grabbed him by the throat and said, 'Jesus Christ, I have been stabbed.' He got off the bed, turned on the light, gave O'Connor a horrible look and collapsed.

After a while, O'Connor went down the stairs quietly, and was just about to open the front door when the doorbell rang. He looked out the spyhole, and could see a man outside. He waited, and watched the man go to a car, get into the back seat and lie down. He left the hotel shortly afterwards, and threw away the knife somewhere not too far away.

In the bedroom where Roche was found, a fingermark was found on the radiator. It was found to have been made by one of O'Connor's thumbs.

Michael O'Connor appeared for trial, after a false start, in June 1983, before Mr Justice McMahon. Defence Counsel was Seamus Egan, the same Seamus Egan that appeared for Peter Pringle. O'Connor pleaded not guilty.

At an early stage, the defence conceded that their client did in fact kill Roche. O'Connor gave evidence himself, and outlined his life, saying he was sexually assaulted many times as a child. He was raped in the Phoenix Park in Dublin at knifepoint, and was revolted by homosexuality. For the defence, consultant psychiatrist Dr Charles Smith told the Court that O'Connor was very strong in his denial of homosexual preferences. He stated that O'Connor was capable of angry responses to homosexual advances. Another psychiatrist, Professor Robert Daly, Professor of Psychiatry at UCC, said he discussed with O'Connor his encounters with the deceased, and he believed O'Connor had severely mixed feelings about homosexuals.

In his address to the jury, the Judge said, 'Put out from your minds all of the recent publicity about homosexuality. There is no question about the sanity of the accused, although there has been evidence of his level of intelligence. If the jury decides the killing was the result of provocation, or has a reasonable doubt, the accused was entitled to the benefit of the doubt. Provocation does not justify murder, but excuses it to a limited extent. They should also take into consideration the background and personality of the accused.'

Michael Mary O'Connor, twenty-six years of age, was found not guilty of murder, but guilty of manslaughter. In passing sentence of five years' imprisonment on O'Connor, the Judge said he believed that Roche was a homosexual, and had enticed O'Connor to take part in homosexual acts with him.

I believe it was a fair and just verdict and sentence, when one takes all the circumstances into consideration.

BOMBING OF THE RADAR TRACKING STATION, SCHULL, 1982

Visitors to Schull, a small town on the road from Skibbereen to Mizen Head, might wonder what the two large buildings are, situated at the summit of Mount Gabriel, inland and to the north. These are visible from some miles away. The lower part of the buildings are circular, and the tops are oval shaped. The buildings are a radar tracking station, used to monitor the movements and the identities of civil aircraft from up to 240 miles away. The station was built in 1979 and 1980, at a cost of £1.6 million.

GAA fans will remember the All Ireland Football Final of 1982. It was between Kerry and Offaly, with Kerry going for five in a row. With one minute to go, Kerry led by two points, and what happened next is history. Seamus Darby of Offaly scored a goal, and destroyed Kerry's dreams. I was at the match, but there was something more important on my mind that day, because it was my twenty-first wedding anniversary, 19 September.

Coming up to midnight on that same momentous night, Martin Ferris, a technician, arrived at the radar tracking station at the top of Mount Gabriel to do his work. The station operated without personnel, but somebody would come every night for maintenance and so on. Ferris was accompanied by a hackney driver, Liam O'Driscoll from Goleen.

When they reached the mountaintop, they were met by five armed men, who were clearly waiting for them, and knew the setup. They forced them into a building there, tied them up, put them lying on the ground, put explosives beside them and ran wires away from the explosives. Possibly the wires did not go anywhere, but they gave the impression that they could detonate them any time they liked. They took the keys from Mr Ferris, and so had access to the station. They went in and planted a great number of explosive devices around the place.

After some time, Ferris and O'Driscoll were put into the hackney and driven halfway down the mountain. Before they were let go, they were photographed. Then the five men drove off in their car. Some time later, as Ferris and O'Driscoll were nearing the bottom of the mountain walking, they saw great flashes of light at the top of the mountain, and heard numerous explosions.

At about 4am, Gardaí on a mobile patrol, somewhere near Charleville on the Limerick Road, stopped a Fiat car with five male occupants. The Gardaí took their names, and the particulars of the car. The Gardaí did not know anything about an explosion at that time. Back in Schull, after the explosion, Gardaí went up to the top of the mountain, and discovered that a great amount of damage had been caused. Parts of the station had been completely destroyed.

Superintendent Farrelly of Bantry, the same man that was involved in the Michael Casey murder investigation, went to the scene and decided again to call for assistance from Garda Headquarters, for an investigation team and fingerprint, ballistics and photographic help. He also contacted the Army, seeking assistance from the Ordnance Corps.

On Monday morning, at about nine or ten o'clock when I went to work, I was sent on the road to west Cork, to Schull. Detective Inspector Christie McCaffrey, Sergeant PJ Brown, Detective Garda Tim Mulvey and Detective Garda Michael Kellegher joined me, and perhaps others. I came across a photograph some time last year with the five of us in it, taken in Schull. We all met up in Schull in the Garda Station on that Monday evening and had a conference. Sergeant Dave O'Keeffe was the Sergeant in charge.

We were made aware of the car stopped outside Charleville at 4am on 20 September, the morning of the explosion. Four of the five occupants of that car were known subversives. They belonged to a proscribed organisation, the INLA. The car was known to be the property of a well-known INLA member. The following morning, I made notes of particulars of the occupants of the car:

their names and addresses, the registration number of the car, and so on. Sergeant Dave O'Keeffe received information from a man residing at the bottom of Mount Gabriel, in the laneway of a narrow road. He had seen a car turn in his yard at his gateway, around 11.30pm on the night of Sunday, 19 September. He had taken the number of the car.

After our conference, I accompanied Sergeant Dave O'Keeffe to see this man. As we approached his house, Dave O'Keeffe saw the man out in the field. It was decided that Sergeant O'Keeffe should speak to this man on his own, as they were known to each other, while I was a complete stranger. Sergeant O'Keeffe got out of the car and went into the field to speak to the man. After about twenty minutes, the Sergeant called me, and when I joined them I immediately noticed that this local man was sweating and shivering with fear. I really thought he was going to have a heart attack.

The Sergeant told me that the man had seen a car and had taken the number, but was afraid to tell us. We coaxed him the best we could, and finally I told him that I believed that the number he had taken down was already in my notebook; that he was not the only person who saw the car that night. I took out my notebook, but I did not open it. We continued to urge him to tell us, and finally he said to the Sergeant, 'I will tell you.' I walked off a little bit, and he told the Sergeant the number. I joined them again, and I knew by Sergeant O'Keeffe that we had the right number. I then produced my notebook, opened it and showed him the number of the car, and I said, 'Now, is that the number?' He nodded his head. I said, 'Listen, you are not the only one that saw that car that night.' His appearance relaxed somewhat. Of course, I did not tell him that the other sighting was on the Limerick border. We had the number; things were looking up at that stage, but in my heart I couldn't see him appearing in the witness box up at the Special Criminal Court to give evidence, though in fact he did when the time came.

When the Army Ordnance Corps came to the scene, they discovered a great number of explosive devices that were not detonated, rigged up around a whole number of places inside this building. Only a part of the explosives had gone off. It took a number of days for them to make safe everything in the building. It was very dangerous, and they had to be very cautious in case the place was booby-trapped. Eventually they had everything checked and were satisfied that it was clear, and then the technical examination was started by the ballistics men, fingerprint men and the photographer.

Detective Sergeant Joe Harte of the Fingerprint Section made a very important discovery. One of the unexploded devices involved a small, plastic funnel. On the funnel was a little sticker, which conveyed to Joe the shop in Limerick in which it was purchased. More importantly, when he examined it, he found a fingermark. It was a good fingermark, with plenty of points for identification.

I believe the five men stopped in the Fiat car were later all arrested. I only dealt with one of them, however, so I cannot say for sure. As I said, four of the men were known, and the fifth man was not known to be connected with any unlawful organisations. His name was John Mortimer Liston, a married man who worked as a fireman in Limerick city, and lived in Castleconnell. He was arrested, and I spoke to him in Henry Street in Limerick, accompanied by another member. I was also present when his fingerprints were taken. He had been arrested under Section 30 of the Offences Against the State Act. Some time afterwards I told him, 'Your fingerprints are taken now, and we have a fingermark on file that was found on a funnel of an unexploded device in the radar tracking station in Schull. If it turns out that this is your fingermark, have you got any excuse for it?' He said, 'It could not be my fingermark; I was not there.' He told me he was at home in bed with his wife all night, and that somebody else who was in the car gave his name.

Joe Harte identified the mark on the funnel as having been made by John Liston's left thumb. Liston was charged with the unlawful and malicious explosion at the radar plant on 22 September 1982. He appeared before the Special Criminal Court in June 1983, and was found guilty. He gave evidence in his own defence, saying that he was at home with his wife that night. His wife also gave evidence on his behalf, saying that he was at home. In relation to the fingermark, he said that he did frequent this particular shop in Limerick where the funnel was purchased, and that he could have picked it up when he was in the shop looking for something else. The shop owner gave evidence, saying that Liston was a customer of his.

The judges of the Special Criminal Court – President of the Court Judge Liam Hamilton, a Judge from the Circuit Court and a Judge from the District Court – did not believe Liston. He was convicted and sentenced to nine years' imprisonment. He appealed his conviction to the Court of Criminal Appeal in October 1984. That Court upheld the conviction.

The INLA issued a statement after the explosion on Mount Gabriel. They admitted responsibility for it, and said they carried out the attack because the station was being used by the North Atlantic Treaty Organisation, as part of an early-warning network against a Soviet strike. They insisted that Mount Gabriel was being used regularly by NATO, in contravention of Ireland's neutrality. Euro Control, the international civil aviation authority, denied this. I am not going to try to figure out who was right and who was wrong, but the damage caused to the radar tracking station could not be justified.

MURDER OF THREE MEMBERS OF THE IRISH ARMY, LEBANON, 1982

Since 1958, the Irish Army, the main branch of our Defence Forces, has had a continuous presence in peacekeeping missions around the world. Since joining the United Nations in 1955, the Army have been deployed on many peacekeeping missions. The first of these missions began in 1958, when a small number of observers were sent to Lebanon.

From 1978 to 2001, a battalion of Irish troops was deployed in South Lebanon, as part of a UN mandate force, UNIFIL. A battalion consisted of approximately eight hundred Army personnel. An Irish battalion, under the command of a Lieutenant-Colonel, would spend six months on duty in Lebanon, and would be replaced at the end of that time by another Irish battalion.

The changing over of a battalion, bringing eight hundred men from Ireland to Lebanon and bringing back eight hundred more, was a big operation. The changeover was not a one-day operation. A planeload would leave Ireland with approximately 250 to three hundred, and fly to Beirut or, because sometimes it was dangerous to land in Beirut, to Ben-Gurion Airport, near Tel Aviv. There would be about the same number of Irish Army personnel waiting at the airport, so the plane would unload and after a few hours the homecoming crowd would get on board and come home. That would be accomplished in one day, and normally that operation would take place midweek. The following week, the same operation would take place, and on the third week, the operation would be complete.

It was a great way of changing the battalion, because the 250 or three hundred that would arrive would have at least two weeks with personnel who had completed their six months there. It helped the new battalion to acclimatise, and get to know their surroundings, their conditions and all aspects of their duty.

In October 1982, the battalion there was the Fifty-first Battalion. They were due to return to Ireland around the end of the month. Their role in Lebanon, like that of previous battalions, consisted of manning checkpoints and observation posts, mounting patrols and providing humanitarian aid to the local population, particularly aiding the orphanage in Tibnin. Tibnin was a small village in South Lebanon, within the region the Irish battalion had responsibility for.

The battalion was divided into four companies. Headquarters Company was based in Tibnin village in their own encampment, popularly known as 'Camp Shamrock'. The other companies were known as A, B and C. They had their own encampments in the area. A Company had responsibility for an area that included a location known as Tibnin Bridge, roughly half a mile away from Camp Shamrock.

By 27 October, the replacement in Lebanon of the Fifty-first Battalion by the Fifty-second Battalion had not been completed. Some of the Fifty-first Battalion had returned home, and some of the Fifty-second Battalion had arrived in Lebanon.

At 2pm on that day, Corporal Michael Whelan completed his tour of duty with three colleagues at the checkpoint at Tibnin Bridge. He handed over the checkpoint to Corporal Gary Morrow, and three of Morrow's colleagues. Corporal Morrow was aged twenty, a native of Lurgan, County Armagh. He was recently married, and resided at Leinster Road in Rathmines. He was attached to Cathal Brugha Barracks, Dublin. He had left Dublin the previous Wednesday with the Fifty-second Battalion. With Corporal Morrow was Private Peter Burke, twenty years old, from Suir Road, Kilmainham in Dublin. He was due home on the following Wednesday, having spent six months there. Also there was Private Thomas Murphy, from Clearmont Park in Glasnevin, Dublin. He was attached to the Fifty-second Battalion, and had only arrived the previous Wednesday, the same as Corporal Morrow. The fourth member of the group was Private Michael McAleavey, twenty-two, from Falls Road in Belfast. He was also there less than a week, with the Fifty-second Battalion.

Tibnin Bridge crosses a small valley, or wadi, in a very remote part of the country. The bridge is surrounded by rough terrain, and a small river or stream flows under the bridge sometimes, though a lot of the time that river is dried up. The road over the bridge comes to a T-junction about fifty or sixty yards away. Immediately opposite this road, there is a bunker or a shelter, built of concrete into the rocks. Army personnel on duty congregate around this bunker. Two other Irish-manned checkpoints were located four or five hundred yards from Tibnin Bridge. They were out of sight, behind rock-strewn hills.

The soldiers were performing duty in probably the most dangerous and volatile country in the world at that time. Every approaching vehicle or person posed potential danger to their lives. At that time, warring factions were roaming South Lebanon and around the Israeli border, and it was highly volatile.

Private Michael McAleavey was not originally rostered for duty at Tibnin Bridge on 27 October. Private Johnston of A Company was detailed for duty, and was endeavouring to get somebody to change duty with him, and Michael McAleavey volunteered. When Corporal Morrow arrived at the checkpoint, he discovered he had forgotten his sub-machine gun. Corporal Whelan loaned him his sub-machine gun. When Corporal Whelan went back to the billet, he found Corporal Morrow's sub-machine gun on Morrow's bed, and he took possession of it.

At 3.45pm, Captain James Sayers, Commander of A Company, called to the checkpoint, and he briefed Corporal Morrow on the routine of the checkpoint. All was normal and correct at the checkpoint at that time, and the other three Army personnel were present. At 8pm, Captain Reverend Sean Conlon, a chaplain attached to the Curragh Camp, passed through the checkpoint at Tibnin Bridge. He stopped and spoke to three of the soldiers there. He saw another soldier on the other side of the bridge. It was dark at this time, and all appeared to be normal. Captain Conlon was the last known person to have passed through or spoken to the soldiers.

At 8.40pm, around forty minutes later, Corporal James O'Connor, a signal officer with A Company, received an incoherent radio call at Battalion Headquarters in Tibnin. There was heavy breathing, and continued repetition of a call sign. He pinpointed the source of the signal as the checkpoint at Tibnin Bridge. He contacted the post by telephone, and it was answered again in an incoherent voice. The voice said, 'We have been hit.' The incoherent voice turned out to belong to Private Michael McAleavey. Asked if anybody was hurt, he said, 'Two dead, one injured.' After a while he said, 'The NCO is missing.' Corporal O'Connor immediately contacted the duty officer at Battalion Headquarters, the hospital and the ambulance. The duty officer was Lieutenant Brian Sweeney, and he immediately went to Tibnin Bridge with a number of troops. He arrived there within five minutes of getting the message.

When he arrived, Private McAleavey was standing on the right-hand side of the bunker, with his rifle pointed in the direction of the bridge. There were two Lebanese civilians, standing with their hands in the air beside a BMW car. Lieutenant Sweeney approached Private McAleavey, and he saw a radio set on the ground at McAleavey's feet. Blood was flowing from the front of the bunker towards the bridge. He saw legs sticking out from the front of the bunker, and asked Private McAleavey what had happened. McAleavey said, 'They came in, the bastards, bastards.' He appeared frightened and shocked.

Lieutenant Sweeney saw two bodies on the ground in front of the bunker. He recognised one as Private Peter Burke. He was lying on his back and appeared to be dead. The other body was that of Private Thomas Murphy. He was lying face-downwards against Private Burke's body, and had injuries to his head. There was a lot of blood on the tarmac and around the bodies. There was a rifle underneath the bodies, and a chair was entangled between both their feet. There were blood stains on the wall above the men's heads, and also further up the wall.

The BMW car belonged to the two civilians, and the headlights were on and illuminating the checkpoint. Lieutenant Sweeney was afraid that the illumination of the checkpoint was creating potential danger to the troops that had just arrived, from the forces believed to have attacked the Irish soldiers. He took Private McAleavey's rifle, went over to the BMW and smashed the two headlights. The place was in darkness again. He returned the rifle to Private McAleavey. He then went to the right side of the bunker, and found another body, lying face-down on the ground. That body was Corporal Morrow.

Later, Lieutenant Sweeney saw Private McAleavey attacking the civilians who were now lying on the ground, kicking and punching them. Other members of the Defence Forces who had appeared at the scene also saw this. They restrained McAleavey, and it took quite an amount of force to hold him. At this stage, other officers had arrived, including Commandant Hudson. He had in his possession a Gustav sub-machine gun. McAleavey made a run at him, and tried to take the gun from him. Again there was a struggle, and McAleavey was pulled away.

Commandant Christopher Moore also went to Tibnin Bridge some time after Lieutenant Sweeney. When he arrived, Private McAleavey had been brought to hospital, as he seemed to be suffering from shock. Commandant Moore organised searches in the vicinity of the bridge and down into the wadi. Some of the troops present reported seeing shadows in the wadi near the bridge. Some of the troops discharged shots towards where the shadows were reported to have been seen.

Commandant Moore arranged for barrels of water to be brought to the scene to wash away the blood, as he wanted the checkpoint re-manned and re-established, and it needed to be in order for the replacement personnel. The Commandant was working on the assumption that there had been an attacking force in the area. Before the road was cleaned up, there was a search of the roadway, and the following morning a number of articles were found, which I shall outline later on.

At midnight, when they were about to call an end to the search for the day, the troops got word of an approaching Israeli patrol. The Israeli party stopped and offered their assistance, but their offer was declined. The bodies of the three soldiers were taken that night to Tibnin Hospital, where McAleavey also was. They were later flown by helicopter to Beirut for post mortem examination.

The following morning, 28 October, the search of the scene and surrounding area was resumed. A large number of men engaged in it, looking for any clues that would help identify the perpetrators of the crime. During that search, spent cartridge cases found around the scene were collected, and eventually found their way to a Swedish ballistics expert.

Private McAleavey was questioned, and gave his version of what had happened the previous night. On his release from hospital three or four days later, he was again questioned, by some officers and by members of his battalion's Military Police. On each occasion, he gave exactly the same story:

He left the checkpoint to go to the toilet, in a galvanised building about ten feet above the level of the bunker and to the rear. While there, he heard shooting, and dived for cover as the shooting continued. When it stopped, he scrambled down the slope to the bunker area, and found his three comrades dead. He then discharged his rifle into the valley, around the bridge area, and under the bridge. He thought that he saw some movements and stopped a car, which contained the two Lebanese civilians.

He continued to recite the very same version of events during all the interviews. He did tell one officer, Commandant Campion, that an Israeli army jeep with Israeli soldiers in it passed through the checkpoint shortly before the shooting. Afterwards he had a bit of an argument with Corporal Morrow in relation to this.

As one might expect, there was great speculation in the following days as to who was responsible. Irish Army officers would not comment, other than to say it could be one of a number of groups. A UN spokesman in Israel said it was difficult to say who was involved, as any number of groups could be responsible. He commented that UN forces manning checkpoints were very vulnerable.

The Lieutenant Colonel commanding the Fifty-second Battalion gave directions four or five days after the incident for Private McAleavey to be accommodated at the Military Police Headquarters at Gallows Green, in Tibnin. With McAleavey being the sole survivor of the shooting, he feared that the perpetrators might wish to silence him, and also felt that he should be kept under observation because the incident may have had an adverse affect on him. The media was of course continually looking for comments from people, and a spokesman for the UN said that McAleavey was not confined to the Irish quarters, but, as the sole witness, was in protective custody.

On 2 November, a UN spokesman stated that the UN Military Police had completed their questioning of the survivor of the attack at Tibnin Bridge, Private Michael McAleavey. The spokesman, Mr Goksel, said that Private McAleavey had given his version of events, and the Military Police were satisfied that he had nothing further to tell them at that moment. There were no plans to question him again, and he was likely to be flown home with the Fifty-first Battalion the next Wednesday. As it turned out, Michael McAleavey remained on in Gallows Green until the end of January 1983.

The bodies of the three slain soldiers, on arrival in Beirut, were brought to the American University Hospital, accompanied there from Tibnin in a helicopter by Commandant Derek Baynes, a medical officer. At the hospital he identified the bodies to the pathologist, a Dr CK Allen, and was present during the examination of the bodies. The pathologist did not carry out full post mortem examinations, as the cause of death was clear – the three had died as a result of bullet wounds to various parts of the body.

The two Lebanese civilians stopped at the checkpoint by McAleavey were detained overnight by the Lebanese police. The following day, they were released. Private McAleavey's FN rifle, and the weapons of the three deceased soldiers, were taken possession of that night by Commandant Rory Campion. Private McAleavey's rifle had two rounds left in the magazine, and one in the breach. All the firearms of the checkpoint personnel, the firearms used and discharged into the valley by Army personnel who came on the scene, and all the discharged cartridge cases found at the scene were handed over to a Swedish ballistics expert for examination and comparisons. The results of the examinations of the bodies, the weapons and the spent cases did not become available until early January 1983.

During the search of the scene, a number of discharged bullets and fragments of bullets were found in the vicinity of the bunker and the surrounding area. All of these were in a very damaged and fragmented condition, as they had struck the concrete walls of the bunker and the surrounding rocks.

Captain Hugo Bonner went to Lebanon on 3 November to assist in the investigation. Colonel Tadgh O'Shea, who at the time was Deputy Judge Advocate-General, travelled with Captain Bonner, in an advisory capacity. While he was there, there were discussions as to who was involved, and different possibilities were discussed. Just one of a number of possibilities was that Private McAleavey was the slayer. Captain Bonner returned to Dublin on 12 November.

The days and the weeks passed, and Private McAleavey remained in protective custody with the Military Police at Gallows Green. He was not confined – he could go out and about around the building, study German, play basketball with the lads and kick a ball around the place, lift weights and go to local shops – but he would always be accompanied by Military Police. At times he didn't like that much, but they insisted that they had to stick with him. After a few weeks, Irish newspapers, which were available to Army personnel in Lebanon, began to print material relating to the deaths of the three soldiers, which was open to different interpretations and speculations. Some of it tended to throw suspicion on one of the Army personnel, and as a result there was a certain amount of unease among McAleavey's colleagues. I can well imagine some thinking that if he was responsible, there could be a repetition of what had happened, with so many firearms readily available.

Colonel O'Shea returned from Lebanon in early January with the post mortem and ballistics reports. Discussions took place with the Adjutant General, and he decided to seek the assistance of the Gardaí in the investigation.

The remains of Corporal Gary Morrow, Private Peter Burke and Private Thomas Murphy arrived at Dublin Airport on the evening of 4 November. The remains of Corporal Morrow and Private Murphy were taken to the Military Chapel at Arbour Hill, where they lay side by side. The remains of Private Peter Burke were brought to Inchicore Church for Mass on the morning of 5 November.

The Army Chaplain, Father Patrick Breslin, said that members of the Defence Forces were inevitably exposed to danger while on overseas duty. The three soldiers who died were not defending themselves or their country, but the cause of peace. He said, there could not be greater or more ideal love, than for a man to lay down his life for a friend. Full military ceremonial funerals were accorded to the three young soldiers. The UN caps lay on top of their coffins, wrapped in the Irish and UN flags. The Lebanese government had remembered and appreciated the supreme sacrifice they made, in the cause of peace. There were two medals for each of the dead soldiers – one for being killed in action, and the other for military service in Lebanon. The President, the Chief of Staff of the Irish Army Lieutenant General Lewis Hogan, Major General William Prendergast, Assistant Commissioner John Fleming, the Minister for Justice and a host of other dignitaries from Church, State and the general public were in attendance, to pay their respects. Corporal Morrow was buried in his native Lurgan in County Armagh. Private Thomas Murphy was buried in Glasnevin Cemetery, and Private Burke was buried in Palmerstown Cemetery.

On 17 January 1983, I got a message to go to Chief Superintendent Dan Murphy's office. He told me that Army authorities were seeking the assistance of the Gardaí in the investigation of the deaths of the three soldiers. He asked me if I was willing to go, and of course I told him that I certainly was. He told me that we were going on the nineteenth, which was in two days' time, and that Detective Inspector Pat Culhane, who was with me in the Pringle case and later in the Livingstone case, Detective Sergeant Gerry O'Carroll and himself would be travelling as well.

My passport was out of date, and there was a bit of a rush the next day to get a new one. Some of the other three were also in the same position. On 18 January, I got a new passport, as well as a special travel document for Israel only. We left Dublin on 19 January, accompanied by two Army officers, and flew to London, where we had to get our visas stamped at the Lebanese Embassy and the Israeli Embassy. We stayed in London that night, and the following day we headed for Beirut.

The four of us were in much the same mind as regards the evidence against the Army chap that we were going to interview. We were also aware that we were going into dangerous territory, from media reports over the years, and hearing about all the atrocities that were committed out there by the various factions.

On landing at Beirut, the situation was really brought home to me, and I think the others as well, as we could clearly see bombed buildings and bombed runways as we taxied in to the terminal. There were holes in the concrete roof of the terminal building. You could look out at the sky, and there were heaps of rubble scattered on the ground as a result of bombings. The building was almost deserted, and you could feel the tension in the air there.

A convoy of UN personnel were at the airport to meet us. They had some jeeps and a minibus, and they escorted us to UN Headquarters in Nacura. Along the route we saw bombed, damaged buildings beside the roadway. The fronts and gables of buildings were scarred from artillery fire, and in many places we saw spent cartridges strewn on the ground. Our journey was uneventful, however.

We arrived in Nacura late in the evening, and were accommodated at UN Headquarters, right on the shore of the Mediterranean. We had dinner in the officers' mess on arrival, and I met a few Army personnel that I had seen around Naas and Newbridge over the years.

The following morning it was down to work, to establishing the facts about the shooting, and gathering all available evidence and information about the suspect, Michael McAleavey. One thing I learned about him that night was that he was a great artist, a great man for sketching, and I will come to that later on.

We had a long conference with Dr Allen, Pathologist at the American University Hospital in Beirut, along with Dr Ian Lynberg of the State Department of Forensic Medicine in Stockholm. We learned that all of the bullets had exited the bodies of the three deceased soldiers. All of the bullets went right through the bodies, as one would expect with a powerful FN rifle at close range. Corporal Morrow had been shot four times, Private Murphy had been shot eight times and Private Burke had been shot six times. Dr Ian Lynberg told us that he was present when a test was carried out with the FN rifle, using cardboard targets to ascertain the effects of shots at various distances.

When Corporal Morrow was shot, one of the four shots hit the right temple. There were markings of burnt powder surrounding the wound, known as tattoo marks, which go into the skin or stay on the skin. Dr Lynberg said that it was difficult to say from what distance this shot had been fired; it could have been fifty centimetres or closer. Private Murphy was shot eight times, and one of the bullets went through the right ear. There were marks around that wound, and Dr Lynberg said again that this shot had been so close that the powder marks had reached the skin.

Private Burke had a bullet wound under the chin, and there were also powder marks surrounding it. The muzzle of the gun in this case could have been very close, perhaps ten to fifteen centimetres. Private Burke also had a bullet wound in the back of his head, from close range, as it also had powder marks surrounding it.

That evening, Detective Superintendent Dan Murphy, Pat Culhane, Gerry O'Carroll and I had our own little private pow-wow. We decided on the approach and strategy we would adapt when we met Private McAleavey. It was decided that Chief Superintendent Dan Murphy and Pat Culhane would interview him first, and then Gerry O'Carroll and I would interview him. It was decided that they would not use up all our ammunition in the first interview; they would leave some vital issue for Gerry O'Carroll and I to put to McAleavey. We were well versed in Private McAleavey's account of the shooting, and his attitude towards authority and being questioned. We also established his status as regards custody in Gallows Green since the incident.

On the night of 21 January, the night after we arrived, we were invited to dinner in the officers' mess, as we had been the night before. Of course, afterwards there were a few drinks. The next morning, we left Nacura early, in a convoy of four or five vehicles. We headed for Tibnin, about thirty-five miles to the north along the 'Burma Road'. The day was very clear and bright, with a blue sky, as was every day while we were there. The journey to Tibnin was a zigzag one. It is very unproductive countryside, where every little pocket of arable land is cultivated – in some cases, pieces as small as a one-vehicle garage. Most houses were built on stilts. The road travelled much of the time along ridges, giving a great view down into the valleys or wadis.

On arrival in Tibnin, we went to Battalion Headquarters at Camp Shamrock. Who was there to meet us, only the Lieutenant-Colonel in command of the Fifty-second Battalion, my former next-door neighbour in Newbridge, Tony McCarthy. He gave us a great welcome, and straight away everything was on a very informal basis. We were accommodated at Camp Shamrock during our stay in Tibnin. Shortly after arrival, we were brought to Tibnin Bridge, about half a mile away, and became familiar with the whole setup there – the bridge, the bunker, the toilet and the three roads leading to and from it.

From our discussions with the Swedish ballistics expert on the previous day, we had also learned that none of the weapons of the three deceased soldiers had been discharged. Obviously they didn't get a chance. An effort had been made over a long period of time, with the aid of a comparison microscope, to compare the spent bullets found at the scene with bullets test-fired from McAleavey's rifle. All the bullets were in such bad condition that it was not possible to establish if any of them had been discharged from McAleavey's rifle. A long, painstaking process, and probably one of the reasons why it took so long for the forensic report to be furnished. You can't look into a microscope for eight hours a day.

Twenty-two out of twenty-four spent cartridge cases found in the immediate vicinity of the bunker were found to have been discharged from McAleavey's rifle. The other two were found to have been discharged from the weapon of Private Curran, who arrived with Lieutenant Sweeney at the scene within five minutes of being notified that an incident had occurred. Private Curran discharged his weapon at the scene, firing it into the wadi when somebody thought they had seen movement. Other spent cartridges were found around the scene and in the locality. Most of them were weathered and showed signs of rust. It was not established what weapons they were from. It came out during the trial that occasionally, out of boredom, some lads would take target practice, firing at a rock or a tree in the valley.

We left Tibnin Bridge and went to the Military Police Headquarters in Tibnin, Gallows Green. This was a roughly built, square building, well away from other houses or buildings, surrounded by very rough terrain with loose rocks and stones scattered around, and a few small trees. Chief Superintendent Dan Murphy and Pat Culhane commenced to interview McAleavey as planned, and that continued for a number of hours.

What transpired during the interview was given in evidence by Chief Superintendent Murphy and Detective Inspector Culhane. Their evidence was that Private McAleavey greeted them with an extraordinary display of aggression. Chief Superintendent Murphy and Pat Culhane were told by McAleavey that he didn't give a fuck who they were, as they were no different to the fucking Military Police. He was told about the great number of spent cases found at the scene, and that they had come from his rifle.

They discussed with him a statement he had made on 30 October 1982, to Sergeant McGrath. McAleavey continued to be agitated, looking very excited and speaking in a very loud and aggressive tone. When Sergeant McGrath's report was produced to McAleavey, he said, 'Do you know who I am? I'm a fucking werewolf, I shoot everybody. I go around shooting up the fucking world.'

As time went on, McAleavey mellowed somewhat, and a stage was reached where he started to cry. When he stopped crying, he was offered a cigarette. He said he didn't smoke, but he needed something now. After some hours, he admitted that he was responsible for the deaths of his three comrades. He made a statement, which was taken down in writing from him.

When that interview terminated and Private McAleavey had some refreshments, Detective Sergeant Gerry O'Carroll and I commenced to interview him. As he had already made a statement of admission, we were not allowed to ask any questions of him, except to clear up any ambiguities in what he had already said. We commenced to speak to him about his younger days in Belfast, and why he had joined the Irish Army. He was calm and talkative, and did not show any aggression whatsoever.

A near neighbour of mine in Naas had told me, some time before I went to Lebanon, that he was a distant relative of McAleavey's. I told McAleavey this, and I think it had an effect on him, that he felt more at ease with us. He started to tell us what had happened before the shooting and during it, and I was taking notes all the time. He was explaining about the bridge and the bunker, and where the three deceased were seated.

I told him that I had heard he was a great man to draw a sketch, and asked would he sketch the positions of himself and his comrades at the time of the shooting. He agreed, and I gave him some paper and a biro. He drew the bridge, the junction, the bunker and the roads leading away from the junction. He indicated, by means of an X on the sketch, where he was standing when he shot his comrades. He marked with three X's, where his three colleagues were seated outside the bunker. At the first X, he wrote, 'This is where I stood when I shot them.' He identified each of the other three X marks, writing the name of the soldier who occupied each chair. He signed the sketch, handed it over to me and said, 'I am sorry I didn't tell the truth to the Military Police that day.'

The interview came to an end around that time. I read the notes I had taken over to him, and he said they were correct and signed them. Before we left him, he said, 'I feel better now that I have told what happened, and I am glad ye came.' We left him around 3.30pm. Shortly afterwards, Captain Hugo Bonner of the Military Police, accompanied by Sergeant Ryan, went in to talk to Private McAleavey. Later that day, Lieutenant Colonel Tony McCarthy charged Private McAleavey with the murders of his three comrades.

Private McAleavey was now in full custody, and he remained in Lebanon until the end of January. When he was awaiting his Court Martial back in Ireland, he was detained at the Curragh Military Detention Centre. Detective Inspector Bill Kavanagh from the Mapping Section, and Detective Inspector Willie Hogan from the Photographic Section, both at Garda Headquarters, had been put on standby to be prepared to travel to Lebanon at short notice. After McAleavey made his admissions, it was clear that he would be charged. Both members were informed, and they left for Lebanon as soon as possible. They joined us in Tibnin. Detective Inspector Bill Kavanagh prepared maps of the scene, as is usual in serious cases, with all the relevant information on them. Willie Hogan took photographs of the scene, and prepared albums. Both gave evidence at the Court Martial.

Detective Chief Superintendent Dan Murphy, Pat Culhane, Gerry O'Carroll and I remained on at Camp Shamrock for two or three days, for the purpose of checking all the statements that were taken in relation to the investigation. Additional statements were taken from some Army personnel. Lieutenant Colonel Tony McCarthy was relieved when McAleavey was charged. He said it had been a great worry over the past number of months, not knowing what had happened.

It came to the stage where we said our goodbyes and shook hands, and all agreed that we would meet again at the Court Martial, which we did.

We left Tibnin with the usual escort, and took the 'Burma Road' back to Nacura Headquarters, where we were wined and dined. Tony McCarthy had arranged for us to be brought on a two-day tour into Israel. The five of us headed south, and when we reached the Israeli border we had a long delay there. We were subjected to a thorough search, including our travel bags, the minibus and anything we carried with us. I had to open my camera, and squeeze some toothpaste out of the tube, in case there was explosive in it. Things were so serious there that any lapse at all could result in somebody being killed. We visited a great many places of interest, including Nazareth and Bethlehem, where we visited many famous historical places. Then into Jericho, on the shores of the Dead Sea, and finally that day we reached Jerusalem, where we stayed the night.

The following night, we went back to Nacura along the coast road on the outskirts of Tel Aviv. We returned to Headquarters, and were wined and dined again. In the canteen the night before we left for home, I saw a large bottle of Bell's whiskey on the shelf. It contained about three-quarters of a gallon of whiskey at least, and cost only about £25. Why did I purchase it? I don't really know, but I thought it would be a great thing to bring home. No one in the house really drank alcohol. I rolled up the bottle in an anorak, put it into my suitcase, and hoped for the best.

We were escorted again to Beirut without any problem. I parted with my suitcase and bottle at Beirut Airport, and it was to go direct to Dublin Airport. We arrived in Heathrow Airport in London some time in the afternoon, and had a few hours to spare before our flight to Dublin. We got the underground train to the centre of London. All the documents relating to the case were in my briefcase, which I had with me, including McAleavey's statement, and the sketch he had made. I stepped out of the train onto the platform, and looked around for the other three. All of a sudden, I realised I had left my briefcase on the floor of the carriage. The door was still open, so I jumped in and grabbed the case. The doors were closing as I jumped out, but I got out with my briefcase. I often think, what would have happened to the case, if the briefcase had been lost?

Anyway, back to Dublin, and when my suitcase arrived on the carousel it looked fine. When I lifted it up, I saw that the underneath part was somewhat wet. My heart sank, and I feared the worst. Then I saw other luggage was wet as well, and discovered that there had been a slight shower of rain outside when the luggage was being unloaded. I went home to Maureen and our three children, and got a great welcome, and I was glad to see them again.

The bottle was intact, and not opened until Maureen and I celebrated our twenty-fifth wedding anniversary, three years later. We went out for a meal at the Hotel Keadeen in Newbridge, which our children had organised. When we arrived home everything looked normal outside – no cars, just one light on in the house. Immediately when we went in, the lights were switched on and the place was packed. So it was a great surprise. I wasn't long in when I took down the big bottle and put it up on the table. I said, 'Here, lads, help yourselves.' We had a great night, and at the end of it there was still a lot of whiskey in the bottle, and it lasted a good number of years after that. Maureen and I never had a drop out of it, but that didn't worry us. The bottle itself is no more. The empty bottle I gave to my son David, and he had a great collection of coins in it, until the force of gravity claimed it and it collided with the ground, a surface much harder than itself.

The Court Martial finally commenced on 18 July 1983, at the Curragh Military Camp in County Kildare. Now, a Court Martial differs from a civilian case in several ways. One of these is that an ordinary civilian Court has a panel for the jury, and they are selected in the Court. A Court Martial jury or panel is selected beforehand, by the Army hierarchy. Also witnesses for the Court Martial are not allowed into the hearing until they are due to give evidence.

Michael McAleavey was the first to be Court-Martialed for murder on overseas peacekeeping duties with the UN. The Court Martial was also the longest and most expensive Court Martial up to that time. The Court Martial has no jurisdiction to try a soldier unless the crime was committed when the accused was on active service. So with this particular case, it had to be proved that Michael McAleavey was on active service when he committed the murders.

The jury or panel in this case was comprised of seven Army officers. The foreman of the jury in this case was Colonel Brendan Cassidy. The prosecutor in the case was Lieutenant-Colonel Martin Cafferty, and the case was presented to the Court Martial on his behalf by Harry Hill, Senior Counsel. Counsel for the accused was one of the best known Senior Counsel in the country at the time, Paddy McEntee, and he had as Junior Counsel Martin Giblin.

Michael McAleavey pleaded not guilty. Harry Hill, Senior Counsel outlined briefly the non-contentious facts, from the time that the four soldiers took up duty at Tibnin Bridge at 2pm on 27 October 1982, up to the time McAleavey was questioned by the Gardaí at Camp Shamrock on 22 January 1983.

The case opened with Detective Sergeant Willie Hogan of the Photographic Section, and Detective Inspector Bill Kavanagh of the Mapping Section. They gave evidence of the scene of the incident. Surprisingly at such an early stage in the proceedings, Detective Chief Superintendent Dan Murphy was called to give evidence. After Dan Murphy said that he cautioned McAleavey, Mr McEntee was on his feet as expected, objecting to any further evidence by the Chief Superintendent, in relation to anything that McAleavey may have said to him. Mr McEntee said that it was up to the prosecution to satisfy the Court that, at the time of that interview, his client's constitutional rights had not been interfered with, particularly his right to liberty and reasonable access to legal advice. He said that the prosecution must also satisfy the Court that anything that was alleged to have been said by McAleavey was given freely and voluntarily, and with no advantage offered for it.

The prosecution called a host of Army personnel in sequence, to cover all aspects of their case. We reached 21 July, when the issue of admissibility of the statements came up for legal argument and adjudication. On that date, Chief Superintendent Dan Murphy, Detective Inspector Pat Culhane, Gerry O'Carroll and I gave evidence to the Court. Some members were cross-examined by Mr McEntee, and some of us were cross-examined by the Junior Counsel, Martin Giblin. We stated that no inducements, no threats and no promises were given to McAleavey in relation to the making of the statements. Every member gave evidence of what actually happened.

A statement made by Private McAleavey to Company Sergeant McGrath on 30 October was read. This was McAleavey's old story, that he went to the toilet, heard shooting, and when the shooting stopped he rushed down and found his colleagues dead. McAleavey held to that story up to 22 January.

On 28 July, Michael McAleavey entered the witness box and gave evidence relating to the admissibility of the statements he had made to the Gardaí. He told the Court Martial that he had broken down and cried when post mortem photographs of his dead colleagues were shown to him by senior Gardaí. He said the Detective Superintendent told him to make a statement, and it would all be over. He said he had made a statement because it seemed the only way to get rid of the uncomfortable situation.

The defence said that if the Court was satisfied that Private McAleavey was denied access to legal assistance, they should exclude the statements he made. If the Court considered that the statements were not made in breach of his constitutional rights, the Court should next consider whether such statements were voluntary. That onus was on the prosecution, and the Court would have to decide, on the evidence, whether psychological pressure was applied on McAleavey, or whether an inducement was offered to him to make the statement.

On 19 July, both the prosecution and defence asked that the Court Martial be adjourned to Lebanon, to hear evidence from some vital witnesses who were unable to travel to Ireland. One of these was Dr CK Allen, the pathologist, and another was a medical attendant at the same hospital. The hospital was not prepared to release their employees to travel to Ireland, but the witnesses would be available to give evidence in Lebanon, if given reasonable notice.

The two Lebanese civilians held up by McAleavey at the checkpoint at Tibnin Bridge that night were also required to give evidence.

On 19 September, the Judge's Advocate said it was not necessary to go to Lebanon to visit the scene, or the accommodation that McAleavey occupied when he was in protective custody. He had considered the submissions made, and had decided that he would not adjourn out of the State to hear evidence. As a result, these prospective witnesses in Lebanon did not give evidence to the Court Martial.

In due course, the jury retired to consider whether they would admit the statements and the sketch. Eventually they came back with the decision that all statements and the sketch map were admissible.

I mentioned earlier that the Court Martial could not try McAleavey for murder, unless he was on active service when the crime was committed. To prove this, and you have to prove it, an Army officer came from Lebanon to show that McAleavey and two of his dead colleagues had been checked into the flight that left Dublin for Beirut in October 1982. The officers who signed McAleavey, Corporal Morrow, Private Murphy and Private Burke into the Army were also called to give evidence.

Now, the Court could not know what was in the statements McAleavey made until the jury had decided whether they were admissible or not. McAleavey made three statements of admission – one to Pat Culhane and Dan Murphy, one to Gerry O'Carroll and I, and then one to Captain Hugo Bonner of the Military Police, and Sergeant Ryan. All of those statements were admitted in evidence.

Now that they were admitted, they could be discussed. First was the statement McAleavey made to Chief Superintendent Dan Murphy and Detective Inspector Pat Culhane. He said that at about 8pm on 27 October 1982, an Israeli army jeep approached the Irish checkpoint at Tibnin Bridge, and an

Israeli officer refused to show his identification. McAleavey lost his temper, cocked his rifle, pointed it at the officer and called him a 'yid' and 'Jew boy'. The Israeli jeep was waved on by Corporal Morrow.

A row broke out between McAleavey and Morrow about the incident. McAleavey told him he was a stupid bastard to let the Israeli through without identification, and also made reference to the fact that Morrow had forgotten his gun and had to borrow one from the outgoing NCO at 2pm. Heated exchanges followed, and Morrow told McAleavey he was only a substitute on the battalion in Lebanon, and he had to crawl to get there. Morrow told him that there would be a vacancy for him on the next flight back to Ireland.

McAleavey said that he started to walk away, and as he did he cocked his weapon, then turned around and opened fire. He started to spray, and just kept his finger on the trigger. 'I fired first at Morrow and then to my left; I then remember running in beside them and mopping them up. The last thing I remember was shooting at Morrow, who was gone around the side of the bunker.'

A number of other witnesses were called, to clear up various matters, and then both Counsel addressed the jury. This took quite a while, with Mr McEntee a past master at his job, and the other man was certainly very good. When they finished, the jury retired to consider their verdict. They came back eventually, and found McAleavey guilty on all counts.

Michael McAleavey was sentenced to life imprisonment for the murder of his three colleagues in Lebanon. He was also discharged from the army with ignimony. He was stripped of his black beret and Army belt, and was transferred from the Detention Barracks in the Curragh to Mountjoy Prison.

Some years later, McAleavey made an application to be transferred to Maghaberry Prison, in County Antrim, to be nearer his family in Belfast. That was eventually granted, and he was transferred on 16 June 2008.

After a while there, he applied for parole, and in March 2010, the independent parole commission decided to release McAleavey on a life licence. A breach of the conditions of that licence will mean that he will be recalled to prison.

I do not hold any ill will towards Michael McAleavey. He served twenty-seven years in prison for his crime. I believe the crime was an outburst bordering on lunacy for about two minutes, caused by his volatile personality. He has expressed remorse for his terrible deeds, and he has satisfied the criteria set out in Northern Ireland for release. I cannot of course speak for the feelings of the relations of the deceased Corporal Morrow, Private Murphy and Private Burke.

MURDER OF JOHN BOB BROWN, LISTOWEL, 1983

We spoke about affairs of the heart before – well, affairs of the heart are not the sole domain of the young. The not-so-young can also get caught up in such affairs, and commit terrible, irrational deeds. For just such a case, we go now to Listowel in County Kerry, in June 1983.

Anne Brown, born on 3 January 1943, lived at Killacrim, Listowel in County Kerry. She started to go out with Jeremiah Sullivan of Lixnaw, County Kerry. The relationship continued for four years, up until June 1983. There was a large impediment to the relationship coming to anything, however – Anne Brown was married, living with her husband John Bob Brown and their six children, four boys and two girls. The eldest was a boy of seventeen, and the youngest a girl aged thirteen months.

They discussed on occasion that they would like it if Bob was out of the way, so they could live together. They agreed on occasion that it would be great if he got into one of his fits and died.

On Monday and Thursday nights, Anne Brown and her daughter Michelle would pick up Bob Brown in the car from Mulvehy's pub in Listowel. Anne Brown saw her husband in Mulvehy's pub some time during the day of Thursday, 2 June. She told him to make his own way home that night. Bob Brown left the pub late, and started to walk home. Somewhere near the creamery on his route home, he was shot dead on the roadway.

His body was found after a short time, and the Gardaí were notified. Garda Daniel Lynch of Listowel was at the scene some time after midnight on 3 June. He saw the body, face-downwards on the road, and recognised it as Bob Brown, who he knew well. The Gardaí believed at first that Bob Brown had been the victim of a hit-and-run accident. Garda Lynch went to the Browns' home at 2.30am, where he told Mrs Brown and her daughter Michelle that Bob had been involved in a traffic accident. Mrs Brown asked if her husband would be coming home, and the Garda told her no, that he was dead.

A post mortem was performed, and the cause of death was discovered to be two gunshot wounds. Of course, straight away it became a murder investigation.

On 3 June, Detective Sergeant Mossy O'Donnell of Tralee and another Garda went to the home of Mrs Brown. They told her that her husband had not died as a result of a traffic accident; he had been shot. They asked her to accompany them to Listowel Garda Station, as they wanted to talk to her. She agreed and went with them, and made a statement, saying that she knew nothing about her husband's death.

Gardaí recovered a spent shotgun cartridge from the murder scene. The Gardaí straightaway had an interest in Jeremiah Sullivan, because information had come to hand that Sullivan and Mrs Brown had been seen together a number of times. So they went to his house with a warrant, and searched the house. They found a legally held shotgun, which they took possession of. The shotgun and the spent cartridge case were sent to the Ballistics Section at the Garda Technical Bureau.

It was found that the striker pin of the shotgun had been filed down. As a consequence, it could not be established by means of the striker pin whether the weapon had been used to discharge the cartridge found at the scene. It appeared that Sullivan knew that the striker pin of a weapon could be compared with a discharged cartridge case.

However, there are other means to compare a firearm and a spent cartridge. The extractor mechanism used to eject the cartridge leaves its impression on the soft brass edge of the cartridge. The face of the breach of the shotgun at the time of discharge, under great pressure, leaves its impression on the brass of the cartridge. All imperfections on the breach face are reproduced on the soft brass. By use of a microscope, they can be compared and photographed. The Ballistics Section established that Sullivan's shotgun was the weapon that had discharged the cartridge found at the scene where Bob Brown was shot.

Sullivan and Anne Brown were arrested on 11 June, under Section 30 of the Offences Against the State Act, as it was a firearms offence. They were brought to Listowel Garda Station, and I interviewed Mrs Brown there that day, accompanied by Detective Garda Martin McCarthy as he was then. Mrs Brown told us she was not at the Western Inn on Thursday night, 2 June, as she had stated on 3 June. She was in a car with Jeremiah Sullivan from 9pm to 11.30pm, at the creamery yard on the Abbeyfeale Road. They discussed many matters, and spoke about her husband Bob, about the amount of drink he was taking and the money he was spending. They had discussed on a number of occasions how they would like to live together, and that they would like if Bob was out of the way so that they could be together.

On that Thursday they did not discuss getting rid of Bob. On many times over the previous two years, they discussed what they would do if Bob ever found out about them. They decided that Jerry should shoot him, in case Bob would shoot one of them. Sullivan asked her to tell the Gardaí, when they came to her, that she was at the Western Inn at Feale's Bridge, Abbeyfeale, with him that night. She was to say that she got home at 11.50pm.

Mrs Brown said she didn't know he was going to shoot her husband that night, Friday, 3 June. Sullivan came to her home at about 9.30pm. He told her he had shot her husband the night before. He told her to stick to her story, about being in the Western Inn with him, and coming home at 11.50pm. She told him she would.

Afterwards, Sullivan came into the room where she was with the Gardaí, and he said to her, 'We are in it together, Anne, we better share it.' Mrs Brown agreed with what he said. 'He definitely does not tell lies,' she said, 'and is straight and honest.'

The following day, I again interviewed Anne Brown with Detective Garda McCarthy. She said she had agreed with Jerry that Bob would be shot. She said that on Monday and Thursday nights over the last three years, she had been going out with Sullivan. 'Bob thought I was going to unislim classes. When Jerry told me on Thursday night, 2 June, to tell the Gardaí we were at the Western Inn, I said to him, "Why would we do that?" He just shook his shoulders and didn't answer me. It sounds stupid, but I didn't ask him why the Gardaí will be calling to me.'

Sullivan was arrested and brought to Listowel Garda Station on 11 June. He made a full confession. He was eventually dealt with at the Central Criminal Court in Dublin, and was convicted and sentenced to penal servitude for life. I did not have any involvement whatsoever with Jeremiah Sullivan during the investigation. I was concerned with his lady friend Anne Brown.

Anne Brown was eventually charged with withholding information from the Gardaí. The case was finally heard before the Dublin Circuit Criminal Court on 21 November 1985. Brendan Grogan, the prosecuting barrister, said that the accused had failed to give the authorities information she had about her husband's murder at the first available opportunity, on 3 June. She knew who had murdered her husband, and she had failed to tell Gardaí.

Barry White, Senior Counsel for the accused, alleged that Anne Brown had been in unlawful custody in the Garda Station, and that she wasn't free to leave. Anything she said there should not be admitted in evidence.

There was a trial within the trial, and the jury was asked to decide on the issue of whether Anne Brown had been free to leave the Garda Station. After deliberating for a little over an hour, the jury returned. Their unanimous decision was that Anne Brown had not been free to leave the Garda Station. When this verdict was announced, Brendan Grogan, barrister for the prosecution, said the State was not in a position to proceed further with the case. The Judge directed the jury to find Anne Brown not guilty. She was discharged.

CHAPTER SIX

INSPECTOR, UNIFORM SECTION

STORE STREET, DUBLIN, 1983

I was Detective Sergeant in the Investigation Section at Garda Headquarters for four years. In November 1983, I was promoted to the rank of Inspector. A year or two before I was promoted, a new regulation came into force, that members of the Detective Branch, on promotion, would revert to the Uniform Section. That meant that anyone in the Detective Branch who gained promotion had to revert to uniform, and had to remain in the Uniform Branch for about two years, before being eligible to return to the Detective Branch. So when I was promoted, I had to go back into uniform. I had been out of uniform since 1961, so to go back into uniform again was strange to say the least.

Now, when a member of the Force is promoted, one consequence, more often than not, is transfer to a new Station. I have known of some members of Garda rank who were promoted to Sergeant, and when notified of the new Station that they were being sent to, applied to be reverted back to Garda rank, rather than leave their present Station, and uproot their home and family. When I was promoted, I was delighted, and would have gone anywhere I was sent. I was sent to Store Street, right in the centre of Dublin city.

On 1 December 1983, I arrived in uniform at Store Street Garda Station, and I was like a fish out of water. I had never served in the Dublin Metropolitan Area. I had very little knowledge of the policing systems there. The Dublin Police Act, one of the main Acts being enforced in the city, was something I didn't know anything about. But I learned as I went along.

When I say I went to Store Street, I mean to 'C' District, dealing with Store Street and Fitzgibbon Street stations.

There were four units – A, B, C and D, and I was Inspector in charge of Unit D. I would work an eight-hour day, either 6am to 2pm, 2pm to 10pm or 10pm to 6am. A few times a month, duty would finish at 10pm, and you'd have to be in again for the 6am shift. I would get home around 10.45pm, and I'd be up at 5am to be in at 5.45am.

For the purpose of policing, C district comprised of the area within a circle, bounded by Capel Street, Bolton Street, Dorset Street Upper and Lower and Clonliffe Road, then down Poplar Row and East Wall Road, as far as the car ferry terminal at the very end of the docks. Then you come back up the North Wall, with the Liffey on your left, straight up the quays and back up to Capel Street Bridge. Everything within that circle was C district.

There is a new Station now at Store Street, about fifteen years old, but when I was there it was the old Station. Included in the Store Street area is the main shopping area for the city – O'Connell Street, Henry Street, Mary Street, Talbot Street and Abbey Street – and of course up the road, in the Fitzgibbon Street area, is Croke Park.

Units at that time paraded fifteen minutes before leaving the Station to go on duty. If you were going out at 6am, you had to be in at 5.45am, and there was a parade. The Station House Officer would brief his officers before they went out, bringing them up to date with happenings, and what to look out for during the day, and allocating them to particular beats. In the Store Street area, there were two twenty-four-hour static posts. A Garda had to go there every shift and relieve the Garda coming off duty.

As Inspector in charge of the unit, I made a point of being in fifteen minutes early. The beats and posts were all entered into an allocation book, and you could look right back and find out who was on what certain beat ten years ago. I would go out and inspect the Gardaí on duty, to see that they were where they were supposed to be. The Inspector had a form to be filled out at the end of his shift, including where he inspected all the members that were on duty.

The biggest problems I would say were in the day time, up around Henry Street and Mary Street, where all the crowds congregate, and all the shopping is. There would be larcenies from shops, unlawful trading and street trading.

Off Henry Street, on Moore Street, there are a number of designated spots or pitches for traders to operate. These spots are marked out on the footpath, about the size of a good-sized kitchen table, with a number painted in the centre of it to correspond with the trader's certificate or licence. Some of these pitches are not great, because there are fewer people around them. The traders want to go where the crowds are, so some with bad pitches, and others with no licence at all, become mobile by means of an old pram and timber trays. The tray goes on the pram, and they fill it up with apples, oranges, bananas or whatever, and away they go, up and down Henry Street and Mary Street. They are often stopped and arrested and brought to Store Street Station, because this is unlawful trading.

There were a number of cars in Store Street Station, but only one van. Some member would arrest a street trader, and the van would go to bring down the prisoner. Particularly on weekend afternoons, it was common to see a pram and goods parked outside Store Street Station, while the trader was being processed inside.

The managers of department stores, and the owners of shops all around the Henry Street area, would complain to the Superintendent in Store Street that the Gardaí were ignoring the street traders. The street traders, they would say, were committing offences – blocking their doorways, and preventing prospective customers from going in, or else setting up in front of their shop windows and obscuring their window displays – and the Gardaí were turning a blind eye to it. The Gardaí were caught between these managers and shop owners and the street traders.

Pickpockets would also have a field day, particularly around O'Connell Street, around the tourist office and anywhere there was a crowd. Protest marches were common, particularly on a Saturday. People would assemble up in Parnell Square and walk down O'Connell Street, taking over half of the road. They could be going to the GPO to have a rally, or over to the Dáil or some government department. That all took up a lot of manpower. There was duty at Croke Park in the summertime, for big matches.

At evening time and nighttime, there were a lot of larcenies from cars, which were being broken into by young criminals. It doesn't take them long to learn. They concentrated mostly on cars with foreign registration numbers, knowing full well that if they were caught, the visitor would be gone back to England, France, Spain or wherever, and wouldn't come back to go to Court. These were everyday occurrences. At nighttime you could also have disturbances on the street outside pubs, and practically every night you'd have reports of alarms going off in different premises.

There was a group of young lads, aged between twelve and fifteen, who would climb up drainpipes and get up on the roofs, and break into the skylights into department stores and shops. It was unbelievable where they could go. I could picture Gardaí getting up on the roof trying to stop these young lads, who were maybe only a third of the weight of a Garda. I was afraid that a Garda could slip on slime and moss up on a roof, on a rainy night, and slide down over the edge onto O'Connell Street and be killed. Or else frighten these young lads into taking chances, and as a result maybe they would fall through a roof, or off a roof.

These young lads were all well known to the Gardaí, as they would be continuously in and out, being charged, and up to the Court. There was no place for juveniles to be detained. I told the members of my unit that they were not under any circumstances to get up on a roof to pursue these fellows, day or night. Anyway, I said, if you do catch them and bring them up to the Court, they will be out the door before you. The lads were enthusiastic, and wanted to catch them, but I said I didn't want anybody to risk their lives.

In Store Street, there was a room just off the public office, used to detain prisoners who would only be in the Station for a short time. There was all sorts of graffiti on the wall, written in biro or marker or whatever, much of it very anti-Gardaí as you could imagine. One piece of graffiti said, 'I always wanted to be a cop, but they discovered I had parents.' Now, you can think that one out for yourself!

I noticed something in the Station that I thought should not be happening, something I'm sure was happening for years, handed down from generation to generation of Gardaí. It was to do with the jargon or lingo the members would use on the radio. Every member going out on duty had a walkie-talkie. I wasn't too long there when I heard someone giving out a message over the radio to a member, that there was a crowd of 'skulls', or a crowd of 'gougers' or 'heads', in such and such a place. Other people in the street could hear the radio as well. In the public office in Store Street, the radio room is quite close. There could be people at the counter, and a radio message would come over the air using those terms: skulls, gougers, heads. It was embarrassing, and I thought it was very unprofessional.

I spoke to the unit a few times about this, and soon there was a great improvement. I told them they should use other terms, like suspects or unruly persons. I remember being out some time around then, and someone on the radio came out with one of those terms, skulls or gougers or whatever, and he said, 'Correction please, "unruly persons".'

There were a lot of good members in Store Street and Fitzgibbon Street, young enthusiastic lads. One man, Sergeant Brian Fenton, was of great help to me at Store Street. He was very cool and level-headed; he knew his job, and advised me on a lot of things while I was there. I am very grateful to him, because as I said, I was like a fish out of water in the DMA.

Another man who stood out to me was Michael Devine, and he was on the motorcycle. He is now a Superintendent in Navan, the last I heard. No matter what incident there was around the place, whether it was in Store Street or Fitzgibbon Street, Michael was generally one of the first to arrive. Wherever he was, or whatever he was doing, he would down tools straight away and go straight to it. I remember one morning we started at 6am, and at about 6.10am there was a call to say there were intruders in a shop on Capel Street. Who was first there? Michael Devine. He was very enthusiastic, a great worker, and it paid dividends for him in the end.

I found it hard really to get used to the type of policing that was done at Store Street. I would go as far as to say, I don't think I got to like it. I always hoped that I would get back into Detective Branch, and back into the investigation of crime. If you had gone to the city straight from the Depot, you wouldn't know the difference, but to go into it after so many years in the Force, I never warmed to it really. I spent three years there, and then a vacancy became available in my old place in the Investigation Section, so I went back there in June of 1986 as Detective Inspector.

MURDER OF MARIE MURTAGH AND TOM TAAFFE, MOYNE, 1986

When a murder, a suicide or a death by traffic accident happens in any town or village, the locals all feel the shock and grief. We have often seen on the television news, a reporter pushing a microphone up to some member of the community, and that person struggling to come to terms with a local tragedy. Very often we hear something like, 'This is a very quiet part of the country; nothing like this ever happened here before.' One community to be shaken like this was Aughnacliffe, a small village in north Longford, practically on the shores of Lough Gowna.

The Parish Priest of Moyne in County Longford in November 1986 was Reverend Father Eugene Cox. On Monday, 17 November, he had a conversation with his housekeeper. He remarked that Marie Murtagh had not opened her shop that day, and said he was concerned about her. Marie and a man called Tom Taaffe were living in a house together. Marie was about forty-five years of age, and Tom was in his mid-fifties. Marie owned the house, a farmhouse with about twenty acres of land. Tom had about thirty acres of land quite close by. She also had a shop, quite close to the church. It was a galvanised, basic building, selling basic household needs. Father Cox decided to go to the house, in case Marie or Tom was ill, because Tom was known to be in bad health.

Father Cox drove to Marie's house at about 7:30pm. On arrival, he saw a light on in the kitchen, and there was a broom handle keeping the back door closed. Marie's Volkswagen van was parked outside. He knocked and got no answer, then pushed in the back door and walked into the kitchen. On the floor, he saw the bodies of Marie and Tom, and quite an amount of blood. They were both dead, and had been dead for quite a while. He notified the local Sergeant, John Linnane, who immediately came to the scene. All the usual preservation procedures were put in place, and all the appropriate personnel were notified.

John and I had soldiered together for some time in Naas. He was a Garda when I was there, and was later promoted to Sergeant and went to Longwood in County Meath, and then to Aughnacliffe.

The previous Saturday evening, Marie and Tom had been seen driving about fifteen or twenty cattle from Marie's land to Tom's. As I understand it, Marie was driving her van and Tom was driving his Cortina car. The last known sighting of them was around 7.45pm, by a local schoolgirl, Elizabeth Grey, who used to work Saturdays in the shop.

On the discovery of the bodies, word spread like wildfire throughout the community. Both deceased were well-liked and well-known members of the community.

Detective Sergeant Brendan McArdle, from the Ballistics Section at the Technical Bureau, went to examine the scene, along with others. Marie Murtagh had had a dog, and it had been in the house when Father Cox entered that Monday night. The dog had licked some blood off the floor and off the bodies, presumably due to hunger and thirst, from having been locked up for over two days.

Dr John Harbison examined both bodies. He found that Marie Murtagh had been shot with a shotgun right through the bridge of the nose, and a second time in the abdomen. Tom Taaffe had also been shot with a shotgun, right through his left eye. Both died from those injuries. The murder weapon was not found at the scene, and was in fact never found. No spent cartridge cases were found at the scene. Brendan McArdle expressed the view that both of them had been standing when they were shot, and all the shots were fired from a range of five or six feet.

Naturally all sorts of speculation was circulating as to what might have happened. The Gardaí, in serious cases like this, do not discount anything that they hear. You cannot afford to ignore anything; you have to examine all possibilities until you are pointed in a certain direction, by information or through examination of the scene. In a rural area such as Aughnacliffe, a number of possibilities would be considered by the investigators, such as agrarian trouble, a besotted or jealous person, or some local deranged person. In this case all options were open.

I was not long back in the Investigation Section when I was sent to assist in this investigation, along with Detective Superintendent Hubert Reynolds, Detective Inspector Christie McCaffrey, Detective Sergeant Tom Dunne, Detective Garda Tom Byrne, Detective Garda John Geraghty and others.

Around 8 December, information was received that a potential suspect was in the area. Members of the investigation team located him, in the company of another man. Both men were arrested under Section 30 of the Offences Against the State Act, on suspicion of the unlawful possession of firearms at Marie Murtagh's house between 15 and 17 November 1986. They were detained at Mullingar Garda Station for questioning.

I interviewed one of the men, with Detective Garda William Staunton and Detective Garda Tom Byrne. The man made a written statement. The other man was also questioned at Mullingar Garda Station, and also made a written statement.

On 10 December, both men appeared at a special seating of Mullingar District Court. They were charged with the murders of Marie Murtagh and Tom Taaffe, and remanded in custody to Mountjoy Prison, to appear at Longford District Court on 16 December. Both men made a number of appearances in the District Court, and eventually the book of evidence was served.

The trial of the two men, at the Central Criminal Court in Dublin, opened on 28 October 1987. One more charge was added to the indictment – that of conspiracy to rob Marie Murtagh. At the opening of the case, Counsel on behalf of one of them requested that the Judge, Mr Justice Barrington, grant his client a separate trial. The Judge acceded to this request.

The trial of the other accused went ahead that day, and his Senior Counsel was Patrick McEntee. Acting on behalf of the DPP was Senior Counsel Fergus Flood. In his opening address to the Court, Mr Flood told the jury that the accused bore the same responsibility for the two deaths as the person who pulled the trigger. On 30 December, the jury were sent home while legal arguments were heard.

In the absence of the jury, the defence Counsel said that his client had been deprived of legal advice, as his solicitor had been refused access to him. If a prisoner requests a solicitor, there is an obligation on a Garda to endeavour to get him a solicitor. What happened in this case, I understand, is that some friends of the accused contacted a solicitor in the Longford area, and asked if he would represent the accused. The solicitor agreed, and telephoned the Garda Station. He spoke to the Superintendent, and requested to speak with the prisoner on the telephone, as he was not in a position to go to Mullingar for some time. The Superintendent recognised the solicitor's voice on the telephone, and there was no question of identity. The Superintendent told the solicitor he would not allow him to speak to the prisoner on the telephone, as the prisoner had not requested him. He told him that when he arrived at the Garda Station, he could have immediate access to the prisoner, if the prisoner agreed to see him. By the time the solicitor arrived at the Garda Station, the prisoner had made written statements of admission.

The Judge found that the Superintendent was wrong in not allowing the solicitor to speak to the prisoner on the telephone, and that he had thereby been deprived of legal advice. He would therefore not allow his statements into evidence. The Judge addressed the jury, telling them there was no evidence to connect the accused with the murders. He directed the jury to find him not guilty of the murder charges, and also not guilty on the third charge of conspiracy to rob Marie Murtagh. The accused walked out of the court a free man.

New issues such as this crop up day-in, day-out at trial, and Garda procedures are shaped on judgments from Superior Courts in such cases.

On 12 January 1988, the trial of the other accused opened at the Central Criminal Court in Dublin. The presiding Judge was Mr Justice Barr. Fergus Flood, Senior Counsel acting for the DPP, outlined the background to the case, and the evidence the State would produce in support of the charges. When he had finished his address, Kevin Haugh, Counsel for the accused, addressed the Judge, arguing that during his address Mr Flood had referred to evidence that may be prejudicial to his client. He asked the Judge to discharge the jury. Having considered the issue, the Judge acceded to this request, and the jury was discharged. The accused was back in custody in Mountjoy Prison, awaiting a new trial date.

On 7 June 1988, the accused again appeared for trial before the Central Criminal Court. The presiding Judge on this occasion was Mr Justice Thomas Gannon. Fergus Flood appeared again for the prosecution, and Kevin Haugh again appeared for the accused. Fergus Flood, in his opening address to the jury, said that en route to the house, the accused knew that if opposition was met, the intention was to rob Marie Murtagh and if necessary to shoot her. The man stayed as lookout in the full knowledge that violence might be used, and this made him a principal in the second degree, and guilty of murder.

After the second day of the trial, the jury was sent home, because there was a trial within a trial, which went on for a few days. This related to the admissibility of evidence. The Judge ruled that the statement made by the accused to Gardaí while in custody was admissable in evidence. Detective Garda William Staunton and I gave evidence of the interview with the accused on 10 December 1986. He had made a statement; it was read over to him and he was cautioned.

He agreed it was correct, and signed it. The statement was read out in court. I was cross-examined by Kevin Haugh, and it was put to me that the accused was exhausted when he made the statement. It was also alleged that during the interviews I had with him, he was called a 'lying dosser', he was pushed against a wall, and he had his jacket pulled off him. I denied all of these allegations, as well as suggestions that our methods of interrogation were designed to frighten him.

On 16 June, the accused gave evidence. He admitted that the statement was made by him. He said he had told the Gardaí lies, because he was under severe pressure. He said he was denied access to a solicitor, despite several requests. He said he was brought from Mullingar Garda Station to Athlone to sleep; the cell he was locked in was cold and damp; the mattress was filthy; and he was not allowed to wash or shave. These allegations were denied, by myself and others. Gardaí involved in investigations and interrogations are well used to allegations such as these being made against them, in an effort to have statements ruled inadmissible.

The Judge eventually ruled that the statement made did not contain sufficient evidence to establish the man's guilt. He called the jury in, and directed them to find the accused not guilty of the murders. The remaining charge of conspiracy to rob was left with the jury to decide on. On 17 June, after deliberating for one hour, the jury returned the verdict that the accused was not guilty of that charge.

When you go into Court with a statement of admission, you would imagine that everything was grand. But sometimes the investigation of the case itself is easier than trying to secure a conviction in the Courtroom. Gardaí involved in investigations and interrogations have to make decisions on the spot, in the instant. But when you go into Court, Counsel can spend days arguing over whether or not you made the right decision. Great caution and care always have to be taken in investigations, and, as can be seen in this case, new issues keep cropping up, sometimes going all the way to the Supreme Court to be decided on.

This was a shocking case – two innocent people were shot dead, in the sanctuary of their own home. Cases like this, you don't just forget them, but they happen and we have to keep going.

MURDER OF CAROL CARPENTER, TALLAGHT, 1988

In May of 1988, there was a reorganisation of the Investigation Section at Crime Branch in Garda Headquarters. As a result, investigating personnel were relocated to Stations in the Dublin Metropolitan Area. I was sent to Tallaght Station in Dublin. I replaced Detective Inspector Paschal Anders, who had been in Tallaght, and he went to Bray, where he resided. Over the ten years up to 1988, the population of Tallaght had grown enormously, to the point where it was on a par with Limerick city, with a population of about 90,000.

The Superintendent in Tallaght was Bill McMunn, and the Detective Sergeant was Kevin Tunny. We covered the Tallaght and Rathfarnham areas, and the Detective Sergeant in Rathfarnham Station was Bill O'Brien. I was lucky when I went to Tallaght to know two Detective Gardaí there, who I had already been stationed with in the Investigation Section in the Bureau. They had transferred to Tallaght quite some time before I arrived. They were of great help to me, and took me by the hand, brought me around and showed me the good areas and the bad areas, the good lads and the bad lads. Tallaght is a very busy Station as regards crime. There was all sorts of crime, and it occurred on a daily basis.

At about 7pm on Friday, 26 August 1988, sixteen-year-old Carol Carpenter left her home at Donaghmore Avenue in Tallaght, to go to the house of Mrs Carol Hughes, also in Donaghmore Avenue, on a message for her mother. Mrs Hughes was able to tell Gardaí that Carol arrived at their house around nine or ten o'clock with a set of tools for Carol Hughes's husband. She stayed at the Hughes's for about twenty minutes, and then left. Poor Carol did not return home that night, or any other night thereafter.

That same night, another young girl, sixteen-year-old Rita Ryan, a neighbour of Carol's, was walking home past Kilinarden Community Centre, in the same locality, at about 11pm. She was approached by a man, who she described as twenty-nine or thirty years of age. He punched her in the face, knocking her to the ground, and then he left. Gardaí were informed, and went to the scene and met Rita. They put her into the Garda car, and drove around the area, hoping that she might identify her attacker, but with no success. Then they drove Rita home, and Rita later went to hospital for treatment of a nose injury.

As Friday night wore on, there was no sign of Carol returning home. Her parents and other members of her family got worried. Her father, Peter, left the house, walked the estate, spoke to a number of people and called to a number of houses, without success. Around midnight or 1am, Peter called to a house on Donaghmore Avenue. The usual occupants of that house were away for a few days, and they had asked a local youth to look after the house for them. They gave him the key to the house, and when Peter called to that house the youth was there. He was Joseph Mark Dowling, twenty years of age, also from Donaghmore Avenue. Carol's father was aware that Joseph Dowling and his daughter were good friends. He asked Joseph if he had seen her, and he said that he hadn't. Dowling left the house and accompanied Carol's father in his search around the estate for some time. Eventually Peter went home, with no sign of his daughter.

Early the next morning, Ann Carpenter, Carol's only sister and the eldest member of the family, reported Carol missing to Gardaí at Tallaght Garda Station. On receipt of that report, the Gardaí started a search for Carol. They searched the area, and contacted her friends, but there was no sign of Carol.

At 4pm on Sunday, 28 August, the body of a young girl was found by a member of the public. It was hidden in a ditch of briars and hedging, which separated open areas of the Donaghmore area. It was only about 500 yards away from Carol's home, and about 200 yards away from the house where Carol's father spoke to Joseph Dowling on the night of 26 August.

During my service in the Gardaí, I have of necessity been to a great number of locations where dead bodies have been found, and are lying in these locations when I have arrived. A very high standard of decorum is usually observed at such crime scenes, by Gardaí and members of the public alike. Out of respect for the deceased and their grieving families, everyone usually behaves in a sombre manner. One exception to this was the scene where the body of Carol Carpenter was found.

On the discovery of the body, Gardaí at Tallaght were naturally informed, and a number of Gardaí went to the scene as quickly as possible to preserve it. The area being very thickly populated, word of the discovery of the body spread very quickly. When the Gardaí arrived, a great number of people were already in the immediate vicinity of the body. Requests for them to leave proved unsuccessful, as they all wanted to have a look. It is always imperative to preserve the scene of a serious crime, and extra Gardaí had to be allocated to the scene.

Crime-scene tape was erected around the area, and members of the public were asked to stay behind the tape. Some youths started to run through the tape into the preserved area, and taunted the Gardaí with a variety of remarks and actions. Superintendent McMunn arrived at the scene, and appealed to the crowd of roughly three hundred to assist the Gardaí in their investigation by remaining behind the tape. He appealed to the parents present to control their children. This had little effect. Youths now started to throw stones at the Gardaí, and in fact caused some damage to a Garda car parked nearby. Some sort of order was restored, after a fairly precarious thirty or forty minutes.

Superintendent McMunn did not mince his words to the media when he spoke to them. He told how four Gardaí had been attacked by as many as four hundred youths. Superintendent McMunn confessed that he was amazed at the poor response from members of the public. They flatly refused to obey Garda instructions to stay back from the area, and repeatedly pressed forward. Some raced after one patrol car when it moved off, and another Garda car was damaged as the crowd surged around it. The writer of the report said:

This is a strange and disturbing state of affairs, reminiscent of scenes in Belfast, where mobs attacked police and firemen on missions of mercy. The problem there is regularly attributed to alienation. Can it really be that the young people of Tallaght have become so alienated from authority that Gardaí, whatever their purpose, are seen as the enemy? A certain feeling of rejection would be understandable – their sprawling suburb suffers from high unemployment and poverty, and is still sadly short of many basic facilities. But that alone would surely not account for the frightening response to the Gardaí investigating Carol Carpenter's murder.

Dr John Harbison visited the scene while the body was in situ, and later carried out a post mortem. I attended the post mortem, and I can say that attendance at a post mortem is not a nice experience, but Carol Carpenter's post mortem was a very harrowing experience indeed. The pathologist itemised all the injuries inflicted on her young body, and gave his opinion that the cause of death was strangulation. Carol had been stabbed numerous times, beaten and raped.

A murder investigation was set in train, and a number of Gardaí attended at Tallaght Garda Station. The perpetrator of the assault on Rita Ryan outside Kilinarden Community Centre was top of the list of suspects. Two men were delegated to pursue that line of enquiry.

Two members were allocated to talk to Joseph Dowling. They met him, and he denied knowing anything about Carol Carpenter's death. In a day or two, it came to light that Dowling had told some youth that he had met Carol Carpenter on the night of her disappearance, and that she had got cigarettes for him in the local shop. This was at variance with what he had told Gardaí.

A shoe was found in the garden of the house adjoining the one Dowling was minding, that Carol's father had called to on the night she disappeared. The shoe was handed over to the Gardaí, and was produced to members of Carol's family. It was identified by the family as identical to shoes that she was wearing on the night she disappeared. Joseph Dowling now became the central focus of the investigation. It was decided to arrest him and question him.

At this stage, the house Dowling was in on that night was in the possession of the Gardaí, courtesy of the returned occupant of the house. During technical examination of the house, a broken portion of a leather belt was found. Another portion was found near to where Carol's body was found in the hedge. It was established that the pieces originally formed the one belt. Blood spatters were found on the fridge in the kitchen, and on the wall. There was blood on the bed upstairs, and blood had soaked into the floorboards in an upstairs bedroom.

Dowling was sought for questioning, and a number of members drove through the estates around Tallaght, trying to locate him. My recollection is that Detective Sergeant Kevin Tunny and I were driving in the Donaghmore area when Dowling was seen by Detective Sergeant Tunny on the roadway. Dowling was arrested and brought to Tallaght Garda Station, where he was questioned by a number of members of the Detective Branch. He initially denied knowing anything about Carol's death, but after an hour or two he admitted responsibility. I remember asking him for a blood sample, and he said he would like to discuss it with his mother. His mother happened to be in the Station, so they conversed, and she decided he should give a blood sample. That sample was taken by a doctor.

Dowling made a written statement, outlining meeting Carol on the road near where he was staying. He said she went and got cigarettes for him, and brought them back to the house. He persuaded her to come into the house. After some time, he started to mess around with her, and she consented for a while. Then she objected, and wanted to leave. I am not going to outline in detail what he said in the rest of his statement. It does not make nice reading, and it serves no purpose to repeat it now. It was not read in Court, so it will remain confidential as far as I'm concerned. In short, Dowling admitted in the statement to everything that the pathologist said had happened to Carol Carpenter.

Carol endured horrendous, unthinkable torture from Dowling, over a period of two or three hours. I very often think of this poor innocent young girl, of what she went through in her last hours, probably knowing that he was going to kill her in the end. When Carol's dad called to the house on that tragic night, his daughter was lying on the floor upstairs. I do not know what condition she was in at that time, and no one will ever know. Dowling waited for quite some time after she was dead. In the early hours of the morning, he brought her out the front door, across the road and over the wall into the park, and down the field about 200 yards to the ditch. He then returned to the house, took off his clothes and washed them in the washing machine, and made an attempt to clean up the house.

Dowling made his initial Court appearance on 2 September in the District Court, presided over by Mr Justice Sean Delap. He made a number of other Court appearances, and eventually came before the Central Criminal Court in Dublin on 1 May 1989, before Mr Justice Richard Johnson. The trial was expected to last about a week.

When the charge of murder of Carol Carpenter was read out to Dowling, he pleaded guilty. It took everybody by surprise, but I suppose it wasn't really surprising, considering the weight of evidence that was against him. Prosecuting Counsel Fergus Flood told the Court that the State was now not going to proceed with the charge of rape. Mr Justice Johnson told Dowling that the law did not allow him any alternative but to sentence him to penal servitude for life, which he did.

DNA analysis in investigating crime was just coming into use in Ireland at this time. I sought permission for DNA analysis to be carried out on certain samples – blood from the floorboards upstairs, blood from the fridge, blood from the bed, blood from Dowling and blood from Carol. My application was granted, and the samples were prepared for dispatch to Cellmark Diagnostics in Abington, Berkshire in England. They were prepared in the Forensic Science Laboratory, either by Dr Sheila Willis or Dr Maureen Smith. I flew over to England with the samples, and went down to Abington on the bus from Heathrow. I came back the same day.

After some time the results of the analysis came back, and I remember that the chances of the blood on the floorboards upstairs being from somebody other than Carol Carpenter were in the region of two or three million to one. These were the first samples that went for analysis abroad. As Dowling pleaded guilty, there was no need for the evidence.

Dowling went off to serve his prison term, and after five or six years he ended his own life in prison. I don't think anybody can imagine the pain, trauma and suffering that the Carpenter family have gone through since the last night they saw Carol, up to today. How do you console a person who has a close and loving member of their family taken away from them in such circumstances? All I can do is pray for them, which I often do, and I remember the relatives and friends of other persons who have been murdered in cases that I have been involved in.

LECTURES AT TEMPLEMORE, 1989

In March 1989, I was on a Superintendent's promotion course at Templemore. There were approximately fifteen or twenty on the course. One morning, a lecturer from Dublin, who was to speak to the class, was not available for some reason or other. I was asked if I would take the class for the day, and give a talk on the investigation of serious crimes – murder, rape, bank robbery, and so on. I did not consider myself in anyway superior to any of my colleagues in that class. I have no doubt that many of them could have given a talk on different aspects of Garda duties, much better than I could. However, I agreed, and I concentrated mostly on investigation of murder.

I went through all aspects of a murder investigation, from the initial report the whole way up to a trial. I dealt with mistakes that had been made on some investigations, the pitfalls, and the responsibility of the member in charge always to keep up to date with all aspects of an investigation. Another matter I dealt with was not allowing any one or two members involved in an investigation to conceal information, and go off on a solo run. All information received should always be passed on to the investigating officer, to let them decide in what direction to go. My talk was all practical common sense, and created a good lot of class discussion, about both actual and hypothetical situations.

Another thing I dealt with was something I had experience of myself at the scenes of serious crimes. Garda members congregate at the crime scene. They could be from outside stations, and they would just go to have a look or whatever. They would stand around, and no one in authority would give them any duties to perform, apart from those of course who were preserving the scene. I told the class that it was my view that somebody in authority should take these men aside, and utilise the manpower available, particularly if the route by which the culprits left the scene was known. Members could go along the road, make enquiries at every house, and see what information they could get as quickly as possible, then report back at an appointed time to the member in charge of the investigation, whether they got any useful information or not.

Gerry Moran, a Meath man and an accomplished footballer in his time, was on a Superintendents' promotion course that I spoke at. On promotion, Gerry was sent to New Ross in County Wexford. Shortly afterwards there was an armed robbery at the Bank of Ireland in New Ross, in which a young female bank official was shot dead. Two hooded raiders arrived outside the bank, on a stolen motorcycle. One entered the bank, armed with a sawn-off shotgun, while the other waited outside on the motorcycle. In the course of the robbery, the shotgun was discharged, with fatal consequences. The raider ran out, and the two of them fled the scene on the motorcycle.

Superintendent Gerry Moran arrived at the scene, and there were a number of Gardaí standing around. He took them in hand straight away, and gave them various directions. He got two of them to go out the road that the motorcycle had travelled after the raid. He instructed them to call to every house. If they got valuable information, they were to return and give it to him; otherwise, they were to continue, and come back at a certain time to meet him. The two members went out along the road, and they came to a house where they got some very valuable information. At the relevant time, a motorcycle of the same description as the motorcycle seen at the bank came from the New Ross direction, and drove into the driveway of a house in the locality. It was seen driving in, and no one living in that house had a motorcycle. They brought the information back to Gerry, there was a mini-conference, and it was decided that they would go to the house and search it.

They did so late that night and armed with a warrant. They found a local youth in the house who was not belonging to the household, and in a follow-up search they found the stolen motorcycle and the sawn-off shotgun. The young man was arrested and subsequently convicted of murder and bank robbery. This was the man that entered the bank and fired the fatal shot.

At the end of the course I was on, a written survey was carried out to establish the view of the class, as to the most beneficial lecture they had received. I was greatly surprised, and I suppose it is fair to say I was pleased, that my lecture was voted the best. As a result, I was asked to continue to give a lecture to all Sergeants, Inspectors and Superintendents on promotion courses. I did so up until the time of my retirement in June 1994.

CHAPTER SEVEN

DETECTIVE SUPERINTENDENT

ROBBERY AT GLENDEVLIN HOTEL, DUNDALK, 1989

In October 1988, I was promoted to the rank of Detective Superintendent, and transferred from Tallaght to Dundalk. I had responsibility for the investigation of crime, ordinary and subversive, in the Louth and Meath Division. Dundalk itself was a busy station as far as the Detective Branch was concerned. It was a favourite haven for subversives on the run from Northern Ireland, and of course it had its own local subversives, engaged in all sorts of criminal activity. This included smuggling, which was rife along the border. Escorting cash and shipments of cigarettes from Carroll's cigarette company in Dundalk took up quite a lot of our time at the Detective Branch in Dundalk. I was always concerned that subversives would get to know the routes and times at which the escorts would take place, and would plan their activities to coincide with the times the Detective Branch would be taken up with such duties.

The Glendevlin hotel was a short distance out the old Dublin road from Dundalk, on the left-hand side as you go out towards Dublin. I believe it has changed hands long, long ago. On Sunday, 9 April 1989, around lunchtime, the hotel was busy with diners and patrons socialising in the bar and the lounge. Three men arrived in the car park outside the hotel in a stolen car. One remained in the car, and the other two, hooded and wearing gloves, ran in to the hotel. They shouted at the customers to lie on the floor, and sought out an employee called Adrian Meade. One of the raiders put a gun to Meade's head and demanded money. They knew exactly where the money was. The raiders walked among the patrons, who were laying on the floor in fear. They eventually took the sum of £13,000, and ran out of the hotel to their awaiting accomplice in the stolen car. They drove away in the Dublin direction, then turned right and headed towards Louth village or Tallanstown.

When the raiders left, a hotel employee telephoned Dundalk Garda Station, and alerted them to what had just occurred. A second man came on the phone from the hotel, and told them that the raiders were using a Cortina car. He had taken note of the registration number, which he gave to the Gardaí. He also gave his name and address. The particulars of the raid and the getaway car were circulated by radio to Garda stations in the vicinity, and to all Garda cars on duty at the time. I happened to be in the Garda Station at the time. One car went immediately to the hotel, preserved the scene and took the names and addresses of all the people they could find.

The raiders stopped at a particular location along the road towards Tallanstown. They got out of the car and set fire to it, then got into another car that was parked nearby and drove off again, heading towards Tallanstown. A young man nearby saw them arrive, and saw them get out and burn the getaway car and get into the other car. He took particular notice of the car they drove away in, and he remembered the make and the colour, and noticed that there was damage to a particular part of the car. The damage was obvious and conspicuous.

Some short time after that, a message was received at Dundalk Garda Station, to the effect that a motorcar was on fire at a location between Dundalk and Louth village. Gardaí went there and found that the car was the one the raiders had left the hotel in. They spoke to the youth, and he gave them the description of the car the men had transferred into. This information was radioed to the control room in Dundalk, and circulated from there. The burned-out car had been stolen in County Cavan some days previously.

This case illustrates some of the things that can go wrong in an investigation, and of course what can go right, thanks to decent, upright citizens, who stand up and assist the Gardaí. Garda John Fahy was a Garda in Blackrock at that time. On that particular day, he was in the Station, and tuned in to radio messages in relation to the robbery. When he heard that the damaged car was heading in his direction, he left the Station in the patrol car, hoping to intercept the fleeing raiders. The Garda patrol car had only been allocated to Blackrock a few days previously, and had not yet been fitted with two-way radio. When John stepped into the car, he was cut off from two-way communications.

Somewhere between Dundalk and Louth village, he caught up with a car travelling in front of him that fitted the description of the one that the raiders were believed to be travelling in. Knowing the raiders to be armed, and being unarmed himself, he kept a good distance from the car, but kept it in view as best he could. He saw the car stop, and two men got out of it and went into a field. The car then drove on, and he continued to keep it in sight. It eventually stopped in the village of Tallanstown. The driver got out and went into a local licensed premises.

The Garda got the registration number of the car, telephoned Dundalk Garda Station, and gave them this valuable piece of information. Gardaí from

Dundalk and the Detective Branch went to Tallanstown, and joined Garda Fahy. They entered the licensed premises and located the driver of the car. He was arrested under Section 30 of the Offences Against the State Act, for possession of firearms at the hotel a short time earlier. He was brought to Dundalk Garda Station, and detained for questioning. His car was also taken possession of and brought to Dundalk Garda Station.

That man was Malachy McPartland, thirty-three, originally from County Armagh but with an address in Dromiskin, County Louth. Garda John Fahy pointed out the spot where he had seen the two men go into the field. A search party was organised, and spent a few hours there searching. They eventually found two men, about two fields in from the road, hiding in a ditch. They said that they were hunting foxes. No dogs, no iron bars, no anything, but their story was that they were hunting foxes. Those two men were also arrested under Section 30 of the Offences Against the State Act, and were also brought to Dundalk Garda Station. They were Paul Jennings, twenty-six, a native of Castlewellan in County Down, with an address in Ravensdale in County Louth, and Oliver Grew, twenty-nine, from County Armagh, and with an address at Bay Estate in Dundalk. All three were known to have been engaged previously in subversive activity, and were known to Detective Branch members in Dundalk. They were questioned from late on Sunday night until late on Monday night. All three denied any involvement in the robbery, or any crime whatsoever on Sunday 9 April.

The youth who saw the men transfer into McPartland's car was brought, with his father, to Dundalk Garda Station. McPartland's car was parked in the yard with numerous other cars – cars belonging to members, patrol cars, crashed cars, stolen cars and all sorts of other cars, perhaps twenty or thirty of them. I brought the youth out to look at these cars, and I brought his father along, because I could foresee that in Court it might be suggested that I may have influenced the young chap in his choice of car. The young lad looked at all the cars, and he settled on one and said, 'That is it.' He said he recognised it by the make and colour, and particularly by the damage in one particular location. It was exactly as he had described, and that was the car that the men had got into.

The car was technically examined, and taken asunder, to see if the firearm or the money was in the car, but they were not. Fingermarks were found on the car, on the outside of one of the doors. The prints were taken of all three men, and these fingermarks were identified as belonging to one of the other two men – not McPartland who owned the car.

A teenage girl who was in the hotel at the time of the robbery turned out to be a very, very important witness. I would say she was the star witness really. The hotel patrons were put lying on the floor, and the men, hooded and wearing gloves, walked among them. One of them stood beside her, and she had a really good look at his shoes. She said to herself that she would know his shoes any-where. She described them as good strong black shoes, embossed on the uppers with a design of a helicopter, green in colour. When Grew was arrested and brought to the Garda Station, he was found to be wearing a pair of black shoes with a green helicopter design, exactly as described by this young girl.

Sunday and Monday were spent questioning the three prisoners, and taking statements from the customers at the hotel, the man who took the registration number of the car, the youth who saw the transfer of the men from one car to the other, and the young lady who saw the pair of black shoes with the helicopter on them. During questioning, McPartland said that he had picked up two strange men at lunchtime on Sunday, when he was driving from Dundalk to his home. He said he had never seen them before; he did not know who they were; they were thumbing a lift and he let them out at a particular spot, where they requested to be let out. Enquiries with the collator at Dundalk Garda Station revealed that some months earlier, an observant and conscientious Detective Branch member had seen McPartland in conversation with Jennings on the main street in Dundalk. Incidentally, the Sergeant in charge at the collator's office was Sergeant Tom Staunton, who was the father of Steve Staunton, the Irish international soccer player. Poor Tom has passed away in the last number of years.

On Monday night at about midnight, I left the Garda Station. The interrogation was still going on, and I went to my accommodation. No sooner was I in the door than I got a phone call from the Garda Station. Terry Hynes, a member of the Detective Branch, was questioning one of the three men, and the man was anxious to make a deal. Terry had brought him to the point where he was worried, and wanted to save his own skin.

I immediately returned to the Station, and I saw him with Terry Hynes. The deal he proposed was that he would recover the £13,000 and the firearm, in return for his release, and that he would never be charged. Naturally, we wanted to get the gun and the £13,000, but it didn't take me long to think about it. I told him that I would be speaking to the DPP early the following morning, and that I was satisfied that he was going to direct that he be charged in relation to the robbery, and that I was equally satisfied that he would be convicted. I told him that if I agreed to his offer, and we recovered the cash and the gun, he could possibly be putting his own life in danger. I told him that he should consider telling Terry Hynes where the cash and the gun were, and when he was charged, inform his solicitor that he had cooperated with the Gardaí, and let his counsel inform the court when the time arose. He considered that, but decided against it.

This sort of situation arises quite often with prisoners, where they want to exchange information for an easing of the charges they are facing. However, the rules say that admissions made as a result of any inducement, threat or promise are not admissible in evidence.

We never did recover the cash or the firearm. We searched the car, and we searched all along the route from the hotel to the field where the men went in. We searched the fields as well, and we didn't find them.

On the morning of 11 April, I went to the office of the DPP in Dublin. I outlined the case, and the evidence available against the three men, to a legal assistant at the office. Directions were received to charge all three with the robbery at the hotel. The three appeared before the Special Criminal Court in Green Street later that day, and were remanded in custody.

Crucial evidence in the case came from Garda John Fahy, the teenage girl, the man who took the registration number of the car at the hotel, and the youth who saw the raiders switching cars. We were all happy that we had a successful investigation. The culprits were in custody, and we had good hopes that they would be convicted. However, the wheels then started to come off the case. The man who said he took the registration number of the Cortina at the hotel contacted Detective Garda Tom Duffy of Dundalk, who had taken a statement from him. He informed Tom Duffy that he had not in fact seen or taken the registration number of the car at the hotel. He said somebody else took it, and told him about it, and he did not know who that person was. It was vital to connect the Cortina car with the hotel. Otherwise we had no case. That was the situation for a week or so. We pondered what to do, and how we were going to get over this situation. We endeavoured to trace the man who had allegedly taken the registration number and passed it on to the man that rang the Gardaí, but without success.

Tom Duffy came into the office to me one morning after that, and he had a big smile on his face. 'You won't believe this,' he said, 'but last night I returned to the Garda Station late, and in the Garda Station, after being arrested for driving while drunk, was the man who originally passed on the registration particulars of the car to the Gardaí.' This man confessed to Detective Garda Tom Duffy that it was in fact he himself who had seen and taken particulars of the raiders' car. He had been approached by a man, and told it would be in his best interests not to give evidence in court. Things were back on track, but only for a while. The teenaged girl had also been contacted, and the youth that witnessed the changeover of the cars had been contacted.

The trial took place at the Special Criminal Court, on 24 October 1989. The three men pleaded not guilty. I and other members of the Detective Branch in Dundalk had spoken to our three vital witnesses that had been intimidated, and they had all agreed to give evidence in accordance with their statements. They all did, and as a result, coupled with other pieces of evidence, all three men were convicted. The court imposed a sentence of nine years' imprisonment on each of them.

On 20 July 1992, all three had their sentences reduced by the Court of Criminal Appeal. Senior Counsel Paddy McEntee appeared for McPartland. He said that McPartland's sentence was imposed on the incorrect basis that he was fully involved in the raid. Eugene Grant, Senior Counsel for Jennings, said that his client's sentence was unreasonable, disproportionate and wrong in principle. Patrick Gageby said that his client was now suffering from muscular dystrophy, which would shorten his life, and that he had no previous convictions. In delivering judgement at the Appeal Court, Mr Justice O'Flaherty said that the Court did not want to make any distinction between McPartland, who provided the getaway car, and the other two. Though the Court reduced the sentence from nine to seven years, it took a very serious view of the gravity of the crime.

The success of this investigation was mainly due to Garda John Fahy, the teenage girl, the man who noted the registration of the getaway car and the youth who saw them switching cars. Garda John Fahy acted in a courageous and admirable way when he pursued the armed raiders. The other three witnesses acted in a similar manner in the face of adversity, and deserve recognition also.

After the conviction of Grew at the Special Criminal Court, I had a conversation with his defence counsel. I said to him that I was expecting Grew's defence to produce an identical pair of shoes with a helicopter on them, to prove to the Court that the shoes were common enough. His reply was, 'It wasn't for the want of trying.' We also endeavoured to find a similar pair of shoes, and were glad we couldn't.

MANSLAUGHTER OF TIMOTHY KIDMAN, SLANE, 1989

In 1989 I was still stationed in Dundalk, and in September of that year, the gamekeeper at Slane Castle and Estate was shot dead. He was shot five times, and his body was dumped into a clump of briars on the Estate. Slane Castle and Estate is located on the banks of the River Boyne, in County Meath.

Timothy Kidman was twenty-eight years of age, a bachelor, and a native of Winchester in England. He had been a gamekeeper at Slane Castle and Estate for some time, having previously been a gamekeeper at a large estate in England. At about 5pm on Saturday, 16 September, Timothy met and spoke to another employee of the Estate, Desmond Ryan. They separated to feed game, and arranged to meet again at 8pm. Timothy Kidman did not turn up as arranged, and Mr Ryan became concerned after a period. Kidman was a good timekeeper, who usually kept to his word. Desmond Ryan went to look for him.

Mr Ryan crossed the River Boyne by boat, to where Timothy lived in a chalet, but there was no sign of him there. Mr Ryan now notified Gardaí, and they immediately went to the Estate. Together with some members of staff, and some members of the local gun club, they searched for Timothy Kidman until it got dark, but there was no sign of him.

The following morning, Sunday, 17 September, at 8.30am, Miss Emer Mooney, secretary at the Castle and Estate, was walking her dog in a field on the Estate, about 200 yards from the bank of the river. Her dog started to bark at a clump of briars, and on investigating, she discovered Timothy Kidman's bloodstained body in the briars.

A phone call was made to Dundalk Garda Station about the finding of a body in the grounds of Slane Castle. That was the message – just a body found. I was in the station at 9am, and was informed that the body had been found, and there were no further particulars, or suspicions of foul play. I went across the road to Mass, and on my return the situation had changed dramatically. Information had now been received that the man in Slane had a number of gunshot wounds. It was believed that he was the gamekeeper at the Estate.

This was the third Sunday in September, and all GAA fans would be well aware of what that meant. The All Ireland Senior Football Final would be played, between Cork and Mayo, and Derry were to play Offaly in the Minor Football Final. I had two stand tickets in my pocket, and my only daughter Maria and I were all set for a great day at the match. But when duty calls you have to respond, and the game would have to go on without us.

I headed for Slane once I had organised some of the Detective Branch members to go to Navan, where an incident room was being set up. On arrival in Slane, I saw a uniformed Garda on point duty at the busy junction in the centre of the village, where the main road from Derry to Dublin goes through. I still had the two stand tickets in my pocket that I was not going to use. I gave them to the Garda, and told him he could do what he wanted with them. I hope someone used them.

I met Sergeant John Clark at Slane Garda Station. John had been stationed there for quite a number of years, and had great local knowledge. He brought me up to date with the situation, and accompanied me down to the Estate to where the body had been found. Then I went to Navan, and met with Detective Sergeant Michael Finnegan and Superintendent Dan Murphy, in whose area the murder had taken place. Michael was later Chief Superintendent in charge of the Louth and Meath Division. Superintendent Dan Murphy incidentally resided in Malahide, Dublin, immediately across the road from James and Grace Livingstone, whom we shall meet in a later chapter. Dan's wife was the nurse that went across the road to Jim Livingstone's house when he was calling for assistance. Detective Sergeant Michael Finnegan, Superintendent Dan Murphy and I had a long discussion on the various possibilities and motives for the murder. We had to have a completely open mind.

I attended the post mortem on Timothy Kidman's body at the morgue at St Mary's Hospital in Navan that night. It was performed by Dr John Harbison, who found that Timothy Kidman had been shot five times. He had been shot once in the right arm, and once in the left arm, and these shots shattered the bones of each arm. He had been shot in the jaw, and the bullet was lodged below his right ear. He had a bullet wound in the chest, which had pierced his lung and damaged his liver. He had a bullet wound to the top of the head, which had fractured his skull. The bullet wound to the chest was a potentially fatal wound. The bullet to the top of the head was received when the victim was alive, and caused fatal brain damage. That is the one that Dr Harbison said killed Timothy Kidman.

The bullets recovered from the body were of .22 calibre. This somewhat shifted the suspicion away from subversives, because they seldom used small-calibre .22 weapons. It did not of course rule them out. Some of the bullets removed were in reasonably good condition, and it was thought that it would be possible to identify the particular weapon they had been fired from.

On Sunday, and through the following days, a search party searched the area where Timothy Kidman's body was found. Some spent .22 cases were found near to where the body was found.

Information started to come in, from various people who saw two youths in the fields around the Estate at about 5pm on the day of the murder. A laneway leads from the Slane–Navan road, a short distance from Slane, down to near where the body was found. A large, black motorcycle, with two youths on it, was seen going down the lane, and coming up again an hour or so later. Having come up the lane, it turned right, towards Slane. One or two persons who saw the motorcycle said the passenger had long, fair hair, which blew in the wind as the motorcycle went by.

I was running the conference daily, and was in touch with all aspects of the case. Some of the Detective Branch members from Drogheda nominated two youths from Drogheda as potential suspects. I asked them to do some background on them. I requested a check be made to see if any .22 rifles had been stolen in the surrounding counties, over the past year or so. The next day, I received a list. About a week before the murder, the home of Raymond Durnin, a butcher from Termonfeckin in County Louth, had been broken into. Some of his wife's jewellery and his .22 Brno bolt-action rifle, together with some .22 ammunition and the magazine for the rifle, were stolen. We were given the serial number of the stolen weapon.

I was aware that all .22 rifles in the surrounding counties had been test-fired during another murder investigation. The test-fired bullets and cases had been retained in the Firearms Section at the Garda Technical Bureau. I contacted Detective Sergeant PC Whelan at the Firearms Section, gave him the serial number and enquired whether Mr Durnin's rifle had been test-fired, and the bullets and spent cases retained. He confirmed that yes, it had been tested, and the bullets and the cases were available. The bullets from Timothy Kidman's body, and the spent cases from the scene, were now compared with the test-fired bullets and cases at the Firearms Section. It was a positive match. The bullets and spent cases from Timothy Kidman's murder had been shot from Mr Durnin's stolen gun.

The question now was, who had stolen the gun? Drogheda Detective Branch was able to pinpoint suspects for the housebreaking, and the larceny of the jewellery and the rifle. Mr Durnin's house had been technically examined after the break-in, by the Scenes of Crime Examiner from Drogheda. On the windowsill, where the culprit entered the house, he found a portion of a palm mark. Now, the palm prints of the two potential suspects that the Detective Branch members had nominated were available. Fingerprint Section at Garda Headquarters identified the mark as having been made by one of the two suspects. There were not sufficient points of similarity for Court purposes, but the fingerprint expert was satisfied enough with the number of points of similarity to make the identification. The two Drogheda youths were now very much suspected in the murder of Timothy Kidman. We still had some work to do on them.

The search through the fields continued, and I arranged to have the Sub Aqua Unit come to the scene and search the River Boyne, only a few hundred yards away. We were looking for the rifle. I told them that if they found it, they were not to tell anybody, but to contact me. They spent a day or two searching the river, and I got a call to go down to the river and meet them. When I arrived, they handed a rifle to me that they had found in the river. It was Mr Durnin's rifle, the murder weapon. I told them not to disclose to anybody that they had found the rifle, and I will explain why later.

I put the rifle into the boot of my car, and drove straight to the Firearms Section at Garda Headquarters. It could have been twenty years since this gun had been test-fired. Parts of it would have got worn in the meantime, leaving distinctive marks, so I asked them to retest it. The retest was positive. They said that yes, this was the gun that fired the bullets into Timothy Kidman's body.

The only persons in the investigation I told of the finding of the gun were Superintendent Dan Murphy and Detective Sergeant Michael Finnegan. The reason was that I did not want the finding of the rifle to get into the public domain and the media, as the culprits might, on reading it, have taken flight and we might never have found them again. Likewise, the identity of Mr Durnin's rifle as the murder weapon was only known to a few members.

Detective Branch members in Drogheda did background checks on the two suspects they had nominated, and discovered that they were suspects for a number of burglaries in the Louth area over the previous month or two. They had a large, black motorcycle, and one of them had long, blond hair. One of them had purchased fifty rounds of .22 ammunition, using his father's firearms certificate, from a firearms dealer in Drogheda a few days before the crime, and it was the same type of ammunition that was used to shoot Timothy Kidman. They also discovered their addresses and who their girlfriends were.

A report appeared in the media that Gardaí were anxious to trace two youths on a black motorcycle seen in and around the scene of the murder on the evening of the murder. That was true – we were looking for them, and anxious to get them. Some days later, Detective John Harrington from the Investigation Section of Crime Branch received a telephone call on the special incident room number, from a male anonymous caller. The caller stated that he had been at the dump at Glenmore, a couple of miles away from the scene, on the afternoon of the murder. He saw two youths on a large, black motorcycle at the dump. The motorcycle was a Yamaha, and part of the registration number was MM 88. We in the incident room discovered that there was no such registration, and we made enquiries in the Glenmore area, in an effort to get more information. These turned out to be negative. In time, we became skeptical of this anonymous caller, and it occurred to us that it could possibly be one of the culprits ringing, to put us off the track.

The investigation was widely reported in the media at home, with some coverage in the UK. One day I received a telephone call in the incident room from a lady connected with the BBC programme 'Crimewatch'. She offered to feature the Timothy Kidman murder case on their programme, in order to assist our investigation. I thanked her, and promised to get back to her if I felt that they could be of assistance. At the time, we knew we were going in the right direction.

In murder cases, where the investigation goes on for a week or more, there is always speculation circulating, as to the culprit, the motive, and so on. The Kidman case was no exception. Speculation arose among locals, and indeed in the media, that Timothy Kidman had discovered an IRA arms dump on the Estate, and had been silenced. Poachers were mentioned, and it was also posited in the media that the deceased could have been an MI5 agent. You have to listen to all sorts of theories, when you are looking for a lead, until you are satisfied you are going in the right direction. When you do, you have to ensure that you stick close to the reliable evidence that you have.

We reached the stage where it was decided to arrest the two suspects and their girlfriends. We suspected the girlfriends of being in possession of infor-mation relating to a scheduled offence – the unlawful possession of firearms. We had a mini-conference at Navan Garda Station. We had already picked a Sergeant and four teams to go to Drogheda the following morning, arrest the two suspects, search their houses, arrest the two girlfriends, and search their houses. We were searching first of all for the black motorcycle, and secondly for evidence relating to the murder weapon. The idea was to search the houses, the yards, and clothing, to see if we could find spent bullet cases that we could identify as having been fired from the gun, or any of the jewellery stolen from the house where the gun was stolen. Everything was arranged, no one was to be told where they were going. They were to be in Drogheda the following morning at 8am.

The conference was held late, to prevent any information in relation to the arrests and search getting to the media. I was in the Garda Station at 10.30

that night, and I received a telephone call from a press reporter. I was asked if it was true that a number of Gardaí were going to Drogheda the following morning, to arrest two youths in relation to the murder of Timothy Kidman. I of course denied it, but it just demonstrates the difficulty in keeping important matters secret in an investigation.

The searches went ahead as planned the following morning. The two youths were found and arrested at the home of one of them – Michael Hodgins, nineteen, from Pierce Park in Drogheda. The other suspect arrested was Shane O'Brien, eighteen, from Balls Grove, Drogheda. Both their homes were searched, and a large black motorcycle was taken possession of, but no trace of spent bullet cases were found in either house. They were both taken to Navan Garda Station, and detained for questioning. The houses of their two girl-friends were searched, and some stolen jewellery was recovered. One of the girlfriends was arrested and questioned, and released later that day.

It was not considered necessary to arrest the other girl, the girlfriend of Shane O'Brien. When the Gardaí arrived at her house and spoke to her and her parents, she immediately volunteered vital information, and was very coop-erative. She said that on the night of the crime, she met Shane O'Brien, and he told her that himself and Michael Hodgins had been in Slane that afternoon, and had shot a man five times. She handed over some jewellery that she had received from Shane O'Brien, which turned out to be stolen from a house in the locality. She made a statement at home in the presence of her parents, outlining what Shane O'Brien had told her, and she gave that vital evidence at the trial.

At Navan Garda Station, both youths were questioned for most of the day. Shane O'Brien, after some time, admitted involvement, and he made a statement after being cautioned. He outlined the events that led up to the shooting. He volunteered to accompany Gardaí to the scene at Slane Estate, and pointed out certain relevant places. He travelled with Detective Sergeant

Sean Gettings of Dundalk and other members. They went down the laneway where the black motorcycle was seen, and he pointed out to them a dump where they left the motorcycle, and a clearing where they had the rifle hidden for use on 16 September.

He pointed out an oak tree, and said that was where they were standing when they saw a man coming towards them. The man was five or six feet away, and he said to Hodgins, 'Shoot him.' Hodgins shot him in the stomach, and the man fell to the ground. He got up, and Hodgins shot him again. The man then ran along a wire fence towards the river, and both of them ran after him. The man went onto a concrete slab overlooking the river, and Hodgins shot him again. Hodgins then went over to the man lying on the ground, put the gun about one foot from his head, and shot him again. Both of them then lifted the body up, and threw it into the bushes. In his statement, O'Brien admitted that it was he who telephoned the incident room at Navan Garda Station and reported a large black motorcycle at the dump in Glenmore. He did this, he said, to try to divert attention away from the black motorcycle that they had in Slane the day of the murder.

Hodgins admitted his involvement some time after O'Brien. It took the placing of the .22 rifle, dripping wet from having been held under a tap, before him on the table, to convince him that we knew he was involved. He then made a full statement, admitting his involvement.

I recall Chief Superintendent John Nolan, the Divisional Officer for the Louth and Meath Division, calling to Navan Garda Station that night. He was on his way back from the west of Ireland, having attended the funeral of his mother. He had shown a great interest in the investigation up to this, and he displayed great dedication in his role as Chief Superintendent, by calling to the Station on such a sad day in his life. He brought members involved in the investigation to a local hotel, for the customary drink that often takes place after major investigations have been brought to a successful conclusion.

The next day, Michael Hodgins and Shane O'Brien were charged with the murder of Timothy Kidman. They appeared before the District Court, and were remanded in custody. On 6 October, both of them applied to the High Court for bail, but their applications were refused. They made a number of District Court appearances, and eventually the book of evidence was served on them. They were remanded in custody to the Central Criminal Court for trial.

On 20 September, hundreds of local people had attended the funeral service for Timothy Kidman at St Patrick's Church in Slane. The small Church of Ireland congregation was swelled to capacity by many Catholic neighbours and friends, as well as family members from Winchester in England.

With the two accused in custody, the investigation continued for some weeks. In his statement, one of the accused admitted disposing of the murder weapon in the River Boyne, and also disposing of a number of rounds of ammunition at the same location. The Sub Aqua Unit returned, and carried out another search of the river, in the area where they located the rifle. In the first instance they had been looking for a big object, and now they were looking for small objects. After some days, they found a number of rounds of .22 ammunition. The purpose of this exercise was to corroborate what the accused had said in his statement, about disposing of the ammunition. The scene and the surrounding area were photographed, and maps of the scene were created by Mapping Section personnel, with relevant areas highlighted, including the lane, the dump, the oak tree where O'Brien said they were first confronted by the deceased, the wire fence he said Kidman had gone along, the concrete slab where Kidman was finally shot in the head, the places where spent .22 cases were found, and the area in the river where the rifle was recovered.

The trial was presided over by Mr Justice Richard Johnson. Seamus Sorohan, Senior Counsel, appeared on behalf of Michael Hodgins, and Barry White, Senior Counsel, appeared for Shane O'Brien. Morris Gaffney, Senior Counsel, prosecuted the case on behalf of the DPP. The court sat for a total of nine days, and the jury arrived at its verdict on 9 March 1990.

A significant part of the prosecution case related to the method of loading and discharging the murder weapon. A firearms expert identified the weapon as a .22 calibre bolt-action Brno rifle, with magazine. The magazine had the capacity to hold five rounds of ammunition. He explained the actions to be taken in order to discharge a round from the weapon. The weapon could be used without the magazine, by opening the bolt and pulling it backwards, then manually placing a round in the breach of the gun. Sliding the bolt forward into position automatically cocked the gun, and it was ready for use. All you had to do then was pull the trigger. To extract the spent case, you simply had to open the bolt, and pull it backwards.

To use the gun with the magazine in place and containing rounds of ammunition, and with no round in the breach, you had to pull back the bolt and slide it forward. The forward movement of the bolt collected a round from the spring-loaded magazine and fed it into the breach, and the gun was now ready to fire. Then you ejected the spent case from the breach by drawing back the bolt, and the forward movement of the bolt collected the next round and fed it into the breach. When the magazine with its full complement of five rounds was placed in the weapon, and no round was in the breach, the bolt had to be operated five times in order to discharge five rounds.

It was not known what state of readiness the weapon was in when Timothy Kidman approached the two accused. Hodgins said that he had just loaded the magazine. If he had loaded the magazine and pulled back the bolt, thereby putting a round into the breach, he then had only to operate the bolt mechanism four times to discharge five bullets. If he had not operated the bolt by the time Kidman appeared, he would have had to operate the bolt mechanism five times. All of this was an important part of the prosecution's case.

Detective Garda John Harkin said that he met Shane O'Brien's solicitor after a consultation with O'Brien. The solicitor told him that O'Brien had stated that he had told Hodgins to shoot Kidman, and that these words had been said to take some of the pressure off Hodgins.

Shane O'Brien's girlfriend gave evidence, telling the Court that she met O'Brien on the night of the shooting. O'Brien told her about the shooting. He said he felt guilty about it, and that the man had begged them not to keep shooting him. She asked how many times the man was shot. He said 'Five times; there was blood everywhere.'

There was also evidence that the black motorcycle used by the two accused had been found at Hodgins's house on the day of their arrests. It had been repainted white, and the petrol tank had been removed.

Now it was half time, and the accused had two very sagacious and experienced counsels on their side, without any time limitations.

Both accused gave evidence in their own defence. Both agreed that what was contained in their statements to Gardaí was indeed what they had told the Gardaí when questioned. In the witness box, however, they gave a different account of the events that day. They claimed that the story about chasing Kidman, and O'Brien telling Hodgins to shoot him, and reloading the rifle three times, was pure invention, and had been agreed on by both of them. They said they told the Gardaí this story because they believed that Shane O'Brien would be in less trouble if it emerged that his only part in the incident was to carry the body six feet or so, and help dispose of it in the undergrowth. Hodgins told the Court that he walked O'Brien into it. O'Brien had done nothing. Hodgins maintained that he did not reload the rifle three times, as he had told Detectives. There was a magazine in the rifle, and he did not have to reload. He said he had panicked when a strange figure came running at him. He was about eight or ten feet away. He had something in his hand, and

Hodgins panicked and fired, and the man fell to the ground. Suddenly he jumped up again. Hodgins was afraid, and emptied all the bullets in the magazine in quick succession. The man never spoke, nor did Shane O'Brien. When he realised the man was dead, he asked O'Brien to help him hide the body.

Shane O'Brien said that he had gone with Hodgins to shoot rabbits and pheasants at the Estate. He had taken a shot with the rifle, and handed it back to Hodgins. Then he noticed a man behind them, running at them, and Hodgins fired a shot at him. He denied that he told Hodgins to shoot him.

On arrest, they had not admitted their involvement for some time. Then they told Gardaí that they ran after Kidman, and O'Brien said he told Hodgins to shoot Kidman.

The jury retired to consider their verdict on 9 March. They returned three times for guidance from Judge Johnson on different points. After five hours' deliberations, they finally returned and found Shane O'Brien not guilty of murder. They found Michael Hodgins not guilty of murder, but guilty of manslaughter. It was a sensational verdict, which took, I would say, the vast majority of the persons in the courtroom by surprise. The verdict caused widespread controversy, with relatives of Kidman and his employer Lord Henry Mountcharles expressing shock and disbelief. In relation to O'Brien, I could understand that the jury had some doubts about his participation.

In the Dáil on 12 March, Fine Gael Justice spokesman Jim O'Keeffe confirmed that Fine Gael would be seeking a second stage reading on the Criminal Justice Bill 1990. The PD Justice spokesperson, Marian Quill, said the tragic case of Timothy Kidman had highlighted inadequacies in relation both to the definition of murder, and the absence of any clear categorisation of the crime of homicide. Present homicide laws needed updating and restating.

I personally could not find any problem with the law as it stood. To me, it was simply the jury getting it completely wrong as far as Hodgins was concerned.

Only one member of the jury was going for a guilty verdict. The jury did their duty according to the oath that they took.

Shane O'Brien was released, and walked free out of the Court. Michael Hodgins was sentenced to a term of twelve years' imprisonment, an indication of the Judge's view of the gravity of his crime.

While in prison, it appears Hodgins became addicted to drugs, or so his Counsel stated at a subsequent court hearing. In prison he learned, however, how to get money without doing an honest day's work. On his release in April 1998, he became involved in the sale of drugs at a significant level. On 16 April 2005, his home in Drogheda was searched by Garda Thomas Quinn and others. He had been under surveillance for some time, suspected of dealing in drugs. When Gardaí arrived at his house, he fled, throwing away a bag containing cocaine. It was recovered, and he was arrested. In the house the Gardaí found cocaine and amphetamines, with a street value of between €13,000 and €16,000. Cash to the amount of €171,000 was found in a briefcase. Hodgins was convicted of dealing in drugs, and sentenced to nine years' imprisonment.

While in prison, in July 2009, Hodgins made an application for the return of the €171,000 to him. He said that the money was his, and that he had saved it since he was released from prison in 1998. Sergeant Tom Quinn told Judge Michael White that the money was concealed inside a panel of the bath at Hodgins's home, and that he believed it to be the proceeds of the sale of drugs. The Judge refused Hodgins's application, and ordered that the money be handed over to the State.

The Kidman case was the only one I was ever involved in where I could not bring myself around to see how the jury came to their verdict. To this day I cannot understand it, but we all had to accept it.

MURDER OF CECIL BLACK, DUNDALK, 1990

In January 1990, I was transferred from Dundalk to the Investigation Section at Crime Branch of Garda Headquarters, as Detective Superintendent. The section had been disbanded in 1988, but had now been re-formed on a much smaller scale, with very few personnel. The town of Dundalk is situated about halfway between Dublin and Belfast, and in 1990 the main road between the two cities passed through the centre of the town.

Cecil Black was in his mid-seventies, a widower, and a publican. He lived alone above his premises, Cecil's Bar, at Park Street in Dundalk, also known as 'Congo Bar'. Cecil's health was not great, and he only opened the premises occasionally, and for short periods of time. He did not have a large clientele, and the premises over the years became in need of refurbishment.

On Saturday, 21 April 1990, Gerard Boylan, also a publican at Park Street in Dundalk, became somewhat worried for the welfare of Cecil. He did not see the pub open on Friday the twentieth, nor on Saturday the twenty-first, which was unusual. Boylan contacted the Gardaí in Dundalk, and Garda John Sweeney was asked to go to Cecil's Bar. Garda Sweeney got no response to his knocking at the front door. He somehow managed to get into the backyard of Cecil's premises, and entered the bar through the unlocked back door.

The public bar was in disarray. Scattered on the floor were papers, broken donation boxes, bottles and a broken glass. There was no sign of Cecil, and no response to Garda Sweeney's calls. Garda Sweeney went up the stairs, which led to Cecil's living quarters overhead.

Garda Sweeney was shocked with the scene that confronted him. He found Cecil lying on the floor, his pants pulled down to his ankles, his feet tied together at the ankles and his hands tied behind his back. There was a neck tie through his open mouth, tied at the back of his neck. His head was completely out of shape, lying in a large pool of blood. It was obvious that Cecil had been dead for some time. The livingroom-cum-bedroom where Cecil was found appeared to have been ransacked, and there was a bloodstained household gas cylinder on the floor beside Cecil's body.

The scene was preserved, and all appropriate Garda personnel were informed. A doctor pronounced Cecil dead, and said he had been dead for twenty-four hours or so. The local priest administered the last rites. Assistance was sought from Garda Headquarters, to carry out a technical examination of the scene. Among others, Detective Garda Moses Morrissey of the Fingerprint Section and Detective Garda Brendan McArdle from the Ballistics Section came to examine the scene. They were there for three or four days. Superintendent Frank Murray of Dundalk sought assistance from the Investigation Section at Garda Headquarters.

On the Sunday, 22 April, I went to Dundalk to assist in the investigation. I was returning to the station I had left only two months earlier. Knowing all the members of the Detective Branch and the geography of the area was of great assistance to me in the investigation. I have always found that it takes quite some time to become acclimatised to a strange location, not knowing the personnel or the geography of the place.

At the crime scene, I met Moses and Brendan, who were hard at work searching for clues. The body had been removed, and a post mortem was being carried out by Dr Declan Gilsenan, an Assistant State Pathologist.

At the station, an incident room was prepared and enquiries had commenced. An appeal had been issued to the local community for information, and questionnaires were being completed for people living in the immediate vicinity of the bar, and by persons known to have been near the scene on Friday.

Another local publican, Noel Ghormley, described Cecil as a lovely, friendly man. He kept his pub open mainly to keep himself occupied, since his wife died a few years earlier. He said that Cecil had opened the pub on the Friday, but he noticed at 6 or 7pm that it was closed, and it did not open on Saturday. Some time on Friday morning, Cecil called to a local butcher's shop to get meat for his dinner. That was the last time that anyone saw him, apart from those who killed him. Park Street was normally busy, with many pedestrians up and down the street, and of course the Dublin–Belfast road passed right outside Cecil's front door.

Once again, a member of the public supplied vital information to the Gardaí, having seen two young men leave Cecil's Bar in the early afternoon of 20 April. What drew their attention was that they banged the front door after them. Then they turned left and walked down towards the Square. They were a bit wild looking and distressed, according to this witness. A description of the men was also supplied, though descriptions as we know can be very far off the mark.

Detective Branch members in Dundalk and the Crime Unit in Dundalk got together and considered all the likely suspects for this terrible crime. The motive for the crime was from the beginning thought to be robbery. Fear of being identified has unfortunately cost injured parties their lives, as we all know the saying, 'Dead men tell no tales.'

Local Gardaí came up with the names of three persons who operated together, and had numerous convictions for crime in the area. The description given of the men leaving the bar on 20 April roughly matched their descriptions. It certainly did not rule them out.

While examining the scene, Brendan McArdle had more success than the perpetrators in their search of Cecil's living quarters. Brendan found a considerable sum of money, in a tin box hidden under the wardrobe. Brendan also discovered unidentifiable footwear marks on the top of the bar counter. It appears that the perpetrators stood on it. Outside the bar counter and touching it, were one or two painted metal pillars or supports, about five inches in diameter, from the floor to the ceiling.

Moses Morrissey examined the supports for finger or palm marks. The footwear marks were in close proximity to the supports. On one support he found a palm mark, a few inches below ceiling level. This was photographed. The fingerprints and palm prints of the three persons nominated by the local members were available. Moses Morrissey identified the palm mark found on the support as having been made by one of these three. Now, I was at least three inches taller than the person who made the palm mark, but when standing on the floor, I could not put my hand into the position of the palm mark. I came to the conclusion that this person had to be up on the counter to have left this mark.

More information was received from the public, that three young men got into a taxi in the square in Dundalk, around the time that the two men were seen leaving Cecil's Bar. We spent considerable time endeavouring to locate the taxi, and finally settled on one. That taxi man was not of much help, saying he had only a vague recollection of bringing people to Oakland Park Estate in Dundalk that afternoon. He couldn't say whether they were male or female. Oakland Park Estate was where the three nominated people lived. Brendan McArdle subjected the taxi to a thorough examination; he collected many samples of material in the hope of getting something to connect with the crime, such as blood. That search was in vain. Around 26 April, the houses of the three – Peter McCaffrey, twenty, of Oakland Park, John Kelly, twenty-six, and Eugene Kelly, twenty-two, brothers also from Oakland Park, were searched by Gardaí. They were looking for bloodstained clothing or footwear, or anything to connect with the crime scene. Items taken were examined, with negative results.

The three young men were arrested, brought to Dundalk Garda Station, and questioned. All three denied any involvement, and they declined to stand in an identification parade. The person who saw the two men leaving Cecil's Bar on the twentieth was willing to view a parade. There was an enclosed yard at Dundalk Garda Station, and I decided to put the three prisoners into the yard together with about fourteen or fifteen other volunteers. We got our witness to view them, conscious of course that a Court would not allow this as evidence. I felt, however, that if one was picked out it might have some effect on him, and perhaps he might admit involvement. However, the three frustrated the exercise, by going into a toilet in the yard and refusing to come out. To take them out would have prejudiced the witness, so we abandoned the attempt. Questioning continued up to the last minute allowed, and then we had to release them without charge.

The three prime suspects were now back on the streets again, and there were no other suspects for the crime. The fact that one of them, John Kelly, had left a palm mark on the pillar, where he had to be on the counter to reach, was a very good indication that he at least was involved. Efforts continued to discover any other customers that may have been in Cecil's Bar on the Friday afternoon, or anyone that may have seen the culprits, but none were found. Time moved on and there was no sign of a break coming. An investigation file was prepared, and sent to the DPP for directions. It was returned, stating that there was evidence that the three suspects were on the premises, but no evidence that they had killed anybody, or committed any offences there. I kept in touch with the Detective Branch in Dundalk for some months regarding progress, but there was none.

Then a Garda in Dundalk contacted me. He had been speaking to Peter McCaffrey's sister, Mary. She gave him some information relating to the crime. She agreed to speak to me with him, but not in Dundalk. An arrangement was made to meet at the railway station or bus station in Drogheda. When we met, Mary was very nervous and afraid of being seen with us. She said that her brother Peter and the two Kellys, John and Eugene, were involved in the murder of Cecil Black. On the evening of Friday, 20 April, her brother arrived at her home in Dundalk in a taxi; he was upset and kept saying, 'We are in trouble now.' He told her what had happened to Cecil Black at his premises earlier that day. He blamed the two Kellys for what had happened.

Mary McCaffrey said she was speaking to us because she knew that her brother and the Kellys should be punished for what they had done. The Kellys intended to go to England very shortly, and were leaving her brother to shoulder the blame. She said that on the evening of the crime, the Kellys burned their footwear and some clothing that they were wearing at Cecil Black's premises.

We were left in no doubt about who was responsible for Cecil's death. It was of no evidential value, however, as Mary said she would not give evidence in Court. The Kellys left Dundalk, and went to England.

Some time afterwards, a member of the Detective Branch in Dundalk informed me that he intended to arrest Peter McCaffrey, in relation to a burglary in Dundalk. This arrest would give us another opportunity to ask McCaffrey questions about the Cecil Black case, when the Detective Garda had completed his questioning in relation to the burglary. McCaffrey had been arrested on numerous other occasions. He was no stranger to interrogation, and not likely to admit anything in relation to Cecil Black to the Gardaí. This was a shocking, brutal murder, of a decent, honest citizen, and we were determined to use every possible means to obtain evidence against the culprits.

McCaffrey was arrested and questioned about the burglary. His detention was extended for a further six hours by the Superintendent in Drogheda. With two hours of the detention time left, the Detective Gardaí were finished with McCaffrey, and he was now available to the investigators of the Cecil Black murder case. I arranged for McCaffrey's sister Mary to be brought to Dundalk Garda Station. Some cases are so serious that one has to embark on unorthodox methods to achieve a successful conclusion. We felt that McCaffrey was unlikely to admit involvement to the Gardaí, but might possibly speak to his sister about it, if he believed he was alone with her in the Station.

We arranged for McCaffrey to be questioned in the basement of the Station, an area used as a cloakroom by the uniform personnel. Each member had a steel wardrobe, to store uniforms and so on. There was a window in this area, and we placed a table and three chairs there. We rearranged the positions of the wardrobes, leaving an enclosed space to accommodate two members lying unseen on the floor. They did not have chairs, because we are afraid that they might creak and give their presence away.

I spoke to Mary in the Station, and she was very cooperative. I asked if she would speak to Peter in the Station, if left alone with him, and she agreed. She was to discuss the Kellys and the Cecil Black case with him; to tell him it was a terrible thing they did to Cecil Black, and to endeavour to get him to tell his side of the story. Mary's husband was in the Garda Station, or came there very shortly afterwards. I selected two very astute members of the Detective Branch, who I knew would not get their feathers ruffled under cross-examination in court. These were Detective Garda Tom Fox and Detective Garda Larry Crowe. The two members went to the basement and lay on the floor, just a few feet away from the table but completely hidden from view. Their function was to listen carefully to the conversation, and note what was said.

I had arranged with a uniform member to come to the basement at a certain time, and to tell me that the Chief Superintendent wanted to speak to me. I would tell him in reply that I would call to see the Chief Superintendent in about half an hour. Then he was to leave and come back, and tell me that the Chief Superintendent said it was urgent, and to come now. I would then ask him to stay in the basement with McCaffrey, and he would say that he could not stay, as he was the only member on duty in the public office.

I brought McCaffrey and his sister Mary to the basement, and we sat at the table. I cautioned McCaffrey that anything he said would be taken down in writing and may be given in evidence. I encouraged him to tell the truth about the Cecil Black murder, and not to be left alone to shoulder the blame, with the two Kellys gone off to England.

The uniformed member arrived as arranged, and we had the conversation as arranged. I told McCaffrey and his sister that I had to leave, but would return as soon as I could. I told McCaffrey that I would arrange for a member to watch the window from somewhere outside, and not to get any ideas about trying to escape. I left Mary and Peter, and I returned after about fifteen minutes. When I got back, the two Detective Garda members had already emerged from their hiding place, and were speaking to McCaffrey. In my absence, Mary had said to Peter, 'That was a terrible thing you did to Cecil Black.' He replied, 'It was, but it is too late now, and I am fucked if I am going to do ten years for it.' Mary left the basement and joined her husband upstairs.

We continued to try to get McCaffrey to tell us about the killing of Cecil Black, but he denied being in the pub. With about thirty minutes to go, I spoke to Mary's husband, and he agreed to speak to Peter. He spoke alone to Peter, then emerged. Peter had told him that if he was charged with the murder, he would make a statement to Gardaí and tell them what had occurred in the bar. Peter's time of detention was now due to expire, and he was released.

Additional statements were sent to the DPP, outlining the new developments in the case. The DPP reviewed the case, and gave a direction to arrest and charge Peter McCaffrey with the murder of Cecil Black.

Peter McCaffrey was arrested in March 1991, and brought to Dundalk Garda Station. He was told he was going to be charged with Cecil Black's murder. Detective Garda Tom Molloy, Detective Garda Jim Lane and I spoke to him. On being told that he would stand alone in the dock for Cecil Black's murder, he said, 'I want to make a statement about what happened.' He asked if his girlfriend could be present when he made it, and we agreed. A short time later, McCaffrey commenced to make his statement to Detective Garda

Tom Molloy and Detective Garda Jim Lane. His girlfriend and I were present. He outlined his version of what had happened in the pub that tragic day. He did not admit to assaulting Cecil Black in any way, but outlined what the Kellys had done.

The trial of Peter McCaffrey opened at the Central Criminal Court in Dublin on 8 October 1991, presided over by Mr Justice Declan Costello. There were three charges on the indictment: murder, robbery and the larceny of cash and alcohol. When the charges were read over to Peter McCaffrey, he pleaded not guilty to murder, but guilty to the other two charges.

A range of witnesses gave evidence, including McCaffrey's sister Mary. The statement that McCaffrey made to Detective Gardaí Lane and Molloy was admitted in evidence and read to the Court. In it Peter stated that he told the other two men to leave Cecil Black alone, and was downstairs in the bar when they killed him upstairs.

The jury deliberated for three hours, then found Peter McCaffrey not guilty of murder. Judge Costello remanded him in custody until 18 October, for sentence on the charges he had pleaded guilty to.

McCaffrey made contact with me before 18 October, and I went to the prison to see him. He said he would give evidence in Court against the Kelly brothers if they were charged with Cecil Black's murder. I had to tell his Counsel, Mr McEntee, about that visit, and that I went there on McCaffrey's request. I also told him of McCaffrey's intention to give evidence against the Kellys.

On 18 October, McCaffrey appeared for sentencing. Mr Justice Costello sentenced him to eight years' imprisonment on the robbery charge and two years' imprisonment on the larceny charge, to run concurrently. Imposing sentence, the Judge said, 'Mr Black pleaded with the criminal involved for his life. Mr Black must have undergone a period of great and intense terror. He was callously murdered, and a great many details of this crime have not been disclosed.' The Judge said that he was taking into account the fact that he was not the ringleader, and that the attack had not been pre-arranged. McCaffrey was sent to Wheatfield Prison.

The two Kellys returned to Dundalk, and were arrested on Saturday, 19 October 1991, and immediately charged with the murder of Cecil Black. They appeared before a special sitting of Dundalk District Court, and were remanded in custody until 23 October. On that date, their solicitor, Dermot Lavery, told the court that he had been instructed by the two accused to make it clear that they had been accessible to the Gardaí at all times. He said they had gone to England, but had been back in the jurisdiction a number of times since the murder, and this had been known to the Gardaí. I believe this was a story told to support an application for bail at a later date.

The evidence of Peter McCaffrey was essential in securing the convictions for murder against the two brothers. The DPP directed that Peter McCaffrey make a deposition to the District Court, in the presence of the two Kellys, to ensure that he was serious in the undertaking he had given, to give evidence when their case came to trial. I saw Peter McCaffrey in Wheatfield Prison prior to making the deposition. He was very depressed, and fearful that the Kellys would be sent to Wheatfield Prison before trial, and intimidate him. McCaffrey's fears were brought to the attention of the Department of Justice, and Wheatfield Prison authorities. The Kellys were not sent to Wheatfield Prison, and perhaps may not have been sent there anyway.

The trial of Eugene and John Kelly opened in the Central Criminal Court in Dublin, on 31 March 1992, presided over by Mr Justice Declan Budd. Prosecution Senior Counsel was Dennis Vaughan Buckley. Seamus Sorohan, Senior Counsel, appeared on behalf of John Kelly, and Barry White, Senior Counsel, appeared for Eugene Kelly. Both accused pleaded not guilty to all three charges – murder, robbery and larceny of cash and bottles of spirits.

Peter McCaffrey appeared in Court as a witness for the State. There was some apprehension as McCaffrey entered the witness box, as to what he might do or say, as all depended on him. He stood by his word; he told the court and jury that he and the Kelly brothers went to Cecil's Bar after a morning drinking session. They ordered pints of lager, and when they said they had no money, Cecil Black ordered them out. There was a scuffle between the Kellys and Cecil Black, and he noticed blood on Cecil's nose. The brothers pushed Black upstairs, and he followed them up after a while. John Kelly told Cecil Black that he was being robbed.

Cecil Black asked Peter McCaffrey to tell the other two men to leave him alone. McCaffrey said he did tell them to leave him alone. Eugene Kelly said, 'We are going to have to kill him, he will be able to describe us.' McCaffrey went down the stairs, and locked the door from the street into the bar. While in the bar, he took some drink, took £60 out of the till, and broke open some donation boxes. After a while, he heard a loud bang from upstairs, and he went up. He saw the Kelly brothers standing over Cecil Black. He noticed that there was blood coming from his head. He pushed the brothers out of the way, and lifted up Cecil's head, and there was a tie around his mouth. He started shouting at him to breathe, but he was dead. McCaffrey went downstairs again, and helped himself to drink.

McCaffrey was cross-examined by Seamus Sorohan, Senior Counsel for John Kelly. McCaffrey denied suggestions that he hoped to get a reduction in his sentence by giving evidence against the Kelly brothers. Barry White, for Eugene Kelly, put it to McCaffrey that the sole purpose of making his statements to the Gardaí was to try to pass the buck from himself to the Kellys.

John Kelly gave evidence in his own defence. He said he was lying when he told Detectives he had never been in the pub where the murder took place. He, Eugene and Peter McCaffrey had simply had a drink in Cecil's Bar on 20 April, and left afterwards.

Eugene Kelly also gave evidence in his own defence, saying that he was lying to the Gardaí when he said he was not in Cecil's Bar that day. He said, 'I was frightened; I knew I had been in the place; I have a bad record.' He admitted he had a number of convictions for burglaries, but said that Mr Black was alive and well when he left the pub, and he had no hand, act or part in his killing.

The trial lasted eleven days, until 14 April 1992. The jury started with the usual number – twelve. During the hearing of the case, the Judge was told that a man on the jury was about to get married in the very near future, and the Judge excused him. That left eleven – six women and five men.

The jury deliberated for two hours, and found John Kelly and Eugene Kelly guilty on all counts – murder, robbery and larceny. The Judge told the two accused that the sentence was mandatory – life imprisonment. John Kelly smiled and said, 'It was a bad jury, your Honour.'

Sentencing for the robbery and larceny was put back until 25 May 1992. On that date, Superintendent Frank Murray of Dundalk outlined all the previous convictions against the two. He agreed that the accused came from a deprived background, their parents having split up twenty years previously. Judge Budd imposed a sentence of nine years for the robbery charge, to run concurrently with the life sentence. The Judge told the two accused that society was entitled to know why two young men would discuss in front of an elderly man how they were going to kill him, and what way they were going to do it.

The murder of Cecil Black was one of the worst, most brutal and barbaric acts I came across in my time in the Garda. The crime would, in my opinion, not have been solved but for the goodness of McCaffrey's sister Mary, and her husband. Some credit must also go to McCaffrey himself, for going into the witness box against the two brothers. I think it shows that he had some conscience. Gardaí in Dundalk, who were very much aware of the activities of the Kelly brothers prior to the murder, were very pleased with the verdict, as were many in Dundalk's community.

Eugene Kelly was released from prison on licence in March 2007, having served a total of fifteen years for Cecil Black's murder. On 19 July 2008, Kelly was under surveillance by the Detective Branch in Dundalk. They saw him at Castletown Road in the town, in conversation with a man in an Audi car. They saw Kelly being handed a package by the man in the Audi. Kelly himself was a passenger in a Toyota Yaris, which then drove away. Gardaí stopped the Toyota, and the package was found to contain a Glock pistol and fifty rounds of 9mm ammunition. Eugene Kelly was arrested and charged with unlawful possession of the firearm.

He appeared before the Special Criminal Court in July 2009, and was convicted. Mr Justice John McMenamin said that the court had taken into account that Kelly had not pleaded guilty, but had fought the case tooth and nail. Kelly was sentenced to ten years' imprisonment. He appealed the conviction and the sentence in the Court of Criminal Appeal, on a number of grounds, but the appeal was refused on all grounds. Kelly clearly did not learn any lesson from the life imprisonment imposed on him for the murder of Cecil Black.

LARCENY OF INCHCLERAUN ISLAND
GRAVESTONES, 1991

My first recollection of being in contact with ancient objects, antiques, old artifacts, and all that sort of material was way back in the early 1960s, when I was in Naas. There was an auction at one of the largest houses in Ireland, Castletown House in Celbridge. The contents of the house were being sold, furniture and all effects. I was on duty there, and I was amazed at the prices that were paid for articles that to me, in my ignorance, seemed like rubbish – old chairs that were falling asunder, selling for thousands of pounds.

Of course, I was aware that old houses around the country, farmhouses and mansions, were being plundered by thieves in search of antiques – brass oil lamps, metal pots, old tools, bits of machinery, furniture, fireplaces and all sorts of things. These items were being sold at auctions around the country, and no doubt some of them went out of the country. Stealing antiques is bad, but stealing pieces of our archaeological heritage is very serious. The next case involves just that – a change from murder, but in a way this case goes back to deaths that had occurred possibly in the fifth, sixth and seventh centuries, and it came to light thousands of miles away from Ireland.

Peter Kenny, sixty-seven years of age, was an Irish man who lived in Australia for a long time. On 6 March 1991, he made a phone call from Miami to the Irish college in Boston, to Robert O'Neill, Director of the Burns Library of rare books and special collections, one of America's most comprehensive collections of Irish historical and cultural materials. Kenny said he was a retired ship's captain, and was trying to find a good home for his possessions. He offered to sell various ancient artifacts to the college, the most important of which were fifth- and sixth-century gravestones. He said that he had other rare Irish antiquities for sale. Kenny told O'Neill that he had owned the artifacts for about forty years – some he had found, some he had bought, and most of them were given to him by deceased members of his family. He claimed that a few of them, including the gravestones, had been in his family from the time of Brian Ború. O'Neill was interested, but he wanted to obtain more information about the items.

About a week later, he received a letter from Kenny, containing details of the items, with photographs and more plausible explanations for how he came by them. O'Neill was suspicious, and he contacted the National

Museum of Ireland and spoke to Eamon Kelly, the assistant keeper of Irish antiquities. That phone call was on 12 March. Eamon Kelly recognised a connection with a situation that the Irish authorities were monitoring at the time. O'Neill faxed Kenny's letter to Eamon Kelly, and Kelly confirmed that the gravestones fitted the description of gravestones that had recently been stolen from an ancient monastic site, on the island of Inchcleraun in Lough Ree, County Longford.

O'Neill contacted the FBI in Boston. Eamon Kelly contacted the Office of Public Works (OPW), which has responsibility for these items, and they contacted the Taoiseach's department, who in turn contacted the Department of Justice. The Department of Justice contacted the Commissioner, and I was tasked with investigating the taking of the gravestones from the island and their presence in Boston for sale.

Detective Sergeant Tom O'Loughlin and I spent a few days making enquiries. I got in touch with the FBI in Boston, and they sought assistance from the Gardaí with the investigation out there, and to bring them up to date with legislation regarding such items. The Department of Justice agreed, and I was on my way to Boston, along with Eamon Kelly and Paul McMahon from the OPW. Their function was to inform the FBI of the importance of these gravestones, and also to identify the materials when Mr Kenny produced them.

The FBI in Boston were in touch with O'Neill a number of times, and on 3 April, Special Agent Darryl Radt and John Newton of the Boston office met with O'Neill. O'Neill agreed to call Kenny the following day, and he authorised the FBI to record the conversation. During this call, it was agreed that Kenny would personally deliver the artifacts to O'Neill in Boston on 15 April. Kenny then called O'Neill, saying he had arrived and was staying in a hotel in Wellesley, Massachusetts. Eamon Kelly, Paul McMahon and I had arrived in Boston by that time.

The FBI organised a sting operation, instructing O'Neill to invite Kenny to come to the library the next morning, 16 April. Federal agents were positioned inside and in front of the building, disguised as students and maintenance workers. The Boston College Police and US Customs were also involved, and Eamon Kelly, Paul McMahon and I were also present. Kenny arrived at the library, with some artifacts in his car. He met with O'Neill and Edward Clark, a wired Special Agent posing as a Boston College benefactor interested in sponsoring the purchase. Kenny wanted $1 million for the whole collection. Bargaining began, and they agreed a price of $435,000. When they agreed on the price, the FBI agent gave Kenny some money.

Kenny said he had the gravestones in a warehouse at the docks in Miami. The following day, Ed Clark and another FBI agent, posing again as another benefactor, flew to Miami with Kenny. He brought them to the warehouse, and produced the gravestones. They then returned to Boston with Kenny and the gravestones.

Kenny at this stage was telling a different story. He said he had brought them from Ireland in his boat, and mentioned a member of the Garda Síochána stationed in County Longford, who was in the process of getting him another archaeological object: a Sheela-na-gig. He gave them the Garda's name. Ed Clark and Kenny telephoned the Garda, and he said, yes, he would be able to get it, and said he would be getting it in a few days' time. The conversation was recorded.

I returned straight away to investigate the Garda in Longford. He had said in the phone conversation that he knew where the Sheela-na-gig was, and that on a certain night he was going to get it, and would then be in further contact.

I went to Longford with Tom O'Loughlin. On the night the Garda was to go to get the Sheela-na-gig, we had surveillance on his home. Around 9 or 10pm, a car arrived. The Garda came out with a stepladder, put it and some tools on the roof and took off with the car driver. Surveillance followed some distance behind, but lost the car they were pursuing. They came to a crossroads, and didn't know which way to go, but there was no great harm done, so they returned to the house and took up their position again. At around 2 or 3am, the car returned, but without the stepladder or anything else. The Garda went in home, and the other man drove off. The Gardaí got the registration number of the car.

There was another phone call from Kenny and Clark in America to the Garda. He told them that he had failed to get the Sheela-na-gig that night. He went to the location, climbed up the stepladder, and was hammering away to dislodge this item from the old castle wall in Tipperary, when the ladder broke. The Garda fell and was slightly injured, and they had to abort the attempt and go home. That information was communicated to me from the FBI. I arranged that the Garda and the owner of the car who picked him up, who happened to be the Garda's brother, be arrested. The Garda was suspended first, and then arrested and brought to Roscommon Garda Station. His brother was arrested in Galway.

I interviewed the Garda in Roscommon with Detective Sergeant Tom O'Loughlin and others. He had nothing to say during the whole interview; he would not talk. I brought him out into my car, and I had brought the first conversation recorded in America with me. I played it in the car, and he still would not say anything. He was eventually released, and on the same day his brother was arrested in Galway and made a full confession. Both brothers were released, and a few days later the Garda resigned. He was not charged, as there was insufficient evidence. His brother was not going to give evidence against him. The brother was charged, and appeared in court in Tipperary some time later. I have an idea that he pleaded guilty, and there was a monetary fine but no custodial sentence given.

Meanwhile back in Boston, Kenny was arrested on 25 July, and charged with smuggling stolen goods into the United States. Kenny pleaded guilty, and was sentenced to four months in federal prison. He had already served that time since his arrest, so he was released.

I am not aware of who actually removed the gravestones from their centuries-long resting place, among the ruins of five churches and a priory on Inchcleraun Island. They were transported to Galway docks and loaded onto Kenny's fifty-four-foot yacht, *Minerva*. Kenny sailed the yacht from Galway to Australia, and on to Miami, arriving there some time in January 1991.

The arrest of Kenny and the recovery of the stolen heritage gravestones received much media coverage, both nationally and internationally. There was also, of course, much reporting on the connection between Kenny and a member of the Garda Síochána.

In Boston, I struck up a very good relationship with FBI Agent Edward Clark. His ancestors came from the Longford and Roscommon areas, and he had never been to Ireland. He made me very welcome in Boston; he was a very homely man. I was invited out to his home one evening for dinner, and I met his wife Cathleen. We had a lovely meal, and a great chat, all centred around the affairs of Ireland.

At the end of August 1991, FBI Agents Thomas Hughes and Edward Clark brought the stolen gravestones with their ancient inscribed markings to Ireland in timber crates. A reception had been organised by the Department of the Taoiseach to mark the occasion, at a hotel near Shannon Airport. Vincent Brady, a Minister of State there on behalf of the government, addressed the reception, stating that anyone stealing items of Ireland's archaeological heritage would be hunted down and caught. He described the illicit removal of thousand-year-old early Christian gravestones as a great insult to the people of Ireland. He paid tribute to the FBI and their agents, the Gardaí and all the others involved in the operation. I invited Edward Clark and his wife Cathleen, in the event of them coming to Ireland on holiday, to stay with us in Naas. A year or so later they did come to Ireland, and came to stay with us for three days. Every Christmas since then, we communicate with each other and exchange greetings.

An article was later published about the case and the investigation. Part of it said:

> The case of the Inchcleraun grave-
> stones carried all the ingredients of a
> riveting spy story, including the most
> elaborate sting operation attempted
> during those frantic years of fight
> against the plunderers of cultural
> heritage. The operation involved
> the Garda Síochána, the National
> Monuments Service of Ireland, the
> Federal Bureau of Investigation, US
> Customs, US Emigration and Nat-

One of the Inchcleraun gravestones

uralization Service and Boston College. The event also stood out because of the huge amount of money at stake, had the traffickers managed to find a real purchaser ready to agree a price for such priceless artifacts as the gravestones are. The Garda Síochána demonstrated in those circum-stances, its ability to effectively deal with this kind of offence on a global scale, by means of far reaching international cooporation with foreign investigator bodies.

Gardaí get the wrong end of the stick in relation to many things, so it is nice to get some recognition for a case that is successfully concluded. The gravestones, on return to Ireland, did not return to the island where they had been for a thousand years. I understand they were brought to the National Museum of Ireland, and as far as I know, that is where they are now.

LARCENY OF ANCIENT MANUSCRIPT PAGES, CHESTER BEATTY LIBRARY, 1991

Chester Alfred Beatty was born in America, and had Irish connections on his father's side. As a young man, he became involved in copper and gold mining, and by the age of thirty-five he had amassed a fortune. He first went to Egypt with his wife in 1913, where he purchased some Oriental manuscripts and one or two Korans. He spent most of the rest of his life putting together one of the finest collections of western and oriental manuscripts in the world.

In 1950, he made his permanent home in Ireland. He brought his collection with him, and set up a library in Dublin. He died in 1967, at the age of ninety-three. On the eleventh anniversary of his death, his collection was bequeathed to the State. The Chester Beatty Library was located on Shrewsbury Road in Ballsbridge in 1991. It is now in Dublin Castle, and has been there for some years.

In February 1969, Dr David James, an Englishman, was appointed the first curator in the Islamic Section of the Chester Beatty Library, at Shrewsbury Road. He remained in that position for twenty years, until February 1989. When David James took up his position in the library, he was given the use of a dwelling house in the grounds. While living there, he had complete access to the library, day and night. He had the keys, and could come and go when he liked. He later purchased a house on Sandford Road in Ranelagh.

At some stage before Dr James left the library, Dr Estelle Whelan from New York was working on a fellowship at the library, and at the same time Pat Donlon also worked there. Dr Whelan was working on a manuscript that was beginning to fall apart. She requested permission to photograph the manuscript, and her request was granted. She photographed it and on her departure back to New York, she brought the photographs with her.

We move on from that period to the summer of 1991. Pat Donlon was then Director of the National Library, and also a member of the Board of Trustees of the Chester Beatty Library. She was in France, somewhere near Fontaine Lou, enjoying a holiday when she received a phone call from New York. It was Dr Whelan, with a story to relate. She had been contacted by the curator of the Museum of Modern Art in New York. The curator had been to London in April, and had viewed a folio from a Koran. He was interested in purchasing it for the New York Museum. The folio was at Sotheby's auction house, and the price was £25,000 sterling. He returned to New York and considered the matter further, and received transparencies of the folio from Sotheby's. He asked if Dr Whelan would view the transparencies, to establish the provenance and genuineness of the folio. Dr Whelan went to the museum, and brought her photographs of the manuscript from the Chester Beatty Library with her. She compared the transparencies from Sotheby's and her own, and was satisfied that the folio on sale in Sotheby's was from the Chester Beatty Library manuscript she had photographed.

As a result of the conversation with Dr Whelan, Pat Donlon's holiday was over. She returned to Dublin the next day, and contacted retired Chief Justice Walsh, Chairman of the Board of Trustees, and another trustee, Joan Duff. They went to the library, and discovered that folios were missing from the manuscript.

Assistant Garda Commissioner Tom O'Leary was an acquaintance of one of the trustees. He was contacted, and they discussed what action the trustees could take. They realised, of course, that other property could be missing, and decided to make an official complaint to the Gardaí, and let them deal with the matter. The Commissioner of the day was contacted, and I was given the task of conducting the investigation.

From the onset, I was conscious that it was of extreme importance to con-duct enquiries in a very discreet manner. Sotheby's were informed that they had an item for sale that was the property of the Chester Beatty Library. I was in contact with a Detective at Scotland Yard. They spoke to Sotheby's, and discovered that the item was given to them for sale by a well-known London collector, Oliver Hoare. He was contacted, and stated that he had purchased the item from Dr David James. This was no surprise, as Dr James was the number one suspect from the beginning.

Sotheby's and Oliver Hoare were asked not to discuss the enquiry. If the media found out about it, Dr James would surely disappear to some far-off unknown place. I travelled to London on a few occasions, and had discussions with police at Scotland Yard, with Sotheby's and with Oliver Hoare. It was important to get Dr James on home ground in this State, in order to arrest, detain and question him. Efforts to trace him in England were without success. In mid-August, I arranged for Sotheby's to hand over the stolen item. The Detective from Scotland Yard that I was dealing with collected it and brought it to Heathrow Airport, where he handed it over to me. The following morning, I travelled to New York with the folio. I spoke to the curator at the Museum of Modern Art, and to Dr Whelan. The curator identified the folio as the one he had seen for sale in Sotheby's. Dr Whelan identified it as the folio from the manuscript at the Chester Beatty Library. Both made statements, and both agreed to come to Ireland to give evidence, if and when required.

We became aware that Dr James would be flying from London Heathrow to Dublin on the night of 20 September 1991. I was concerned that the Gardaí were not in possession of a photograph of James. We did have a description, but a description alone was not much use, when 100 passengers disembark from an aircraft and pass you by within a few minutes. You could pick out perhaps a dozen that might fit the description, or perhaps none. I contacted Pat Donlon, and she volunteered to go to the airport with us, and identify Dr James. She contacted Joan Duff, who also agreed to go.

Detective Garda Hogan and I arrived well before the time of arrival, and had discussions with airport security. We got permission to go behind the scenes, to where we could see the passengers disembark, and come down the ramp. They gave us a nice spot, where Detective Hogan and I and the two ladies were out of sight, but with a clear view of the passengers.

The flight arrived on time, and the passengers disembarked. One of the ladies said, 'Oh, I think that's him, I'm not sure.' After a few seconds, she said, 'Yes, it's him, definitely, that's him.' Detective Hogan and I left the two ladies, joined the passengers and continued with them to the luggage claim hall, as if we had been passengers as well. We stood close to Dr James as he collected his luggage. As he walked away, we stopped him and identified ourselves. We told him the enquiries we were involved in, and that we believed he could assist us. He agreed to speak to us there in the baggage hall.

We went to a quiet area and sat down, and he was told he was free to leave the airport at any time. He agreed to stay and talk to us. We told him that we believed he had taken a folio from a Koran at the Chester Beatty Library while he was curator there, and had sold it to Oliver Hoare. He was told that we now had the folio in our possession, having got it from Sotheby's. He initially denied that he had taken any items from the Chester Beatty Library, but he only adhered to that denial for five or ten minutes. He then admitted to taking the folio and selling it to Oliver Hoare. He said, 'I knew this day would come, and that I would have to face the consequences.'

He started to outline to us other materials he had taken from the library, over a number of years. I was under no obligation to arrest Dr James. He had been cautioned, and he volunteered to talk and to make a written statement. I decided that if he wanted to talk there and then, I would let him talk. Airport security kindly gave us an office, and over the next couple of hours, Dr James made a statement.

Dr James listed many pages from ancient manuscripts that he had stolen, beginning in 1986. Some had been sold on his behalf by Oliver Hoare, as well as several other dealers and collectors, and some were in his flat in London. He had received tens of thousands of pounds for the pages, which included folios from Korans, manuscripts of poetry, calligraphy and art. Dr James gave permission to the Gardaí to enter his flat in London, and to take possession of the property stolen from the Chester Beatty Library.

After making his statement, at about 1.30am, Dr James was arrested and brought to Bridewell Garda Station. Later that morning, he was interviewed again. He made another statement, giving more details on the stolen pages, and later that day, he made a third statement, in the presence of his solicitor, Mr Illio Miloko. Dr James listed more items stolen from the library, including rugs and small paintings. Some items had been sold to dealers, some were in his London flat and some in the house on Sandford Road in Dublin. Dr James said that these items were taken between 1983 and 1989, while he was employed at the Chester Beatty Library. He now deeply regretted the thefts, and said that he would cooperate fully in the recovery of items, and in making restitution where possible. This third statement was signed by David James and Illio Miloko.

While Dr James was on bail, on 4 October he made another statement at Garda Headquarters, listing three other items – two large Koran pages and one small manuscript page – that he had stolen and sold in Copenhagen.

There was great relief all round when Dr James was arrested and placed in custody. The trustees and staff at the Chester Beatty Library, along with art lovers around the world, were shocked to learn of the long list of material James had taken from the library. There was security in place at the Chester Beatty Library, to prevent burglaries, but how does one prevent theft of materials by a trusted employee, when he has keys to the premises and unlimited access? You have to trust somebody.

Some days after Dr James was remanded in custody, Detective Liam Hogan and I travelled to London. We made contact with local police in London, who had no interest from a criminal point of view in the material at Dr James's apartment. They volunteered to give us any assistance we required. It had been agreed that Dr James's wife would meet us at the apartment.

We met her, and she was in no way hostile. She assisted us in every way in our search of the apartment, and the retrieval of the Chester Beatty Library property. The search took a few hours. The local police sent a car to collect us when we had finished. All the property was packed into the car, with some difficulty. It was locked into a cell in the police station overnight, and I held the key to the cell.

The next morning I telephoned Joan Duff, and discussed the safety of the materials, as I had to remain in London for a few days, pursuing some of the dealers that David James had sold material to. Joan Duff made contact with the Director of the British Museum in London, and she kindly facilitated us in storing the material at the Museum. Joan Duff also arranged for a London valuer to examine the material, and value it. The estimated value that was given to me was the value of the property I put on the charges preferred against Dr James. Towards the time of the trial of Dr James, the Chester Beatty Library raised the issue of the value of the materials, saying that it had been grossly undervalued.

In London, we located some dealers who had purchased items from Dr James, and had sold them on to other dealers. They in turn agreed to pursue those dealers. It took quite some time to finally locate some of the items. We returned to Dublin, with the materials occupying a passenger seat on the flight, paid for by the Chester Beatty Library. On arrival in Dublin, the materials were brought to Garda Headquarters and stored for a few days. David James came to Garda Headquarters, and identified the materials taken from the library. We had taken one or two bits that he said were his own.

Dr James's first appearance in Court was on 23 September, and he was charged with one or two counts. More charges were added, and some were withdrawn. Eventually in total, there were thirty-six separate charges of larceny from the Chester Beatty Library. Dr James was granted bail after a few Court appearances. There were no objections from the Gardaí, and indeed he proved useful in the recovery process. When we required information regarding recovery of some property, he was always very cooperative.

Eventually at a Dublin District Court, he pleaded guilty to the thirty-six charges. He was sent forward for sentencing to the Dublin Circuit Criminal Court, which was adjourned to give James the opportunity to continue in the recovery of stolen materials.

Eventually the moment of truth came for Dr James at Dublin Circuit Criminal Court on 14 January 1993. Dr James was sentenced to five years' imprisonment, thirty-eight months of which were suspended.

The total value of the property stolen, as outlined in the charges, amounted to £455,340 sterling. Property with an estimated value of £385,340 sterling was recovered. When one considers the long list of materials Dr James said he stole, I believe it is reasonable to assume that he has overlooked some items. I believe he did not intentionally withhold any information. The sentence imposed on Dr James was about what I had expected. From the very outset one could say that he admitted his guilt, cooperated fully and was of enormous assistance in the recovery of the material. On the other side, of course, he betrayed the trust of his employers, and he committed a long series of offences over a period of years.

The recovery process continued for a long time. Detective Garda Liam Hogan, Detective Sergeant Tom O'Loughlin and I travelled to London again and again, meeting with dealers, who were continually in and out of the country. The London dealer Oliver Hoare was of enormous assistance, and telephoned me on a number of occasions with information. I have no doubt that he was a big loser financially in this whole affair. I also travelled to Copenhagen in pursuit of items, and after long negotiations, the David Collection handed over some material that Dr James had stolen.

On my retirement in June 1994, some material was still outstanding, and I'm sure some material is still outstanding today. I handed over all the information I had in my possession regarding the outstanding material to the Chester Beatty Library, so that they could continue to make their own enquiries.

I understand that Dr James, on release from prison, went back to London. Unfortunately, I believe his marriage broke up. Anyone that has committed a crime that I have dealt with, and that has admitted it, I never hold a grudge against them. They admit it, they go into Court, they serve their sentence and pay their debt to society. I don't go around holding grudges. Dr David James died in November 2012, at his home in Ronda in Spain.

MURDER OF SIOBHAN BRENNAN, CARRICK-ON-SHANNON, 1991

Detective Garda Andy Brennan was stationed at Carrick-on-Shannon in November 1991. He was married to Nora, and they had three children – Lorraine, aged sixteen, Siobhan, aged fifteen, and Andrew, aged ten. Siobhan, a third-year student at the vocational school in the town, had worked at Glancy's supermarket in Carrick-on-Shannon for a year or so, on a casual basis.

On Sunday, 10 November 1991, Siobhan worked at short notice at Glancy's, and finished work there at 8pm. She walked away from the supermarket with two friends, Marie Burns and Anne-Marie O'Rourke, also casual workers at the supermarket. They walked up Bridge Street, and departed from Siobhan at about 8.50pm. She told them she was going straight home, and was looking forward to going to Dublin the following morning with friends.

Siobhan's journey home to Summerhill from Bridge Street was about half a mile, through a bright, built-up, residential area. That night, when Siobhan had not come home, her family became worried. They contacted her friends and other locals, to see if anyone knew her whereabouts. There was no further sighting or word of her after she had left her two friends at 8.50pm.

Andy Brennan contacted the Garda Station and reported his daughter missing, and a search was organised in the area. It proved unsuccessful. At 7.30am on Monday, 11 November, Siobhan's body was found in a layby on the Carrick-on-Shannon to Longford town road, at a place called Clonart South, eighteen miles from Carrick-on-Shannon. Gardaí went to the scene immediately and preserved it. The body was identified at the scene, by a Garda who knew Siobhan personally. The body was fully clothed with the exception of one item. On the discovery of the body, murder was immediately suspected, and a murder investigation commenced.

Superintendent Tom Hughes was responsible for the investigation. He contacted Crime Branch for assistance, and members from Fingerprint Section, Photographic Section, Ballistics Section and Mapping Section went to the scene. That Monday morning, I was on annual leave, and was playing golf with the Carlow Kildare Garda Golfing Society. I remember I was walking down a fairway when my mobile phone rang. It was the Chief Superintendent at Crime Branch. He told me of the finding of the body of Siobhan, and asked was I available to travel to Carrick-on-Shannon. Of course I agreed, as any member of the Investigation Section would. I packed up my golf clubs, and headed home to Maureen. I told Maureen about the situation, and organised for some members of the Investigation Section in Dublin to meet me as soon as possible in Carrick-on-Shannon. When I arrived at the scene that afternoon, Siobhan's body had been removed to hospital for a post mortem examination. The scene was being preserved and searched. I spent some time there, and then went on to Carrick-on-Shannon, where I met up with Superintendent Tom Hughes.

A conference was held that night, and the following morning. It transpired that a jacket worn by Siobhan on the night of 10 November, along with her glasses, had not been found with the body. At the layby a small river, the Finn, flowed under the road. There was a wall, about three feet high, on the right-hand side of the layby as one faces Longford. The river emerged from under the layby. From the top of the wall down to the river was approximately seven to ten feet. Siobhan's body was found beside this wall. A search of the layby revealed all sorts of bits and pieces of things, as one would expect to find in such places. A great amount of material was collected, and two of these items turned out to be of great evidential value. One was a black polythene bin liner, found beside the body. The other was a light fitting to illuminate the rear number plate of a motor vehicle.

The post mortem on the body of Siobhan was carried out by Dr John Harbison. His opinion was that Siobhan had died from strangulation, and he found no evidence of sexual assault.

On Tuesday, 12 November, President Mary Robinson called to the Brennan family home, and offered condolences to the family on her own behalf, and on behalf of the people of Ireland.

From Monday morning, Gardaí sought information from the public. Conferences were held daily, and statements and questionnaires were being completed. As the days went by, the occupants of three different motor vehicles were being sought for interview. One was the occupant or occupants of a red car, which was seen doing handbrake turns near the fire station, just off Carrick-on-Shannon's main street, at 9pm that night. The second was a large white van, seen at 10pm that night, parked in the layby at Clonart where Siobhan's body was later found. The third was a car seen parked in the layby at 3am on the Monday morning. It had a roof sign, and may have been a taxi. A lot of enquiries went into trying to trace the occupants of those three vehicles.

The light fitting found in the layby was established to be a standard fitting on a particular make of car. Of course there was no evidence that it was connected with Siobhan's murder at this stage, but at least we established the make of car that it came from. Friends of Siobhan were also of great interest in the investigation. One friend of Siobhan's, a young lady who resided on St George's Terrace in the town, happened to be away from Carrick-on-Shannon, certainly during the earlier part of the night. She had a boyfriend in Carrick-on-Shannon.

Garda Sub Aqua members came to Carrick-on-Shannon to assist in the investigation. They searched the Finn river, and downriver from the layby they found Siobhan's missing jacket. Local members of the Detective Branch interviewed the boyfriend of Siobhan's friend at St George's Terrace. They also interviewed the girl, of course. They found that the boyfriend owned a car of the make that the light fitting found in the layby came from. They noted that his car had a new light fitted. He said that he knew Siobhan through his girl-friend, and they decided to ask him to come to Carrick-on-Shannon Garda Station for an interview, and to take a statement from him. He agreed, and came with no problem. He denied any involvement in Siobhan's murder.

Members of the Fingerprint Section had found identifiable fingermarks on the black polythene bin liner found at the layby. The young man in the station, Kevin Mary Liam O'Connor, twenty-one years old, consented to give his fingerprints. They were compared with the fingermarks found on the poly-thene bag, and it was found that he had left the marks on the bag. O'Connor, who came voluntarily to the Garda Station, was now the prime suspect for

Siobhan's murder. It was necessary to have him arrested and detained, for the proper investigation of the crime.

At the time, according to the Criminal Justice Act of 1984, a person could be detained in custody for the investigation of a crime, if he was brought in custody to a Garda Station. O'Connor had not been brought in custody to a Garda Station, and so he could not be detained there. If he were detained, any statement he might make would be inadmissible at a subsequent trial. O'Connor was told that he could leave the Station, and he left. When he was fifty yards down the street, he was stopped and arrested, on suspicion of the murder of Siobhan, and brought in custody back to the Garda Station. That part of the 1984 Act has now been changed, and it is now in order to arrest someone in the Garda Station and detain them there.

O'Connor was again interviewed, by Detective Garda Bernie Hanley and I. We told him that his fingerprints had been found on the polythene bag, and that we believed a light fitting found in the layby had come from his car. We asked him to tell us the truth about Siobhan. He asked if he could talk to his girlfriend first, to tell her what he had done. We asked him to tell us now, while somebody went to get his girlfriend. He admitted to us that he had killed Siobhan.

He made a written statement, saying that at about 9pm on Sunday night, 10 November, he saw Siobhan walking home alone on the outskirts of the town. He stopped and spoke to her, and she sat into his car. On some pretext he got her to come to her friend's flat. He knew his girlfriend would not be there. On arrival at the flat, he started to mess around with her, and it reached a stage where she refused to engage in activity he wished her to engage in. The activity was of course sexually oriented. She told him she was going to tell his girlfriend what he had done to her. Again, as we have encountered in the past, he sought to protect himself from complaints, and so decided to kill Siobhan.

He put his hands around her neck, and strangled her. He got a dinner plate and pushed the edge of it firmly against her throat, and held it there until he was sure she was dead. Then he got a black bin liner, and pulled it over her head. He dragged her down the stairs and put her into the boot of his car. Then he tidied up the flat, and drove to his home on the outskirts of Leitrim village, about four miles away. He collected his mother and somebody else, and drove them back to Carrick-on-Shannon to bingo, with Siobhan's body still in the boot.

While they were at bingo, he drove to the layby at Clonart South, with the intention of throwing Siobhan's body into the River Finn. He took her body out of the boot, and was in the act of getting it over the wall and into the river, when a car came along the roadway. He let the body go and it fell onto the layby beside the wall. He left it there, returned to Carrick-on-Shannon to collect his mother and passengers, and drove them home to Leitrim village.

He then went to his girlfriend's flat. He invited her to Longford town to attend a dance. She agreed, and they travelled the route he had travelled earlier in the night with Siobhan's body, and passed by the layby. On arrival in Longford, he said it was now too late to go in, and they sat outside the dance hall. This was some time after midnight. They drove back to Carrick-on-Shannon, again passing the layby. The next day, his mother passed a remark to him, about the rear light fitting missing from his car. He drove to Roscommon town, to the main dealers of the car he was driving, and got a new light fitted.

O'Connor spoke to other Gardaí in Carrick-on-Shannon after he had made this statement, and made more admissions to them. O'Connor spoke to his girlfriend, again in the presence of Gardaí, and told her that he had killed Siobhan. He said he wanted to tell her himself; he didn't want her to hear it from somebody else.

Kevin Mary Liam O'Connor appeared before a special sitting of Carrick-on-Shannon District Court, presided over by Mr Justice Bernard Brennan, on 17 November, and was remanded in custody to Charlestown District Court until the following Wednesday, 22 November.

O'Connor's trial for the murder of Siobhan Brennan opened at the Central Criminal Court in Dublin on 22 June 1992, presided over by Mr Justice Paul Kearney. O'Connor replied, 'Yes,' when asked by the Court registrar if he was Kevin O'Connor, and he replied, 'Guilty,' when the murder charge was read out to him. He was sentenced to imprisonment for life. The whole proceedings were over in two or three minutes, but the pain and suffering of the parents, brother, sister, relations and friends will linger on for years.

FATHER PATRICK RYAN, 1992

This case is somewhat connected to two other very serious crimes, which received national media headlines in 1975 and in 1992. On 3 October 1975, Dr Tiede Herrema, Chief Executive of the Ferenka factory in Limerick, was on his way to work when he was abducted by a number of people. He was kept in different locations, and eventually arrived at a house in Monasterevin with two of his captors, Eddie Gallagher and Marian Coyle. He was there a short time when Gardaí discovered the location. Gardaí went to the house at daybreak one morning and a siege took place, which lasted seventeen days.

I was a member of one of the first groups of Gardaí that went to the house. I spent a part of each of the next seventeen days in the hallway of that house. I was not there when the siege came to an end. I recall I was at home getting ready to go to Monasterevin, when a newsflash on television stated that the siege was over.

In January 1992, I went to Waterford with other members of the Investigation Section, to assist local Gardaí in a major investigation. The AIB cash pool in Waterford had been robbed by a number of hooded and armed men, who took £2.5 million in cash. The night before the robbery, two of the culprits had bored a hole in the flat concrete roof and gained access to the building. They hid inside the suspended ceiling of the one-storey building, in the cash pool area. The staff had no access to this area above the ceiling. The raiders remained there until the afternoon.

That afternoon, a stolen Hiace van drove into the yard of the premises. There were four men in the van, all armed and hooded. When they arrived, the other two culprits came down through the ceiling, also hooded and armed. They loaded the cash into the van, fired some shots and drove away.

As they made their escape, some miles from Waterford, they came to a Garda checkpoint. They drove through, firing shots at the unarmed Gardaí. They drove to a disused quarry at Glenmore, near Mullinavat in County Kilkenny, where they abandoned the van. They left in two stolen cars that they had parked there. One car had been stolen in Dublin city, the other in Dublin Airport. No one was ever charged in relation to the robbery.

It got great publicity for quite a while, and the media consistently attributed the robbery to the Provisional IRA. Knowing what I knew then, and what I know now, that is not my belief. During the course of the investigation, it was discovered that the van was stolen in Monasterevin a few days before the crime. The owner was a small building contractor, who was working in Dublin during that time. He used the van every day, going up and down to Dublin. One evening, it was parked outside his house, and he had a visitor.

The owner of the van was PJ Bailey. Bailey was connected to the kidnapping of Dr Tiede Herrema. When Herrema was kidnapped, he was brought to a few different locations, and was eventually picked up in a car by PJ Bailey. He picked up Dr Herrema, Eddie Gallagher and Marian Coyle, and brought them to his brother-in-law's house at St Evan's Park, Monasterevin. For his part in the kidnapping, he was sentenced to five years' imprisonment.

His visitor that night in 1992 was Father Patrick Ryan. Born in Tipperary in 1930, Father Ryan was a member of the Palatine order, ordained in 1954. He spent ten or eleven years in Africa, then went to the United States for a number of years, and eventually, around 1970, found his way to a parish in London.

He brought himself under notice there, and it is alleged that in the early 1970s, he had evolved into an Irish republican activist, and become the Quartermaster of the Provisional IRA, an allegation which he has denied. In 1972, one of his functions was collecting funds for missionary work in Africa. His superiors noticed that, for all the hard work he was doing, he was sending less and less money to the missions. They challenged him on this, and he openly said that he was sending the money to a more worthy cause, the republican movement in Ireland. He refused to stop doing this, and was given leave of absence for six months, and suspended from his normal duties for two years.

In the following years, he is alleged to have travelled throughout Europe collecting funds for the Provisional IRA. He admitted to collecting funds, but said it was for the nationalist community in want, and denied that he ever raised funds to buy arms or anything like that.

When Bailey was leaving for work the morning after his visit from Father Ryan, he discovered that his van was gone. He immediately contacted the Gardaí in Monasterevin.

When members investigating the crime in Waterford discovered that Father Ryan had been in Bailey's house the night the van was stolen, he immediately became a person of interest. Father Ryan was sought for interview, and it was eventually established that he had a room in a farmhouse in County Tipperary.

I went to that house with a number of Gardaí, including Detective Gardaí Bernie Hanley and Tom Byrne. The house was owned and occupied by an elderly lady. Also living there was her married daughter and the daughter's husband.

Father Ryan was not there, but we saw a caravan, and we were told that Father Ryan had brought it there. When he arrived with the caravan late at night, he did not have a key – he had to get in and out through the window. We took particulars of the caravan, and we left.

We discovered that a caravan of the same description had been stolen from Rooskey in County Roscommon on 30 March. It was the property of John Bidwell, an electrical contractor from England, working at a hotel renovation. He had brought his caravan from England to live in while he was here. He went back to England on a weekend off, and when he returned his caravan and everything in it was gone. He put a value on it of £10,000.

I returned to the farmhouse with a number of Gardaí, in possession of a warrant to search the house and outbuildings. John Bidwell was with us, to identify his caravan and property. When we arrived, however, the caravan was no longer there. We searched the house and the outbuildings, and found an amount of stolen property, particularly property of Mr Bidwell that had been in the caravan – clothing, a microwave, bedding and a great lot of items. A great lot of other property was found, including a lot of expensive tools from a van that had been stolen in Dublin a day or so before the caravan was stolen.

Somebody in Rooskey had since seen the caravan, being towed by a Hiace van. The van was eventually found abandoned, between Cahir and Cashel. Also found at the farmhouse were some rounds of ammunition in a small box, in good condition. Items were found belonging to about four or five different injured parties. Most of the property had been stolen in Dublin, from different locations and at different times.

The elderly lady came from an old republican family. After the search, her daughter was arrested. Father Ryan was there during the search. He took out his mobile phone and rang a number of people, and as it turned out some of them were local media people. He told them that the Gardaí were there, and that he was being harassed, and continuously watched wherever he went. The lady arrested was brought to Clonmel Garda Station. She was not too long in the Station when she put her hand in her pocket, took out £10,000 and handed it to the Gardaí. She said that Father Ryan had asked her to mind it for him when the Gardaí arrived. That lady was very helpful, and told us what we wanted to know in relation to the caravan and other matters, and she was released.

The £10,000 was folded in a particular way, in bundles of £500. It was brought to the cash pool in Waterford, shown to the staff and they examined the way it was folded. They said that the cash stolen from them would not have been folded in that particular manner. We could not prove where the money came from.

Some time during the search, Father Ryan left, but some days later he was arrested under Section 30 of the Offences Against the State Act, suspected to be in possession of the ammunition that was found. He was brought to Clonmel Garda Station and questioned, but he refused to discuss anything about the caravan or the articles found in his bedroom in the house. He also denied knowing anything about the robbery in Waterford. He was released without charge.

A file on the stolen caravan and all the other stolen items was prepared for the DPP, together with statements from the daughter of the elderly lady, and the son-in-law. That file contained a recommendation that Father Ryan be charged with offences relating to the stolen property, and that the trial be before the Special Criminal Court. The file was returned in due course, saying that there were potential witness difficulties in the case against Father Ryan. A setback, but we were not finished yet.

I went to Clonmel to discuss the matter with the local Superintendent and the local Sergeant. The local Sergeant was on good terms with the household, and he went to them. The daughter and the son-in-law said they were prepared to go to Court and give evidence. The elderly lady was not in a good enough state of health to travel to Dublin for trial. The family was very annoyed with

Father Ryan when they discovered that he had brought stolen property to their home, and they had since told him to leave. The willingness of the two witnesses to give evidence was reported to the DPP, and the DPP directed that Father Ryan be charged with five charges, in relation to receiving the caravan, the tools and other items, and that he be brought before the Special Criminal Court. The caravan was never recovered.

On 26 August 1993, I arrested Father Ryan, in a car park in Parnell Street in Dublin. He appeared before the Special Criminal Court on 27 August, presided over by Mr Justice Liam Hamilton. Justice Hamilton asked the State Solicitor on what basis did the DPP feel that the charges should be brought before the Special Criminal Court, and not the District Court or Circuit Court. The State Solicitor agreed that it was hard to fathom the basis on which the Director certified that these Courts were inadequate. I certainly cannot second-guess the DPP's thinking. Father Ryan was remanded on his own bail.

His trial took place at the Special Criminal Court in April 1994, presided over by Mr Justice Frederick Morris. All prosecution witnesses gave evidence in accordance with the statements they had made to the Gardaí, including the householder's daughter and son-in-law. At the conclusion of the prosecution's case, counsel for the defence, Patrick Gageby, said that the defence was not going into evidence. There was insufficient evidence to prove beyond a reasonable doubt that his client handled the property, or knew it had been stolen. Father Ryan was convicted on four of the five charges, while the fifth charge was withdrawn.

The Judge heard that Father Ryan had handed over £10,000 to an occupant of the house to mind for him when the Gardaí arrived. As the caravan, valued at £10,000, was never recovered, he ordered Father Ryan to compensate the caravan owner, Mr Bidwell, for his loss. The £10,000 in possession of the Gardaí was handed over to Mr Bidwell. Sentencing was adjourned until 21 June.

On 21 June, Justice Morris told Father Ryan, 'The court sees no reason to deal with you any differently than any other convicted person by reason of calling or vocation.' He sentenced Father Ryan to three years' imprisonment, which was suspended, and Father Ryan undertook to sign a £1000 bond, binding him to the peace, and to be of good behaviour for a period of five years.

When the court convicted Father Ryan, the Palatine order had said that they did not regard him as a member of the order. It is only fair of me to say, that I do not have any reason to believe Father Ryan was involved in the AIB cash pool robbery in any way.

MURDER OF GRACE LIVINGSTONE, MALAHIDE, 1992

The murder of Mrs Grace Livingstone, at 37 The Moorings, Malahide in Dublin, on Monday, 7 December 1992, received great media attention for a long, long time. Grace Livingstone was fifty-seven years of age, and the mother of two children – Tara Anne, aged twenty-two, and Conor, aged twenty. She was murdered in her own home, between 2pm and 6pm in the afternoon. Grace Livingstone's husband, James Livingstone, was a Senior Inspector of Taxes with the Special Revenue Branch. Jim and Grace were to travel to Castleblaney, County Monaghan, that evening, to attend an anniversary Mass for Jim Livingstone's late brother, Father Peadar Livingstone. The Mass was due to commence at 8pm.

In the morning, Grace Livingstone was first up, and got breakfast for her husband and son. Jim and herself discussed the trip to Castleblaney that evening. He said he would be home early, and they decided they would have something to eat, and be ready to leave around 6pm to travel to Castleblaney. Jim Livingstone left home at 8.25am and drove to work, taking his son Connor with him.

Grace Livingstone would be alone in the house all day. She went to 9am Mass in Malahide, and afterwards went shopping to her local supermarket. She came home again, and her neighbour at number 38, Garda Bernard Owens, spoke to her in her driveway at 11.45am. Anne Watchorn, a nurse living across the road, spoke to Grace Livingstone in the porch of Mrs Livingstone's house for fifteen or twenty minutes, and left at 2.10pm. That was the last known sighting of Grace alive.

Having left home, Jim Livingstone picked up a work colleague, Art O'Connor. They dropped off Conor in O'Connell Street, then continued on to their base at Setanta House in Nassau Street in Dublin city. Jim Livingstone remained in the city in his office all day. At 5pm, himself and Art O'Connor left the car park at Setanta House, and drove straight to O'Connor's home, at Charlesfort Avenue in Malahide.

Late on the night of 7 December, Art O'Connor was interviewed by Gardaí. He was asked what time Jim Livingstone had dropped him off at his home. Mr O'Connor estimated that he was home around 5.50pm. Jim Livingstone said that he arrived home having dropped off Art O'Connor, and he put the time at about 5.50pm. The driving time from O'Connor's to the Livingstones' is only about five or six minutes.

Livingstone said that he entered his house by the front door, using his key. He entered the kitchen, and the light was off. Now this was wintertime, approaching 6pm, so it was dark outside. The light was off and there was no sign of any cooking, where he had expected there would be a meal ready. His wife was nowhere downstairs, so he went up the stairs. On the landing, he saw his .22 rifle leaning against a door jamb.

He entered the main bedroom, the light was off and he saw his wife lying on the bed. He thought she had become ill and vomited on the bed. He put on the light in the bedroom and then discovered it was blood on the bed, not vomit.

Grace was lying on her stomach in the centre of the bed, her head facing the top of the bed, and her feet protruding over the end of the bed. Her hands were bound behind her back with black insulating tape, about two inches wide. Her ankles were tied together with the same type of material, and the same type of material was bound around her mouth. She had a serious head injury, and there was a lot of blood around her head.

Jim Livingstone said that when he realised the seriousness of the situation, he rushed across the road to a neighbour and friend, Anne Watchorn, whom he knew to be a nurse. He rang the doorbell and got no response. Mrs Watchorn was actually at home, but happened to be out in the garden at that time. Jim Livingstone did not delay at the door. He went next door to a Mrs Margaret Murphy, who he also knew to be a nurse. He rang the doorbell and Cathal, Mrs Murphy's son, came to the door. Jim Livingstone told him to tell his mother to come over urgently to his home, and then he walked away. Mrs Murphy got the message straight away and immediately went across the road to the Livingstones'.

When she went into the house, Jim Livingstone was on the phone in the hallway, and she heard him say that there had been a terrible accident. She took it he was on the phone looking for an ambulance. Jim Livingstone did telephone for an ambulance. He got through to Tara Street Fire Station, and spoke to a fireman there named John Keogh. He requested an ambulance be sent to his home. He said when he came home there was a woman battered or injured. That 999 call was received at 5.58pm.

Mrs Murphy went into the main bedroom upstairs, and saw the deceased lying on the bed, bound as I have described. She felt for a pulse, and found none. She told Mr Livingstone she had got a slight pulse, just to comfort him somewhat. She said the blood had started to congeal, and the bleeding seemed to have stopped. She noticed the body was still quite warm, and the bedroom was quite warm.

The fireman John Keogh telephoned Garda control and gave them the information he had got from Mr Livingstone. Garda Control telephoned Malahide Garda Station and relayed the message. The Gardaí at Malahide sent Detective Garda Frank Gunne and Garda Catherine Moran to Livingstone's house. Before they arrived, Mr Livingstone himself contacted Malahide Garda Station to report what he had found on his return home. He was told that the Gardaí were on their way.

Frank Gunne and Catherine Moran arrived at the Livingstones' house at 6.15pm. On their arrival, Reverend Father John Keegan was entering the house, and he administered the last rites to the deceased. They had a conversation with Mr Livingstone, and he told them what he had found when he arrived home. He told Frank Gunne that one of his shotguns was missing out of his wardrobe in the bedroom. Detective Garda Gunne asked Mrs Murphy, who was still in the house, to contact Dr Barry Moodley, the Livingstones' family doctor.

Dr Moodley arrived at 6.35pm, and pronounced Grace's death. He saw what appeared to be a gunshot wound at the base of the skull. He noticed a lot of blood on the bed, some of which had clotted. He found the body to be slightly warm. Detective Garda Gunne asked him how long he thought Mrs Livingstone was dead. He made a professional estimation, that Mrs Livingstone was dead for approximately two hours.

Mr Livingstone asked Detective Garda Gunne and the others who were there if they got the smell of a discharged firearm in the bedroom. He said he didn't get it. Detective Garda Gunne and Garda Moran did not get it either. Mr Livingstone asked Detective Garda Gunne to check his bedside locker, to see if there was a .45 revolver there, in a leather holder, with twelve rounds of ammunition. The Gardaí checked, and found that the revolver and ammunition were still there. This weapon turned out to be unlawfully held by Mr Livingstone.

Garda Moran, accompanied by Mr Livingstone, looked around and checked all the windows and doors downstairs, to see if there were signs of a forced entry, and there were not. They looked upstairs, and found the window in Conor's bedroom open – not forced, just open. The scene was preserved from the time Detective Garda Frank Gunne and Garda Catherine Moran arrived, and everybody coming to the scene after that had a note taken of their name and the time of arrival.

The Moorings is an estate off the road from Malahide to Portmarnock, about half a mile from Malahide. The Livingstones resided there, on a cul-de-sac with about nine or ten houses on each side of the road. Their house was number 37, about halfway down on the left-hand side. The driveway into the house is not more than the length of two cars parked bumper-to-bumper. The houses are well below the level of the road and the footpaths. There is a steep drop of about three or four feet from the footpath down to the houses. The driveway is on the left-hand side of the house, and it stops at what was once a garage, converted into a room by the Livingstones. To the right of this room is a glass-fronted porch, and inside the porch is the door into the Livingstones' house.

Jim Livingstone that night accompanied the Gardaí voluntarily to Malahide Garda Station, where he was questioned by two members of the Detective Branch. He was there until the early hours of the morning. He made a long statement, detailing the events of that day and what he found when he came home that evening. He left the Garda Station and went to stay with neighbours that night. Gardaí had possession of the house for the next five days, and they carried out meticulous searches of the house, the garden and the surrounding area.

Around 8.30pm on the day of the murder, members of the Garda Technical Bureau arrived at the Livingstones' house to carry out a technical examination. Detective Sergeant Brendan McArdle of the Ballistics Section, Detective

Garda Myles Fitzgerald of the Fingerprint Section and Detective Garda Peter O'Connor of the Photographic Section were later joined by Detective Garda Eamon Murphy from the Mapping Section. Forensic scientist Dr Maureen Smith also visited the scene, and the State Pathologist Dr John Harbison arrived at 11.30pm.

On the same night, Gardaí interviewed Ena Brennan, a seventeen-year-old girl. She lived four or five doors away from Mrs Livingstone on the cul-de-sac, and on the same side of the road. She made a statement that night, telling Gardaí she was walking home from school at about 4.30pm that day, and had been talking to a number of school pals at the entrance to the cul-de-sac. She left them and walked down the cul-de-sac, towards home. She would pass the Livingstones' house on her way home. But before she left the girls, she and the rest of them saw a young man walking up the hill towards them, from the direction of a pedestrian entrance to the Malahide–Portmarnock Road. That would be maybe 200 yards from them. There was another row of houses behind the Livingstones', and he could have been coming from those houses. Anyway he came up the road and passed within ten feet of them, turned to his left and entered the cul-de-sac, walking slowly with his head down.

Ena Brennan said the strange young man walked down the cul-de-sac towards the Livingstones' home and her own house, which was beyond the Livingstones'. She described him as about six feet tall, with mousey-coloured hair, thick and collar-length with a longish fringe, with a long, beige mack coat and black boots. In a subsequent statement, she said he was about twenty years of age. She said, 'I walked by him on the road, and he was outside number 41, 40 or 39 when I passed him.' From where the girls were, as you walk down the cul-de-sac, on the left-hand side, the houses decrease in number – 41, 40, 39, 38 and then the Livingstones' is 37. This young man was never located. Who was he? No one knows only himself.

Another one of the girls – Hillary Maguire, seventeen, who lived not too far away – said she was at the corner of the cul-de-sac for a chat with the other girls, and she saw a man, about nineteen years of age, heading into Ena Brennan's road, where the Livingstones also lived. She said he was about ten feet away from her, was about six feet tall, with a fawn trench coat which went below his knees. She said he had blond hair, parted in the middle, a thin build and was average enough looking. The other girls said much the same thing.

On the same night, when Mr Livingstone went to Malahide Garda Station, he handed over to the Gardaí the clothing that he was wearing all day. He took them off and they were put into evidence bags and sealed, and delivered to the Forensic Laboratory for examination. Examination of them proved negative for firearms residue or bloodstaining.

On the morning of 8 December, Philip McGivney of Swords, a landscape gardener, thirty-six years of age, called to the Gardaí at the Livingstones' home. Later that morning, he made a statement to the Gardaí. He said that on 7 December, he was working at number 27 The Moorings, the opposite side of the road and a house or two to the right as you come out of the Livingstones' driveway. His van was parked outside number 27. He stopped work when it got dark – his watch was not working, so he did not know the time, but it was dark. He got into his van, which was facing into the cul-de-sac, and moved forward, intending to turn at the bottom of the cul-de-sac. There were young lads playing football on the road, so he turned at the driveway of a house on his left, before he reached the young lads.

He identified the Livingstones' driveway as the one he had turned in the previous evening. He said he turned the front of the van into the driveway, and with the headlights of the van he could clearly see a young man in the porch of the Livingstones' house. He was bending down and picking up a potted plant, which he took to be a yucca plant. There was a yucca plant in the Livingstones' porch. The man was about twenty, or early twenties, average height, with dark, collar-length hair and a thin build. The glass porch door was closed, but the door from the porch into the hallway was open. He saw the man walk from the porch, through the hall door and into the house. He said he was sure there was no car in the driveway, because he could clearly see the driveway and the front door. When he went home, he said he looked at the clock, and he reckons he would have left The Moorings at 4.40pm.

Jim Livingstone's next-door neighbour, at number 36, said she was upstairs in her bedroom, to the front of the house, and at 4.20 to 4.30pm, she heard a loud noise, which sounded to her like an empty oil tank being dropped on the ground, or someone hitting an empty oil tank. She said the sound came from the direction of the Livingstones' house. The distance between their houses, like all the houses on that road, is no more than eight or ten yards. There is no driveway between them, just a hedge.

Another lady, who lives across the road from the Livingstones at number 30, made a statement on 8 December. She was out of her house between 2.30 and 4pm, but she was in the front room of her house from 1.40 to 2.30pm, and again from 4pm onwards. She heard a loud noise outside, coming from the direction of number 29, her neighbour on the right as you go in to her house. The noise was loud enough for her to tell her daughter to keep away from the window. She said it was not dark at the time, and thought it may have been prior to 2.30pm that she heard the noise. Her house is across the road from the Livingstones', four or five houses to the left as one comes out of the Livingstones'.

Margaret O'Sullivan of Sea Park, a road that runs parallel to The Moorings, said that on the afternoon of 7 December, she was at home watching 'Emmerdale Farm' on television, which finished at 4.30pm. She said some time after that, she was in the back garden, checking clothes on the clothesline. She heard a noise, which to her sounded like a banger, and remembered being a bit annoyed that there were still bangers around, so long after Halloween. She said the noise came from the direction of The Moorings. Now, she was out in the open, in the garden. Across the road from the Livingstones live Mrs Watchorn and Mrs Murphy. Their back gardens adjoin Mrs Sullivan's back garden – their houses are back-to-back. She puts the time of hearing that noise at shortly after 4.30pm.

In mid-January, a man contacted the incident room at Malahide Garda Station, and subsequently came to the Station and made a written statement, outlining his observations on the evening of the murder. He said between 4pm and 5pm, he was driving from the city towards Malahide. He came to the left turn that takes you on to the Swords to Malahide road at around 4.05pm. He intended to take the left turn, when a car turned right directly in front of him onto that road. The car was being driven in an erratic manner, and the driver was deranged-looking.

He followed this car, as it was going in his direction anyway. When it came to the roundabout at Swords, instead of turning left and going around the roundabout, it took the short cut, turning right onto the Balbriggan Road. He followed that car nearly to Balbriggan. It was a small, old, red car, an Opel Cadet or a Fiat, and not in great condition. He took a mental note of the number plate, and he told Gardaí the number he remembered. The number he gave turned out either to be a false number, or incorrectly remembered. But that car and driver were never located. It was coming out of Malahide at a crucial time, and the driver's behaviour was so erratic that this man decided to follow him. He described the driver of the car as about thirty or thirty-five, with thick, black hair down to his collar and halfway down his head. He kept turning his head from side to side in a disturbed fashion. He was gibbering and grinning.

Another man who made a statement to Gardaí said he parked his car, some time after 5pm, in the car park on the side of the Malahide to Portmarnock road, beside the sea opposite The Moorings. This is nearly across the road from the pedestrian entrance, near to where the girls saw a man walking up the hill towards them. He said that he saw a young man come running, over the fence into the car park, and up into the top corner of the car park. He got into a small, red car that was parked there. He drove away at speed, going through potholes as if he had no respect for his car. On leaving the car park, the car turned right towards Malahide, less than half a mile away. If this car carried on straight through Malahide, it could possibly be the car that was seen driving erratically into the Swords to Malahide road, and went the wrong way around the roundabout. The description he gave of the car and the driver was much the same as the other man had given.

He had telephoned the Gardaí with this information, and the task of interviewing him was given to a Detective Sergeant. This Detective Sergeant knew this man and had some dealings with him previously, and was of the view that he was unreliable. He did not go to see him, but merely spoke to him on the phone. Maybe he was very unreliable; maybe he was telling lies; but the case that the Detective Sergeant was investigating was very, very serious. However, this man will turn up again later on.

Detective Garda Myles Fitzgerald of the Fingerprint Section arrived at the scene around 8.30pm. He took possession of the tape that was used by the culprit to bind the deceased's hands, ankles and mouth. There were fingermarks on it. All persons known to have been in the house that night, including Jim Livingstone, were fingerprinted. Some marks remain unidentified on that tape. At least one of them is an identifiable fingermark, and it is still unidentified. This mark was found about fourteen inches from one end of the tape, on the adhesive side of it. It was obvious that the insulating tape was new, and had not previously been used. No similar tape was found in the Livingstones' house, or on any object therein – on electrical fittings or whatever. A search for the remainder of that tape, the reel and the core, was carried out in the house and the garden, and surrounding areas. There was no sign of it. Detective Garda Myles Fitzgerald, on taking the tape into his possession, put it into a box and treated it with great care, and no other person had access to it.

Now we come to the time of death of Grace Livingstone. The actual time of death, if known, would have been a great help in this investigation. The actual time of death cannot be definitively established by examination of a body in any case. All that can be established is the approximate time of death. Dr Moodley was at the scene at 6.35pm, and his professional opinion was that Grace Livingstone had died about two hours previously. The blood was partially congealed, the body was still partially warm, and he formed that opinion. Dr John Harbison came to the house at 11.30pm, and was told that the body had been quite warm at 6pm. Some time around 12.30am, he started taking the temperature of the body. He took it a number of times through the next hour and a half or so, and came to the conclusion that Mrs Livingstone had died at 6pm or thereabouts.

On the bed where the deceased was found lying, there were six pillows. Two of the pillows, according to Mr Livingstone, were a particular blue colour, belonging to Conor's room, and were missing from his bed. How or why they got from Conor's room into his parents' room, no one knows. Perhaps Mrs Livingstone brought them in herself. One pillow is of some significance, as there was a lot of firearms residue on it. It was suggested by those investigating the case that the culprit held the pillow over the gun to deaden the sound. Two Detective Sergeants from the Ballistics Section and I could not agree with this – if the pillow was anywhere near, or certainly in front of, the muzzle, the material would be damaged, part of it would be blown away. There were no burn marks on the pillow, and no damage to the material; the only damage was staining from the firearms residue. The Ballistics men spent a long time thinking about this, and we agreed that the most likely thing was that immediately after the gun was discharged, it was thrown down on the bed, and the muzzle was in contact with the pillow. There would be no danger of it being damaged or burnt in a scenario like that.

Jim Livingstone had said that a shotgun was missing from his bedroom, and that shotgun was found later on the night of 7 December, in a hedge on the Livingstones' front lawn. It was handed over to Garda Myles Fitzgerald, the fingerprint man.

When I was in Garda Headquarters, prior to being called into this case, there was a conference every Tuesday morning in Assistant Commissioner Ned O'Dea's office with members from Crime Branch. Happenings from the previous week would be discussed. I remember the Livingstone case coming up a number of times. I wasn't there every Tuesday, as I could be around the country anywhere. But if I was in Headquarters on a Tuesday morning, I would attend the conference. Chief Superintendent Brendan Burns would update the Commissioner, and he would be in touch with various cases around the country, seeing how they were going. When this case was discussed, it always centred around Mr Livingstone himself – he was always the main suspect.

When Jim Livingstone's house was searched, a number of guns were found. He had eight in total – three shotguns, two .22 rifles, one .45 Weber revolver, one .177 air pistol and one .77 rifle. The three shotguns were licensed, as was one of the rifles. Jim Livingstone's father had been in the RIC, and when he retired he set up a jeweller's shop, and also became a firearms dealer in Castleblaney, County Monaghan. Jim Livingstone became very interested in guns as a result of his father's occupation. He also joined the FCA, where he became a Commandant. At least two of the firearms in the house were found to be incapable of discharging a shot.

At 7.40am on 3 March 1993, Jim Livingstone was arrested at his home by a Detective Sergeant from Coolock, under Section 30 of the Offences Against the State Act, for possession of a firearm on 7 December 1992, with intent to endanger life. He was brought to Swords Garda Station, and detained for questioning. As Livingstone left his home in handcuffs, television cameras were waiting to record the event. The arrest was screened on television news during the day. Livingstone was released from custody without charge at midnight on 4 March.

Livingstone himself nominated a number of persons as suspects, whom he had dealings with in the course of his work. There were known drug dealers, racketeers and persons with IRA connections. He believed that someone he had dealt with was responsible for his wife's murder. These people were investigated, and some were questioned, but nothing came to light as a result.

On 25 August 1993, the complete file of the investigation was given to Chief Superintendent Pat Culhane. A copy of the file was sent to Crime Branch at Garda Headquarters, and eventually reached Deputy Commissioner Tom O'Reilly.

The murder of Grace Livingstone continued to receive extensive media coverage. A lot of the coverage expressed views that in my opinion were becoming slanted in a particular direction. The language used was ambiguous and adverse to Jim Livingstone's interest. Investigators spent a lot of time at Setanta House, interviewing Jim Livingstone's work colleagues. They searched lockers and presses that he had access to. His work colleagues began to shun him, many clearly holding the view that he was responsible for his wife's death. The Revenue Commissioners became uneasy about his position and situation, and the feeling went right to the top of the department. Some of the members of the first investigation team were, in my view, not very discreet about where they expressed their views about the case.

Deputy Commissioner Tom O'Reilly contacted me through his clerk, and I was instructed to go to his office. When I went there he said, with a big smile on his face, 'I have a nice job for you.' The smile of course meant that it was not a nice job, and that was exactly how it turned out. He discussed the Livingstone case with me, and expressed his reservations about the investigation and its findings. He instructed me to carry out a review of the investigation, and come back to him with my views. That was in late August 1993.

I contacted Chief Superintendent Pat Culhane – the same Pat that was with me when we questioned Peter Pringle in Galway. Anyway, I informed him of my instructions, and we met in his office in Whitehall. A Detective Superintendent from the Division was also present, who had been a member in charge of running the investigation. We discussed the case at length, and the Detective Superintendent left me in no doubt that he believed Jim Livingstone was responsible for his wife's death. The Chief, Pat Culhane, gave his opinion, which was essentially in agreement with the Detective Superintendent, but not nearly as forceful or dogmatic. I was promised all the cooperation I needed, and the investigation file and all other documentation was handed over to me at Malahide Garda Station.

The review was carried out from Malahide Station, and I was accompanied by Detective Sergeant Tom O'Loughlin, Detective Garda Barney Hanley from the Investigation Section for some short time, and other members from the Coolock District on and off. I had another meeting with Pat Culhane, accompanied by Detective Sergeant Tom O'Loughlin. By this stage, I had read the complete file, and gone through all the documentation relating to the case.

I had found, to my amazement really, that questionnaires were not carried out in the immediate vicinity of the crime, as would normally be carried out, as outlined in the Garda manual of investigation technique. Only a few people in the cul-de-sac where the crime took place were interviewed, where standard practice was that everybody in the area that afternoon should have been recorded and located. Where they were, who they met, what they saw, what they heard or recalled.

During the review, we located many people from the cul-de-sac who had not been spoken to by the Gardaí. One man who was two or three houses away from the Livingstones' that afternoon was never spoken to, and we located him in Galway. He was of no help, but he should have been included in the initial enquiries. We took his fingerprints just in case. Then there was the man who reported the erratic driver, and of course what the landscape gardener saw.

I met the Detective Superintendent from the first investigation, who was continually telling me that Jim Livingstone was the culprit. I put several facts to him, that he had available during his investigation. The loud noise that was heard by the ladies at approximately 4.40pm: He said, we are near the sea here, and occasionally you hear loud booming sounds coming from the sea. The fingermark on the tape: He said, someone in the Fingerprint Section at Garda Headquarters must have picked it up to look at it, and left their mark on it. The man seen by the landscape gardener in the porch of the Livingstones' house, between 4 and 5pm on the evening of the murder: He said, that man made a mistake, the person he saw was Mrs Livingstone. The young man seen by a group of school children at approximately 4.30pm: He said, we couldn't find him; he could be anybody from around the locality.

I put it to him that nobody in the locality reported hearing a shot, or a loud noise, at around 6pm. He said, Livingstone used a pillow, to put over the gun and deaden the sound. We discussed the absence of firearms residue on Jim Livingstone's clothing. He said that the clothing was in bags in the Forensic Science Laboratory for a few days, and when they came to examine it it was too late; it had faded away. I checked this with the Forensic Science Laboratory, with the individual who examined the clothing, and they completely discounted that notion.

I asked the Detective Superintendent to outline to me the reason he suspected Mr Livingstone. He outlined an amount of little instances and remarks made by Livingstone on the night of the crime. I told him I did not believe that any one of them, or all of them collectively, should be any reason whatsoever to suspect Livingstone. I asked him why questionnaires were not carried out in an appropriate manner. He told me that what happened in Livingstone's house happened after Livingstone returned home. He told me in no uncertain manner to go back to Garda Headquarters, that they were well able to investigate their own crimes there. The meeting came to a very acrimonious ending.

Detective Sergeant Tom O'Loughlin and I met with Dr Moodley one evening in his surgery, and discussed the time of death of Grace Livingstone. He said he had had several discussions with the State Pathologist, Dr Harbison, on this matter. He said he was aware of Dr Harbison's opinion, but it was his professional opinion that Mrs Livingstone had been dead for approximately two hours when he saw her body in her home at 6.35pm.

I discussed the matter with Dr Harbison. I reminded him of his opinion, which was 6pm or thereabouts, while Dr Moodley was saying time of death was approximately 4.30pm. His reply was, 'I could not argue with Dr Moodley's opinion.' When Reverend Father John Keegan saw the body of the deceased at 6.15pm, he also had the impression that she had been dead for some time.

Jim Livingstone remarked to persons in the bedroom on the night of the murder about the absence of the smell one gets after a firearm has been discharged. I asked Nurse Murphy, Detective Garda Frank Gunne, Garda Catherine Moran and Dr Moodley whether they got the smell when they were there. They all said they did not. To establish the significance, or evidential value, of the absence of the smell of a discharged firearm in the bedroom, I organised a test in the bedroom. The same shotgun that was used to kill Grace Livingstone was discharged in the bedroom. This test was also designed to establish whether the people who had heard a noise on the afternoon of the murder could hear the noise created by the shotgun being fired in the bedroom. It would also establish what firearm residue would be found on a person's clothing after discharging this weapon.

We performed two tests. Test one was carried out at 4.30pm one afternoon, with the persons who heard the noise on 7 December in exactly the same locations as they were on that afternoon. It happened that a near gale was blowing, and the trees in the immediate vicinity of the house created so much noise that the shot was not heard by any of the four neighbours.

Ten minutes after the discharge of the shot, I brought Nurse Murphy to the bedroom of the deceased. On entering the room, she said she could get a strong smell, which was not there when she entered the bedroom on the evening of 7 December. Twenty minutes after the discharge of the shot, Garda Catherine Moran entered the bedroom, and twenty-five minutes after the discharge, Detective Garda Frank Gunne entered the bedroom. Both members, independently of each other, said they got the strong smell of the discharged firearm on the landing and bedroom, which had not been there on the evening of the murder.

Both members returned to the house for a further test. An hour and a half after the discharge, they each returned to the bedroom alone. Garda Catherine Moran could still get the smell. Detective Garda Gunne, a few minutes later, got the same result. A member from the Ballistics Section who carried out the tests, and discharged the murder weapon, sent his special sterile suit that he wore for the occasion to the Forensic Science Laboratory for examination. It was found to have firearms residue on it. Another member put on special sterile sleeves over his jacket, and he went into the room five minutes after the discharge of the firearm. He remained in the room for approximately one minute. Subsequent tests on the sleeves proved positive for firearms residue. That was the first test.

A second test was carried out in the bedroom, the same as before, using the same firearm. Weather conditions were something similar to 7 December.

On this occasion, only three of the four persons who had heard a noise were available, and they were in the same positions as they had been on 7 December. All three heard the sound of the firearm being discharged, and they all said that it was similar to the noise heard by them on 7 December. A Garda from Malahide Station stood outside the door of the absent fourth person's house, and clearly heard the sound of the firearm being discharged. Jim Livingstone cooperated fully in the carrying out of both tests.

Jim Livingstone's shotgun, which was missing from the house and found in the hedge in the front lawn, was handed over to Detective Garda Myles Fitzgerald, the fingerprint expert. He examined the gun closely for fingermarks and palm marks, with negative results. He opened the gun, and discovered two cartridges in the breach. The two cartridges were the same – 12-gauge Eley cartridges, both number four. The one in the right-hand barrel had been discharged, while the one in the left-hand barrel was a live cartridge. He removed the cartridges and examined them for fingermarks, again with negative results.

Myles Fitzgerald examined the interior of the Livingstones' house, and found numerous palm marks and fingermarks. He spent quite a while, and eventually eliminated all those marks as having been made by persons with legitimate access to the house, with one exception of course – the fingermark found on the insulating tape.

Around March 1994, I reported back to Deputy Commissioner Tom O'Reilly, and informed him of how my review was going. He told me to continue, and also to endeavour to establish who was in fact responsible for the crime. Tom O'Loughlin and I decided to establish whether Jim Livingstone could in fact be eliminated completely as a suspect, so we could concentrate on other lines of enquiry.

We went through all the known facts, which I have already outlined, and in addition we considered the fact that, on Livingstone's return home that evening, he said there was no sign of cooking in the kitchen, though he and Grace had arranged that when he came home that evening, they would have a meal and leave the house around 6pm. Jim Livingstone said when he returned home, the kitchen was dark. There was dirt or dust swept into a little heap on the kitchen floor, a dustpan lying beside it and the sweeping brush not too far away, lying up against the kitchen units. It would appear that Grace was disturbed, or didn't get back to finish it.

In the report from the State Pathologist is a list of the clothing that the deceased was wearing. He itemised them as they were removed from the body. There were white shoes, somewhat worn, the soles of one of them being tacked on by three tacks at the toe; socks, one on inside out; an apron, tied rather loosely with a simple bow at the back; corduroy slacks; two cardigans; and a silk camisole. Mrs Livingstone's state of dress when found indicates to me that some time earlier in the evening she was prevented from having the meal pre-pared, and being in a more ready state of dress for the trip to Castleblaney. No matter how we looked at the question of the time of death, together with the observations by various people that evening, we could not find any credible evidence whatsoever that the deceased was alive when Jim Livingstone came home at about 5.50pm.

In the investigation file is a list of about twenty-five reasons why Jim Liv-ingstone was the main suspect up until 25 August 1993, when the file was completed. I went through each and every one of the reasons given, and came to the conclusion that, alone or collectively, they did not represent a shred of credible evidence to suggest that Livingstone had any hand, act or part in his wife's death. Having said that, of course, it was right and proper that Jim Liv-ingstone should have been a person of interest from the beginning. But after three or four days, it should have been obvious that the investigation should have concentrated on other possibilities. The file states that the investigation team were satisfied that Mr McGivney, the landscape gardener, was an honest person, and his sightings of a young man at 37 The Moorings were, in his belief, correct. However, it was the belief of the investigation team that Mr McGivney actually saw the deceased, Mrs Livingstone, in the porch on the day of the murder.

As the investigation proceeded, Jim Livingstone was the only real suspect. The man seen in the porch never made it to be classed as a suspect. The young man seen by the young girls, the driver of the car coming from Malahide and driving erratically, and the driver of the car alleged to have driven out of a car park near The Moorings that afternoon, and driven towards Malahide, also failed to be classed as suspects, and were never located.

We decided to have the crime featured in an upcoming 'Crime Line' programme, and to seek assistance from the public. That programme was shown on the night of 16 May 1994 – the crime was seventeen months old at that time. There was a reconstruction of sightings of the young man in the cul-de-sac, of the car driving erratically and other events, which I have described. The focus was particularly on the period between 4.30 and 5pm, because that is the time I believe this crime happened.

A caller contacted Gardaí in the studio that night with information. An appeal was made at the end of the programme for him to come forward, and he did so. He came to Malahide Garda Station the following morning, where Tom O'Loughlin and I spoke to him. This was the man who had contacted Malahide Garda Station some time after the crime, and said he had been in a car park 300 yards away from The Moorings, and had seen a man run to a red car, and drive out of the car park towards Malahide. A Detective Sergeant was given the task of seeing him, but considered him unreliable and didn't go to see him. He stayed with us for most of the day, and we went through everything with him, partially on account of his possibly being unreliable. At the end of the day, he gave his fingerprints voluntarily. His prints were not the prints on the tape.

Another person who saw the 'Crime Line' programme and contacted the review team was a lady from Swords. She had an encounter on an evening early in December; she could not fix the date, but it was definitely between 4 and 5pm and closer to 5pm. She knew this because there is only one key to her house, and she had it; her husband would be home from work at five o'clock, and she always had to be home to let him in. She was driving home after shopping in Woodies for Christmas decorations. She was entering the Swords roundabout from the Balbriggan direction, when a small red or orange car came from the Malahide to Swords road. She said it was an old car, and it did not go the proper way around the roundabout. It should have gone left, but it turned right, and was heading for her. She had to slam on her brakes; her car cut out and a truck behind her blew its horn. She got a fright. She said the car was the same type as her neighbour's car, a Datsun Cherry. She described the driver as youngish, with collar-length hair flopping around, and he was shaking his head from side to side. She said first of all she thought it was a woman with the hairstyle.

Another development came from the 'Crime Line' programme. A man from County Meath had contacted Ashbourne Garda Station on the evening of 8 December 1992, the evening after the murder. He had been coming out of Limerick city that morning at about 9 or 10am, and was driving to Dublin. He picked up a hitchhiker, and described him as about twenty, tall and thin, with a long coat and black boots. This description is similar to that given by the girls of the young man seen in the Livingstones' cul-de-sac, though descriptions can be notoriously wrong. This hitchhiker had an English or Scottish accent.

The driver said that when news came on the car radio of the murder of Mrs Livingstone in Malahide, this man's demeanour changed suddenly, and he got very upset. The driver became suspicious of him. The hitchhiker told him he had left Dublin that morning at 3am, and got lifts to Limerick. He said he went down there to have a look around, and was on his way back to Dublin to collect his dole money. The driver picked up little bits of personal information about him – where he was from in the UK, his occupation, and the area in Dublin where he lived. The driver got suspicious and afraid of him, and dropped him off in Roscrea, telling him he wasn't going any further for a while, because he had a number of calls to make. The driver said that this wasn't true; he just wanted to get rid of him.

On the driver's way home that evening, he called to Ashbourne Station and reported the meeting with the hitchhiker, and gave a description of him. The Ashbourne Gardaí passed this information on to the incident room at Malahide. No member of the Gardaí had contacted the driver of the car, up to the night of the 'Crime Line' programme, seventeen months after the crime. The motorist happened to see 'Crime Line' that night, and contacted the Gardaí a second time.

This time he contacted Gardaí in Kerry, where he happened to be. They took a statement from him, and sent it to the review team at Malahide. Detective Sergeant Tom O'Loughlin went to see him, and got all the information from him again, first-hand. The hitchhiker he described was considered very important, so Detective Sergeant O'Loughlin and three other members from Coolock went to the Social Welfare offices in Dublin and, with the cooperation of Social Welfare staff, they went through the records.

After quite a number of days, they found him. Without a name, they found him, and they got an address in Dublin. They went to the address, which turned out to be the young man's grandmother's home. The chap had come over from England, and was not staying with his grandmother, at the address on the social welfare system, but had stayed in a boarding house with a group of other people. When the Gardaí called after seventeen months, he had gone back to England, and had been gone quite a good while.

Police in England were contacted in the locality where he lived, and they knew of him. They interviewed him, and he was willing to talk to the Gardaí. Detective Superintendent Ted Murphy and Detective Sergeant Tom O'Loughlin went to see him. By now, I was retired, as I retired in June 1994. When they went to see him, he admitted he was the man that got the lift from Limerick, and agreed with everything that was said, but didn't admit to being upset about hearing of the murder. He said he was not wearing a long coat and boots at the time, as he had never had a long coat. As it transpired, some people that knew him, where he worked, and where he stayed, said they remembered seeing him with a long coat and boots; most of the others said they never saw him in a long coat and boots, so it is hard to know either way. Anyway, he denied having anything to do with the murder. He had a girlfriend in Dublin when he was there, whose sister lived 200 yards away from the Livingstones' house in The Moorings. His fingerprints were taken, and were not the fingerprints found on the tape.

He had a conviction in England. One night around 11 or 12pm, he met a young lady on the street. He approached her, and invited her back to his apartment for sex. She continually walked away from him; he punched her in the face, knocked her down and kicked her. The police arrived, and he was arrested, charged and convicted of assault. He would have been very interesting to find here in Ireland, where he could have been arrested and interrogated.

I always think about this fingermark on the tape – and you will recall that the member in charge of the initial investigation said that somebody picked it up in Headquarters. Now, it is possible that when preserving the scene, somebody, a member of the Gardaí or otherwise, went into that scene and picked up the tape, and their name was not recorded by the people in charge of the scene. It is very, very unlikely, but you can never say definitely. You can never know how important a piece of evidence like this is – if the fingermark was known to have been left by the culprit, it was important for elimination purposes, and of course for the identification of the culprit. On the other hand, if it was not left by the culprit, the chances of the real culprit being eliminated by reason of the mark not being his would be very real indeed.

The first investigation discovered that on the evening of the crime, five people from some organisation in the city were out collecting money in the Moorings, from about 4 to 6pm, and they were all interviewed and their fingerprints taken. Unfortunately, the part of the finger that the fingerprint expert required was not taken. When the review team decided to re-fingerprint the collectors, only four were available. The fifth was a UK youth, and had returned home.

He was another interesting character, this UK youth. He came to Dublin in September of 1992, and began working as a collector with this group in October or November. The other four collectors gave information that this UK youth had stolen property from houses in Newbridge, County Wicklow, and in Castleblaney in November 1992, and in Malahide in early December 1992. That was all while collecting from houses. They said he was continually taking cannabis, and on some days was in no condition to collect. He return to England before Christmas 1992. Detective Sergeant Tom O'Loughlin and Detective Superintendent Ted Murphy went to England and interviewed him. He denied committing the crimes alleged by his fellow collectors, and of course he denied involvement in the murder of Grace Livingstone. Some collectors pointed out houses that they alleged he had stolen property from. The occupiers of these houses acknowledged that property had been stolen. This young man had several previous convictions in England, for theft and possession of drugs. When he came to Ireland, he was avoiding a Court appearance in the UK. His prints were taken, and proved negative.

Now back to the man who called the 'Crime Line' programme on 16 May 1994, and who came to Malahide Garda Station the next morning, and spent the day talking with us. When he went home that evening, he had a caller to his home. It was a journalist, the late Veronica Guerin. She wanted to know what information he had given to Gardaí, and if Gardaí from the review team had criticised the first investigation team. The following morning this man returned to Malahide Station. He was angry that Veronica Guerin had got to know he had been at the Station.

On 17 May 1994, the Garda Press Office contacted me, and asked if I would agree to be interviewed by RTÉ reporter Tom McCaughren about the Livingstone case, and particularly in relation to the 'Crime Line' programme the previous night. I agreed, and went to Montrose to be interviewed. I was asked what time I believed Grace Livingstone had been murdered, and I said it was my belief that the crime happened between 4.30 and 5pm. Later in the interview I was asked if I was satisfied that Jim Livingstone was in Dublin city at that time. I said I was satisfied, and that he did not leave the city before 5pm. The interview was screened on RTÉ News that evening. I received a phone call from Chief Superintendent Noel Conroy, later Commissioner Noel Conroy. He said that the Minister for Justice required an updated report on the Livingstone murder the following morning. He asked me to have it in his office early in the morning.

I made out a report from the information and documents I had in my possession at that time. I outlined the investigation as I saw it at that time – the loud noise that was heard, the strange man seen by the girls, the man in the porch, and so on. In conclusion, in that report I said, that there was no credible evidence that Jim Livingstone murdered his wife. What credible evidence there was strongly indicated that he did not. I handed that report to Chief Superintendent Conroy the following morning, and it was typed and delivered to the Secretary of the Department of Justice. Later that morning, I received a call from the member in charge of the first investigation. He expressed his anger at me for stating that the murder had happened between 4.30 and 5pm. He said, 'We will never be able to charge him now.' That conversation did not last very long.

Reports in the media alleged that a dispute had arisen between the first investigation team and the review team. There was a difference of opinion certainly, but as far as I was concerned, it was a professional difference of opinion, with both parties expressing their beliefs in private. The fact that it reached the media was a result of someone being imprudent.

The first investigation team in their conclusion considered that James Livingstone was a prime suspect for the murder of his wife Grace. The team said they had not been in a position to prove conclusively one way or another his involvement in the murder, nor his innocence. Jim Livingstone was eventually released, and the investigation was scaled down.

When Tom O'Loughlin and I commenced the review, I telephoned Jim Livingstone and told him I would like to see him. He said, 'Okay, no problem, I will go to Malahide Garda Station to see you.' So I suggested we meet at his home, that he had seen enough of the Garda Station. Tom O' Loughlin and I went to his house, and spent a couple of hours with him. We told him we were engaged in a review of the investigation. He was delighted, and promised his full cooperation. He told us he hadn't had any contact with the Gardaí for a number of months, and he was aware that he was the main suspect in the case. He told us of his torment, suffering and sadness over his wife's death, compounded by being regarded as the main suspect for her murder. He broke down a number of times, and shed tears.

During the review, I had a phone call from Veronica Guerin. She wanted to talk about the case. I declined, as the matter was under investigation. I retired on 24 June 1994, and the review continued. Some time after I retired, she rang me again, and I agreed to see her.

We met at the Ambassador Hotel one morning. Over coffee, we discussed many criminals around the city that she had been writing about. Eventually she got down to why she was there – the Livingstone case. She was aware that I had made a report, and she wanted to know if I could tell her the contents of it. She told me that some members of the first investigation didn't have access to it. I told her I did make a report, but that I could not tell her what was in it, as the matter was still under investigation.

She told me that she had interviewed Jim Livingstone, and she expressed her own views on the case. She brought up the fact that I had said in the 'Crime Line' programme that the murder happened between 4.30 and 5pm, and that Jim Livingstone was in work at that time. She asked why I thought the crime had happened at that time. But the matter was still under investigation, so I could not tell her.

Shortly after I retired, in June 1994, I got a personal letter from Jim Livingstone, wishing me well in my retirement. Part of it said, 'On a very personal note, I wish to thank you for the professional way in which you approached the investigation into my wife's murder. Certainly if your concept of the pursuit of justice had been applied at an earlier time, a lot of suffering to me and my family could have been avoided. Probably the pursuit of the murderer would have been more positive, and more credible to the Gardaí.'

Around January 2003, eleven years after the murder of Grace Livingstone, I received a phone call from Jim Livingstone. He asked if I would talk to him if he came down to Naas, and I agreed. We met, again at the Ambassador Hotel in Kill. He told me that he had instituted a civil action against the State, regarding the manner in which Gardaí had investigated his wife's murder. I later learned that his daughter Tara Beauchamp and son Conor had also made a civil action against the State. Jim Livingstone was bringing proceedings for recovery of damages for false imprisonment, abuse of legal process, abuse of power and/or misfeasance of public office, conspiracy, conversion and/or detinue, slander and breach of his rights, under the European Convention of

Human Rights. He and his two children were claiming for the intentional and/or negligent infliction of emotional suffering, negligence, breach of duty, breach of statutory duty and breach of their constitutional rights; and also for severe personal injury, distress, trauma, damage, including damage to reputation, loss, embarrassment and inconvenience.

Jim Livingstone told me of his long fight to clear his name. He spoke of the distress and torment that he had been living under since the death of his wife. Jim Livingstone poured out his heart to me at the Ambassador Hotel that morning, and I felt great sympathy for the situation he was in. At that time, his civil claim had been before the Court for eight years, and he was finding it difficult to move it on any further. He asked me if I could help him in any way to clear his name, and I felt morally bound to help him. When I heard that Livingstone had lodged a civil claim in 1995, I was conscious that I would likely be subpoenaed to give evidence in the High Court. I told Jim Livingstone that I would help him in any way I could, and he was delighted. He asked if I would talk to his solicitor, and I agreed.

Very soon after that, I got a letter from the solicitor acting for Jim Livingstone, Gerard Charlton. We met at the Ambassador Hotel in Kill one morning, for about three hours. I told the Solicitor that I would give evidence in relation to the review. I could not go into any detail about the review, however, until the High Court decided to grant discovery of documents in the case, including the report I had made to the Commissioner that went to the Department of Justice. It had not been released up to that time. I had a number of meetings with Gerard Charlton over the next couple of years. He had other business interests around the Naas area, and was there fairly often.

In late 2007, or early 2008, the High Court decided to release all documentation held by the State relating to the Livingstone case. One of the documents released was my report on the review. When Mr Charlton was in possession of it, I was quite at liberty to discuss its contents, and I knew that when the High Court hearing came, I would be called to give evidence.

The High Court hearing eventually came in early April 2008. It was expected to take eight weeks. I was subpoenaed to attend the Court, and I was there throughout the whole proceedings. On the fourth day of the hearing, after a number of witnesses had given evidence, and my report that had gone to the Commissioner and the Minister for Justice was read into the record of the Court, and when Mr Livingstone had been in the witness box for quite a while, but had not yet got into evidence about happenings in his house, the State asked the Court for an adjournment. John Rogers, former Attorney General, was the leading Senior Counsel on Jim Livingstone's team. Both parties had a consultation, and then the Court was informed that the case had been settled.

The State issued a statement, saying that Jim Livingstone was entitled to the unreserved and absolute presumption of innocence in relation to his wife's death. Jim Livingstone was completely vindicated by the clear and unambiguous language of that statement. The rest of the terms of the settlement were never known to me.

Jim Livingstone and his family were entirely satisfied with the result. Their relief was crystal clear from their expressions and body language at the conclusion of the Court action. I was somewhat torn, between showing loyalty to the Garda Force, which I had served in for thirty-nine years, and in which my two sons are still serving, and having to give evidence in a civil action against the State. Regardless of my personal feelings, it was my duty to tell the truth in relation to the investigation. I was delighted that Jim Livingstone was vindicated, and also delighted that I did not have to give evidence.

At the very time that Jim Livingstone's High Court hearing was in progress, another High Court case was in progress in Dublin. Livingstone's solicitor, Gerard Charlton, was not in attendance at Livingstone's civil action, as he was attending another hearing, in the Four Courts. He and his neighbour, broadcaster

Pat Kenny, were crossing swords in relation to a plot of land overlooking Wood-lock Harbour – it was the property of Mr Charlton, but Pat Kenny was claiming it by reason of squatter's rights. This case was also settled after a number of days. I do not claim to know the settlement terms, but I do know that, like Jim Living-stone, Mr Charlton was very satisfied with the outcome.

The Livingstone case was, for me, an unpleasant task to say the least. Another member of the review team, and at least one member of the team that examined the scene, were subjected to what I would describe as harsh and inappropriate action. I must mention one member of the first investigation team, who did not agree entirely with the views of the others. That member was Detective Inspector John Gallagher. To me, he always had an open mind and listened to other views and opinions. He was later Detective Superintendent John Gallagher, now retired.

This was a crime that to me was very solvable, and should have been solved. But I have no doubt that the first investigation team really believed they were fulfilling their duties properly.

CONCLUSION

I am about to conclude, in the knowledge that sometimes I get carried away by my feelings. That's just the way I am, and I hope to stay that way. I have mentioned many crimes that may not have been solved but for the assistance of good, civic-spirited people. There must be a great many people around the country who have information relating to unsolved serious crimes. It does not matter how old the crime is, it is never too late; the Gardaí will always welcome it. People may have been prevented from giving information at the time of a crime for some reason, and perhaps that reason has now passed. Just think – if the injured party in the crime was a member of your family, a relation or a friend, you would hope a person in possession of information would pass it on to the Gardaí. If you have such information, or know someone who has, do not take it to the grave with you.

During the course of investigations, Gardaí often receive anonymous letters, or anonymous phone calls, perhaps naming certain individuals for particular crimes. They also get a number of bogus anonymous letters and phone calls. How are they to decide which is which? Gardaí like to speak to a person who provides information – to establish how they know something; how sure they are; and how the Gardaí should proceed to investigate it. If you want to remain anonymous, you can go to an intermediary, a go-between between yourself and the Gardaí. If the Garda wants to follow up on anything, they can do it through this person. There is a great saying: 'If there is a will, there is a way.'

I hope you have derived some pleasure from reading my book, and understand why I put pen to paper in the first place. Now back to my much-neglected household chores, gardening and more golf, for as long as God only knows.